W9-BAA-123

Italian
phrase book

Berlitz Publishing / APA Publications GmbH &
Verlag KG, Singapore Branch, Singapore

PRONUNCIATION

This section is designed to make you familiar with the sounds of Italian using our simplified phonetic transcription. You'll find the pronunciation of the Italian letters and sounds explained below, together with their "imitated" equivalents. This system is used throughout the phrase book: simply read the pronunciation as if it were English, noting any special rules below.

THE ITALIAN LANGUAGE

Italian evolved from Latin, just as French, Spanish, Portuguese, and Romanian. What is known as standard Italian today dates back to last century, when the great Italian novelist Alessandro Manzoni (1785-1873) gave Italy a national language by resolving that it should basically be Tuscan Italian with a heavy contribution from the Italian used in the other regions of Italy. The language spoken and written in Tuscany had taken precedence over the regional forms from the twelfth century to Manzoni's times because of the political, artistic and social prominence of Florence.

There are approximately 64 million speakers of Italian. These are the countries where you can expect to hear Italian spoken (figures are approximate):

Italia Italy

Italian is the national language, spoken by almost the entire population (59 million). Other languages: Sardinian in Sardinia (1.5 million); Rhaeto-Romanic in Friuli, near the border with Slovenia and Austria.

Svizzera Switzerland

Italian is one of the four official languages, spoken by about 800,000 people in the southern part of the country, particularly the canton of Ticino (capital: Bellinzona). Other languages: German in the north (5 milllion); French in the west (1.3 million); Romansch in the east (50,000).

Italian is also spoken amongst large Italian emigré communities, particularly in the United States (**Stati Uniti**), with almost 1.5 million speakers, and Canada (**Canada**), with over half a million speakers.

The Italian alphabet is the same as English, with the addition of accents which indicate stress only (see below). However, the letters **j**, **k**, **w**, **x** and **y** only appear in foreign words.

English has absorbed numerous Italian words, for example: **balcony**, **studio**, **umbrella**, **volcano** as well as terms in the fields of food (e.g. **broccoli**, **maca-roni**, **pizza**, **spaghetti**) and music (e.g. **concerto**, **piano**, **solo**, **trio**, **viola**).

CONSONANTS

Letter	Approximate pronunciation	Symbol	Example	
c	1) before **e** and **i**, like *ch* in *ch*ip	*ch*	**cerco**	<u>*chay*rko</u>
	2) elsewhere, like *c* in *c*at	*k*	**conto**	<u>*k*onto</u>
ch	like *c* in *c*at	*k*	**che**	*k*ay
g	1) before **e** and **i**, like *j* in *j*et	*j*	**valigia**	va*lee*ja
	2) elsewhere, like *g* in *g*o	*g*	**grande**	<u>*g*ran</u>day
gh	like *g* in *g*o	*g*	**ghiaccio**	<u>*g*ee</u>acho
gl	like *lli* in mi*lli*on	*ly*	**gli**	*ly*ee
gn	like *ni* in o*ni*on	*ny*	**bagno**	<u>*ba*nyo</u>
h	always silent		**ha**	ah
r	trilled like a Scottish *r*	*r*	**deriva**	deh<u>*r*eeva</u>
s	1) generally like *s* in *s*it	*s*	**questo**	<u>kway*s*to</u>
	2) sometimes like *z* in *z*oo	*z*	**viso**	<u>vee*z*o</u>
sc	1) before **e** and **i**, like *sh* in *sh*ut	*sh*	**uscita**	oo<u>*sh*eeta</u>
	2) elsewhere, like *sk* in *sk*in	*sk*	**scarpa**	<u>*sk*arpa</u>
z/zz	1) generally like *ts* in hi*ts*	*ts*	**grazie**	<u>graa*ts*eeay</u>
	2) sometimes like *ds* in roa*ds*	*dz*	**romanzo**	ro<u>man*dz*o</u>

VOWELS

a	1) short, like *a* in c*a*t	*a*	**gatto**	<u>*ga*tto</u>
	2) long, like *a* in f*a*ther	*aa*	**casa**	<u>*kaa*sa</u>
e	1) can always be pronounced like *ay* in w*ay*, but without moving tongue or lips	*ay*	**sera**	<u>*say*ra</u>
	2) in correct speech, it is sometimes pronounced like *e* in g*e*t or, when long, more like *ai* in h*ai*r	*eh*	**bello**	<u>*beh*llo</u>
i	like *ee* in m*ee*t	*ee*	**vini**	<u>*vee*nee</u>
o	can always be pronounced like *o* in g*o*	*o*	**sole**	<u>*so*lay</u>
u	1. like *oo* in f*oo*t	*oo*	**fumo**	<u>*foo*mo</u>
	2. like *w* in *w*ell	*w*	**buono**	<u>b*wo*no</u>

b, **d**, **f**, **k**, **l**, **m**, **n**, **p**, **q**, **t** and **v** are pronounced as in English

Two or more vowels

In groups of vowels **a**, **e** and **o** are strong, and **i** and **u** are weak vowels. The following combinations occur:

two strong vowels	pronounced as two separate syllables	**beato**	*bay-aato*
a stong vowel and a weak vowel	1) the weak one is pronounced more quickly and with less stress than the strong one; such sounds are diphthongs and constitute only one syllable:	**piede**	*peeayday*
	2) if the weak vowel is stressed, then it is pronounced as a separate syllable	**due**	*doo-ay*
two weak vowels	pronounced as a diphthong; it is generally the second one that is more strongly stressed	**guida**	*gweeda*

STRESS

Stress has been indicated in the phonetic transcription by underlining the letters that should be pronounced louder than the others.

Generally, the vowel of the next to last syllable is stressed. When a final vowel is stressed, it has an accent written over it (**caffè**). Normally, when the stress falls on the syllable before the next to last one, it is not indicated by an accent.

PRONUNCIATION OF THE ITALIAN ALPHABET

A	ah	**N**	_ehnnay_
B	bee	**O**	o
C	chee	**P**	pee
D	dee	**Q**	koo
E	ay	**R**	_ehrray_
F	_ehffay_	**S**	_ehssay_
G	jee	**T**	tee
H	_aaka_	**U**	oo
I	ee	**V**	voo
J	ee _loongga_	**W**	voo _doppeea_
K	_kaappa_	**X**	eeks
L	_ehllay_	**Y**	ee _grayka_
M	_ehmmay_	**Z**	_dzaytah_

cane

BASIC EXPRESSIONS

GREETINGS/APOLOGIES

ESSENTIAL		
Yes.	**Sì.** *see*	
No.	**No.** *no*	
Okay.	**D'accordo./Va bene.** *daakordo/va baynay*	
Please.	**Per favore.** *pehr favoray*	
Thank you (very much).	**(Mille) grazie.** *(meellay) graatseeay*	

Hello/Hi!	**Salve./Ciao!** *saalvay/chaao*
Good morning.	**Buongiorno.** *bwon jorno*
Good afternoon.	**Buonasera.** *bwona sayra*
Good evening.	**Buonasera.** *bwona sayra*
Good night.	**Buonanotte.** *bwona nottay*
Good-bye.	**Arrivederci.** *arreevaydehrchee*
Excuse me! *(getting attention)*	**Scusi!** *skoozee*
Excuse me. *(May I get past?)*	**Permesso?** *pehrmehsso*
Excuse me!/Sorry!	**Scusi!/Sono spiacente!** *skoozee/sono speeachehntay*
It was an accident.	**È stato un incidente.** *eh staato oon eencheedehntay*
Don't mention it.	**Prego.** *praygo*
Never mind.	**Non importa.** *non eemporta*

COMMUNICATION DIFFICULTIES

Do you speak English?	**Parla inglese?** *parla eengglaysay*
Does anyone here speak English?	**C'è qualcuno qui che parla inglese?** *cheh kwalkoono kwee kay parla eengglaysay*
I don't speak . (much) Italian	**Non parlo italiano (molto bene).** *non parlo eetaleeaano (molto baynay)*
Could you speak more slowly?	**Può parlare più lentamente?** *pwo parlaaray peeoo layntamayntay*
Could you repeat that?	**Può ripetere?** *pwo reepehtayray*
Pardon?/What was that?	**Prego?/Cosa ha detto?** *praygo/kosa ah daytto*
Could you spell it?	**Come si scrive?** *komay see skreevay*
Please write it down.	**Lo scriva, per piacere.** *lo skreeva pehr peeachayray*
Can you translate this for me?	**Può tradurre questo?** *pwo tradoorray kwaysto*
What does this/that mean?	**Cosa significa questo/quello?** *kosa seenyeefeeka kwaysto/kwayllo*
Please point to the phrase in the book.	**Per piacere, indichi la frase nel libro.** *pehr peeachayray eendeekee la fraazay nel leebro*
I understand.	**Capisco.** *kapeesko*
I don't understand.	**Non capisco.** *non kapeesko*
Do you understand?	**Capisce?** *kapeeshay*

ON THE STREET

Buongiorno! Come sta? *bwon jorno komay sta*
(Hi. How are you?)
Bene, grazie, e Lei? *baynay graatseeay ay layee*
(Fine, thanks. And you?)
Bene, grazie. *baynay graatseeay*
(Fine . Thanks.)

Where?

Where is it?	**Dov'è?** *doveh*
Where are you going?	**Dove va?** *dovay va*
to the meeting place	**al punto d'incontro** *al poonto deenkontro*
[point] downstairs	**al piano inferiore** *al peeaano eenfayreeoray*
from the U.S.	**dagli Stati Uniti** *daalyee staatee ooneetee*
here	**qui** *kwee*
in the car	**in automobile** *een owtomobeelay*
in Italy	**in Italia** *een eetaaleea*
inside	**dentro** *dayntro*
near the bank	**vicino alla banca** *veecheeno alla banka*
next to the apples	**accanto alle mele** *akkanto allay maylay*
opposite the market	**di fronte al mercato** *dee frontay al mayrkaato*
on the left/right	**a sinistra/a destra** *ah seeneestra/ah daystra*
there	**là** *la*
to the hotel	**in albergo** *een albehrgo*
toward Florence	**verso Firenze** *vehrso feerehnzay*
outside the café	**fuori del bar** *fwooree dayl baar*
upstairs	**al piano superiore** *al peeaano soopayreeoray*

When?

When does the museum open?	**Quando apre il museo?** _kwando apray eel moozeho_
When will the train arrive?	**Quando arriva il treno?** _kwando arreeva eel trayno_
in 10 minutes	**fra dieci minuti** _frah dee-ehchee meenootee_
after lunch	**dopo pranzo** _dopo prandzo_
around midnight	**verso mezzanotte** _vehrso mehdzanottay_
at 7 o'clock	**alle sette** _allay sehttay_
before Friday	**prima di venerdì** _preema dee vaynayrdee_
by tomorrow	**entro domani** _ayntro domaanee_
early	**di buon'ora** _dee bwonora_
every week	**ogni settimana/tutte le settimane** _onyee saytteemaana/toottay lay saytteemaanay_
for 2 hours	**per due ore** _pehr doo-ay oray_
from 9 a.m. to 6 p.m.	**dalle nove alle diciotto** _dallay novay allay deechotto_
immediately	**immediatamente** _eemaydeeatamayntay_
in 20 minutes	**fra venti minuti** _frah vayntee meenootee_
always	**sempre** _sehmpray_
never	**mai** _maee_
not yet	**non ancora** _non ankora_
now	**ora/adesso** _ora/adehsso_
often	**sovente/spesso** _sovayntay/spehsso_
on March 8	**l'otto marzo** _lotto martso_
on weekdays	**nei giorni feriali** _nayee jornee fehreeaalee_
sometimes	**qualche volta** _kwalkay volta_
soon	**presto/fra poco** _prehsto/fra poko_
then	**poi** _poee_
within 2 days	**entro due giorni** _ayntro doo-ay jornee_

What kind of ...?

I'd like something ...	**Vorrei qualcosa ...**	*vorrehee kwalkosa*
It's ...	**È ...**	*eh*
beautiful/ugly	**bello(-a)/brutto(-a)**	*behllo(-a)/brootto(-a)*
better/worse	**migliore/peggiore**	*meelyoray/paydjoray*
big/small	**grande/piccolo(-a)**	*granday/peekkolo(-a)*
cheap/expensive	**a buon prezzo/caro(-a)**	*a bwon pretso/kaaro(-a)*
clean/dirty	**pulito(-a)/sporco(-a)**	*pooleeto(-a)/sporko(-a)*
dark/light	**scuro(-a)/chiaro(-a)**	*skooro(-a)/keeahro(-a)*
delicious/revolting	**delizioso(-a)/disgustoso(-a)**	*dehleetzeeozo(-a)/deesgoostozo(-a)*
easy/difficult	**facile/difficile**	*faacheelay/deeffeecheelay*
empty/full	**vuoto(-a)/pieno(-a)**	*vwoto(-a)/peeayno(-a)*
good/bad	**buono(-a)/cattivo(-a)**	*bwono(-a)/katteevo(-a)*
heavy/light	**pesante/leggero(-a)**	*paysantay/laydjehro(-a)*
hot/warm/cold	**molto caldo(-a)/caldo(-a)/freddo(-a)**	*molto kaldo(-a)/kaldo(-a)/frayddo(-a)*
modern/old-fashioned	**moderno(-a)/antiquato(-a)**	*modayrno(-a)/anteekwato(-a)*
narrow/wide	**stretto(-a)/largo(-a)**	*straytto(-a)/lahrgo(-a)*
old/new	**vecchio(-a)/nuovo(-a)**	*vehkkeeao(-a)/nwovo(-a)*
open/shut	**aperto(-a)/chiuso(-a)**	*apehrto(-a)/keeooso(-a)*
pleasant/nice/unpleasant	**gradevole/bello(-a)/sgradevole**	*grahdayvolay/behllo(-a)/zgradayvolay*

quick/slow	**veloce/lento(-a)** *vaylochay/laynto(-a)*
right/wrong	**guisto(-a)/sbagliato(-a)** *joosto(-a) zbalyaato(-a)*
tall/short	**alto(-a)/basso(-a)** *alto(-a)/basso(-a)*
vacant/occupied	**libero(-a)/occupato(-a)** *leebayro(-a)/okoopaato(-a)*

How much/many?

How much is that?	**Quanto costa?** *kwanto kosta*
How many are there?	**Quanti ce ne sono?** *kwantee cheh neh sono*
1/2/3	**uno(-a)/due/tre** *oono(-a)/doo-ay/tray*
4/5	**quattro/cinque** *kwattro/cheenkway*
none	**nessuno(-a)** *nayssoono(-a)*
about 20 euros	**circa venti euro** *cheerka vayntee ayooro*
a little	**un po'** *oon po*
a lot of traffic	**molto traffico** *molto traffeeko*
enough *(adv./adj.)*	**abbastanza/sufficiente** *abbastantsa/sooffeecheeayntay*
few/a few of them	**alcuni(-e)/alcuni(-e) di loro** *alkoonee(-ay)/alkoonee(-ay) dee loro*
more than that	**più di quello(-a)** *peeoo dee kwayllo(-a)*
less than that	**meno di quello(-a)** *mayno dee kwayllo(-a)*
much more	**molto di più** *molto dee peeoo*
nothing else	**nient'altro** *neeayntaltro*
too much	**troppo(-a)** *troppo(-a)*

Why?

Why is that?	**Perchè?** *pehrkay*
Why not?	**Perchè no?** *pehrkay no*
because of the weather	**a causa del tempo** *a kowsa dayl tehmpo*
because I'm in a hurry	**perchè ho fretta** *pehrkay o fraytta*
I don't know why	**non so perchè** *non so pehrkay*

Who?/Which?

Who's there?	**Chi è?** *kee eh*	
It's me!	**Sono io!** *sono eeo*	
It's us!	**Siamo noi!** *seeamo noee*	
someone	**qualcuno** *kwalkoono*	
no one	**nessuno** *nayssoono*	
Which one do you want?	**Quale vuole?** *kwalay vwolay*	
one like that	**uno(-a) come quello(-a)** *oono(-a) komay kwayllo(-a)*	
that one/this one	**quello(-a)/questo(-a)** *kwayllo(-a)/kwaysto(-a)*	
not that one	**non quello(-a)** *non kwayllo(-a)*	
something	**qualcosa** *kwalkosa*	
nothing	**niente** *neeayntay*	
none	**nessuno(-a)** *nayssoono(-a)*	

Whose?

Whose is that?	**Di chi è quello(-a)?** *dee kee eh kwayllo(-a)*
It's …	**È …** *eh*
mine/ours	**mio(-a)/nostro(-a)** *meeo(-a)/nostro(-a)*
yours *(formal)*/ yours *(familiar)*	**Suo(-a)/tuo(-a)** *soo-o(-a)/too-o(-a)*
his/hers/theirs	**suo(-a)/di lui (di lei)/loro** *soo-o(-a)/dee looee(di layee)/loro*

How?

How would you like to pay?	**Come desidera pagare?** *komay dayzeedayra pagaaray*
by cash	**in contanti** *een kontantee*
by credit card	**con carta di credito** *kon karta dee kraydeeto*
How are you getting here?	**Come arriva qui?** *komay arreeva kwee*

by car	**in automobile/macchina**
	een owto<u>mo</u>beelay/<u>mak</u>keena
by bus	**in autobus** *een <u>ow</u>tobooss*
on foot	**a piedi** *a pee<u>ay</u>dee*
extremely	**estremamente** *aystrayma<u>mayn</u>tay*
quickly	**presto** *pr<u>eh</u>sto*
slowly	**lentamente** *lehnta<u>mayn</u>tay*
too fast	**troppo veloce** *<u>troppo</u> veh<u>lo</u>chay*
totally	**totalmente** *total<u>mayn</u>tay*
very	**molto** *<u>molto</u>*
with a friend	**con un amico/un'amica**
	kon oon a<u>mee</u>ko/a<u>mee</u>ka

Is it …?/Are there …?

Is it …?	**È …?** *eh*
Is it free? *(unoccupied)*	**È libero(-a)?** *eh <u>lee</u>bayro(-a)*
It isn't ready.	**Non è pronto(-a).**
	non eh <u>pronto</u>(-a)
Is there …?	**C'è …?** *cheh*
Are there …?	**Ci sono …?** *chee <u>sono</u>*
Is there a bus into town?	**C'è un autobus per il centro?**
	cheh oon <u>ow</u>tobooss pehr eel <u>chayn</u>tro
Are there buses to the airport?	**Ci sono autobus per l'aeroporto?**
	chee <u>sono</u> <u>ow</u>toboos pehr la-ayro<u>por</u>to
Here it is/they are.	**Eccolo(-a)/eccoli(-e).**
	eh<u>kko</u>lo/eh<u>kko</u>lee
There it is/they are.	**È là/sono là** *eh la/<u>so</u>no la*

IN A STORE

Come desidera pagare? *<u>ko</u>may day<u>zee</u>dayra pa<u>gaa</u>ray* *(How would you like to pay?)*
In contanti, per favore. *een kon<u>tan</u>tee pehr fa<u>vo</u>ray* *(Cash, please.)*

Can/May?

May I have …?	**Posso avere …?** _posso avayray_
May we have …?	**Possiamo avere …?** _posseeamo avayray_
Can you tell me?	**Può dirmi …?** _pwo deermee_
Can you help me?	**Può aiutarmi?** _pwo aeeootaarmee_
Can I help you?	**Posso aiutare?** _posso aeeootaaray_
Can you direct me to …?	**Può indicarmi la via per …?** _pwo eendeekaarmee la veea pehr_
I can't.	**Non posso.** _non posso_

What do you want?

I'd like …	**Vorrei …** _vorrehee_
Do you have …?	**Ha …?** _ah_
We'd like …	**Vorremmo …** _vorrehmmo_
Give me …	**Mi dia …** _mee deea_
I'm looking for …	**Cerco …** _chayrko_
I need to …	**Ho bisogno di …** _beezonyo dee_
go …	**andare …** _andaaray_
find …	**trovare …** _trovaaray_
see …	**vedere …** _vaydayray_
speak to …	**parlare a …** _parlaaray ah_

18

OTHER USEFUL WORDS

fortunately	**fortunatamente** *fortoonata<u>mayn</u>tay*
hopefully	**con (la) speranza di** *kon (la) spay<u>ran</u>tsa dee*
of course	**naturalmente** *natooral<u>mayn</u>tay*
perhaps/possibly	**forse/possibilmente** *<u>for</u>say/posseebeel<u>mayn</u>tay*
probably	**probabilmente** *probabeel<u>mayn</u>tay*
unfortunately	**sfortunatamente** *sfortoonata<u>mayn</u>tay*

EXCLAMATIONS

At last!	**Finalmente!** *feenal<u>mayn</u>tay*
Damn!	**Maledizione!** *malaydeetsee<u>o</u>nay*
Go on.	**Continui.** *kon<u>tee</u>nooee*
Good Heavens!	**Santo Cielo!** *<u>san</u>to chee<u>ay</u>lo*
I can't believe it!	**Incredibile!** *eenkray<u>dee</u>beelay*
I don't mind.	**Mi è indifferente.** *mee eh eendeeffay<u>ray</u>ntay*
No way!	**Assolutamente no.** *assoloota<u>mayn</u>tay no*
Really?	**Davvero?** *dav<u>vay</u>ro*
Rubbish.	**Stupidaggini.** *stoopee<u>dad</u>jeenee*
That's enough!	**Basta!** *<u>ba</u>sta*
That's true.	**É vero.** *eh <u>vay</u>ro*
How are things?	**Come vanno le cose?** *<u>ko</u>may <u>van</u>no lay <u>ko</u>say*
Fine, thanks.	**Bene, grazie.** *<u>bay</u>nay <u>graat</u>seeay*
great/brilliant	**magnifico** *man<u>yee</u>feeko*
great	**benissimo** *bay<u>nees</u>seemo*
fine	**bene** *<u>bay</u>nay*
not bad	**non c'è male** *non cheh <u>ma</u>lay*
okay	**abbastanza bene** *abba<u>stan</u>tza <u>bay</u>nay*
not good	**non bene** *non <u>bay</u>nay*

ACCOMMODATIONS

Early reservations are essential in most major tourist centers. If you haven't booked, most towns and arrival points have a tourist information office (**azienda di promozione turistica** or **ufficio turistico**).

The Italian tourist organization **E.N.I.T.** publishes an annual directory of all the 37,000 hotels in Italy, with details of prices and facilities.

There is a wide range of accommodation options available, from **locande** (country inns) and **rifugi alpini** (mountain huts) to converted historic buildings, and the following:

albergo/hotel _albayrgo/otehl_

Hotels in Italy are classified as **di lusso** (luxury class), or **di prima**, **seconda**, **terza**, **quarta categoria** (first, second, third, fourth class).

Note: especially near railway stations, one often finds **alberghi diurni** ("daytime hotels"). These have no sleeping accommodations, but provide bathrooms, rest rooms, hairdressers, telecommunication, and other similar services. Most close at midnight.

motel _motehl_

Increasing in number and improving in service; the Automobile Association of Italy has a list of recommended motels.

pensione _paynseeonay_

Corresponds to a guest house; it usually offers **pensione completa** (full board) or **mezza pensione** (half board). Meals are likely to be from a set menu. **Pensioni** are classified first, second, and third class.

ostello della gioventù _ostehllo daylla jovayntoo_

Youth hostel. They are open to holders of membership cards issued by the International Youth Hostel Association. The Italian Association of Youth Hostels (**AIG**) publishes a complete guide of youth hostels in Italy. Information can also be obtained from any **CTS** (**Centro Turistico Studentesco**). Reservations are advisable.

RESERVATIONS

In advance

Can you recommend a hotel in …?	**Può consigliarmi un albergo a …?** _pwo konsilyarmee oon albayrgo ah_
Is it near the center of town?	**È vicino al centro?** _eh veecheeno al chayntro_

How much is it per night?	**Quanto costa una notte?**
	kwanto kosta oona nottay
Is there anything cheaper?	**C'è qualcosa di più economico?** _cheh_
	kwalkosa dee peeoo aykonomeeko
Could you reserve me a room there, please?	**Può prenotarmi una camera, per piacere?** _pwo prehnotaarmee oona kamayra pehr peeachayray_
How do I get there?	**Come ci arrivo?** _komay chee arreevo_

At the hotel

Do you have a room?	**Avete camere libere?**
	avayteh kamayray leebayray
I'm sorry. We're full.	**Mi dispiace, siamo al completo.**
	mee deespeeachay seeamo al komplayto
Is there another hotel nearby?	**C'è un altro albergo qui vicino?** _cheh oon altro kwee veecheeno_
I'd like a single/. double room	**Vorrei una camera singola/doppia.** _vorrehee oona kamayra seengola/doppeea_
A room with …	**Una camera con …**
	oona kamayra kon
twin beds	**due letti**
	doo-ay lehttee
a double bed	**un letto matrimoniale**
	oon lehtto matreemoneeaalay
a bath/shower	**bagno/doccia**
	baanyo/dotcha

AT THE HOTEL RECEPTION

Avete camere libere? _avayteh kamayray leebayray_
(Do you have any vacancies?)
Mi dispiace, siamo al completo. _mee deespeeachay seeamo al komplayto (I'm sorry, we're full.)_
Grazie. _graatseeay (Thank you.)_

RECEPTION

I have a reservation.	**Ho una stanza prenotata.** *o oona stahnzah prenohtahtah*
My name is …	**Sono …** *sono*
We've reserved a double and a single room.	**Abbiamo prenotato una camera doppia e una camera singola.** *abbeeaamo praynotaato oona kamayra doppeea ay oona kamayra seengola*
I confirmed my reservation by mail.	**Ho confermato la prenotazione per lettera.** *o konfehrmaato la praynotatseeonay pehr lehttayra*
Could we have adjoining rooms?	**Possiamo avere camere adiacenti?** *posseeamo avayray kamayray adjachehntee*

Amenities and facilities

Is there (a) … in the room?	**C'è … nella camera?** *cheh naylla kamayra*
air conditioning	**l'aria condizionata** *lareea kondeetseeonaata*
TV/telephone	**la televisione/il telefono** *la taylayveezeeonay/ eel taylayfono*
Does the hotel have a(n)…?	**L'albergo ha …** *lalbayrgo ah*
laundry service	**il servizio di lavanderia** *eel sayrveetseeo dee lavandayreea*
satellite TV	**la televisione via satellite** *la taylayveezeeonay veea sataylleetay*
solarium	**il solarium** *eel solareeoom*
swimming pool	**la piscina** *la peesheena*
Could you put … in the room?	**Può mettere … nella camera?** *pwo mayttehrray … naylla kamayra*
an extra bed	**un letto supplementare** *oon lehtto soopplaymayntaray*
a crib [child's cot]	**una culla** *oona koolla*
Do you have facilities for children/the disabled?	**È attrezzato per i bambini/i disabili?** *eh attraytsaato pehr ee bambeenee/ ee deesabeelee*

How long?

We'll be staying …	**Ci fermeremo …**	*chee fehrmayraymo*
overnight only	**solo per una notte**	*solo pehr oona nottay*
a few days	**per alcuni giorni**	*pehr alkoonee jornee*
a week (at least)	**una settimana (minimo)**	
	oona sayteemaana (meeneemo)	

I don't know yet.	**Non so ancora.**	*non so ankora*
I'd like to stay an extra night.	**Vorrei fermarmi per un'altra notte.**	*vorrehee fehrmaarmee pehr oonaaltra nottay*

YOU MAY SEE

SOLO CAMERA … EURO	room only … euros
COLAZIONE COMPRESA	breakfast included
RISTORANTE	meals available
COGNOME/NOME	last name/first name
INDIRIZZO/DOMICILIO/	home address/street/
VIA/NUMERO	number
NAZIONALITÀ/PROFESSIONE	nationality/profession
DATA/LUOGO DI NASCITA	date/place of birth
NUMERO DI PASSAPORTO	passport number
NUMERO DI TARGA DEL VEICOLO	license plate [registration] number
LUOGO/DATA	place/date (of signature)
FIRMA	signature

YOU MAY HEAR

Posso vedere il suo passaporto, per piacere?	May I see your passport, please?
Per piacere, compili questo modulo/firmi qui.	Please fill out this form/sign here.
Qual è il suo numero di targa?	What's your license plate [registration] number?

PRICE

How much is it …?	**Quant'è …?** kwan<u>teh</u>
per night/week	**per notte/per settimana** *pehr <u>not</u>tay/pehr saytteema<u>ma</u>ana*
for bed and breakfast	**per il pernottamento e la colazione** pehr eel pehrnotta<u>may</u>nto ay la kolatsee<u>o</u>nay
excluding meals	**pasti esclusi** *paastee aysk<u>loo</u>zee*
for American Plan (A.P.) [full board]	**per la pensione completa** *pehr la paynsee<u>o</u>nay komp<u>lay</u>ta*
for Modified American Plan (M.A.P.) [half board]	**per la mezza pensione** *pehr la <u>mehd</u>za paynsee<u>o</u>nay*
Does the price include …?	**Il prezzo include …?** *eel <u>preh</u>tso eengk<u>loo</u>day*
breakfast	**la colazione** *la kolatsee<u>o</u>nay*
sales tax [VAT]	**l'IVA (Imposta Valore Aggiunto)** *<u>lee</u>va (eem<u>po</u>sta va<u>lo</u>ray ad<u>joo</u>nto)*
Do I have to pay a deposit?	**Devo pagare un anticipo?** *<u>day</u>vo pa<u>gaa</u>ray oon an<u>tee</u>cheepo*
Is there a reduction for children?	**Ci sono sconti per i bambini?** *chee <u>so</u>no <u>skon</u>tee pehr ee bam<u>bee</u>nee*

DECISIONS

May I see the room?	**Posso vedere la camera?** *<u>pos</u>so vay<u>day</u>ray la <u>ka</u>mayra*
That's fine. I'll take it.	**Va bene. La prendo.** *va <u>bay</u>nay. la <u>pray</u>ndo*
It's too …	**È troppo …** *eh <u>trop</u>po*
dark/small	**buia/piccola** *<u>boo</u>eea/<u>pee</u>kola*
noisy	**rumorosa** *roomo<u>ro</u>za*
Do you have anything …?	**Ha qualcosa di …?** *ah kwal<u>ko</u>za dee*
bigger/cheaper	**più grande/più economico** *pee<u>oo</u> <u>gran</u>day/pee<u>oo</u> ayko<u>no</u>meeko*
quieter/warmer	**più tranquillo/più caldo** *pee<u>oo</u> trank<u>wee</u>llo/pee<u>oo</u> <u>kal</u>do*
No, I won't take it.	**No, non la prendo.** *no non la <u>preh</u>ndo*

PROBLEMS

The … doesn't work.	**… non funziona.**	*non foontsee<u>o</u>na*
air conditioning	**L'aria condizionata**	*laareea kondeetsee<u>o</u>naata*
fan	**Il ventilatore**	*eel vaynteela<u>to</u>ray*
heat	**Il riscaldamento**	*eel reeskalda<u>mayn</u>to*
light	**La luce**	*la <u>loo</u>chay*
I can't turn the heat [heating] on/off.	**Non posso accendere/spegnere il riscaldamento.**	*non <u>po</u>sso atchayn-dehray/<u>spay</u>nyehray eel reeskalda<u>mayn</u>to*
There is no hot water/ toilet paper.	**Non c'è acqua calda/carta igienica.**	*non cheh <u>a</u>kwa <u>ka</u>lda/<u>kar</u>ta eej<u>ay</u>neeka*
The faucet [tap] is dripping	**Il rubinetto perde.**	*eel roobee<u>neh</u>to <u>pehr</u>day*
The sink/toilet is blocked.	**Il lavello/water è bloccato.**	*eel la<u>veh</u>llo/<u>va</u>teyr eh blok<u>aa</u>to*
The window/door is jammed.	**La finestra/porta è bloccata.**	*la fee<u>nay</u>stra/<u>por</u>ta eh blok<u>aa</u>ta*
My room has not been made up.	**La mia camera non è stata rifatta.**	*la <u>mee</u>a <u>ka</u>mayra non eh <u>staa</u>ta ree<u>fa</u>tta*
The … is broken.	**… è rotto(-a).**	*eh <u>ro</u>tto(-a)*
blind	**la tapparella**	*la tappa<u>reh</u>lla*
lock	**la serratura**	*la sehrra<u>too</u>ra*
There are insects in our room.	**Ci sono insetti nella nostra camera.**	*chee <u>so</u>no een<u>seh</u>tee <u>nay</u>lla <u>no</u>stra <u>ka</u>mayra*

Action

Could you have that taken care of?	**Può farlo(-a) controllare?**	*pwo <u>far</u>lo(-a) kontrol<u>laa</u>ray*
I'd like to move to another room.	**Vorrei cambiare camera.**	*vor<u>reh</u>ee kambee<u>aa</u>ray <u>ka</u>mayra*
I'd like to speak to the manager.	**Vorrei parlare con il direttore.**	*vor<u>reh</u>ee par<u>laa</u>ray kon eel deeray<u>to</u>ray*

REQUIREMENTS

In the hotel

Where's the …?	**Dov'è …?** *do<u>veh</u>*
bar	**il bar** *eel baar*
restroom [toilet]	**la toilette** *la toeh<u>leh</u>teh*
parking lot [car park]	**il parcheggio** *eel par<u>kay</u>djo*
dining room	**la sala da pranzo** *la <u>sa</u>la da <u>pran</u>dzo*
elevator [lift]	**l'ascensore** *lashayn<u>so</u>ray*
shower	**la doccia** *la <u>do</u>tchaa*
swimming pool	**la piscina** *la pee<u>shee</u>na*
tour operator's bulletin board	**la bacheca dell'agente di viaggio** *la ba<u>kay</u>ka daylla<u>jayn</u>tay dee vee<u>ad</u>jo*
Does the hotel have a garage?	**L'albergo ha un garage?** *lal<u>bayr</u>go ah oon ga<u>razh</u>*
What time is the front door locked?	**A che ora chiudete?** *ah kay <u>o</u>ra kee<u>oo</u>dayteh*
What time is breakfast served?	**A che ora è servita la colazione?** *a kay <u>o</u>ra eh sayr<u>vee</u>ta la kolatsee<u>o</u>nay*
Is there room service?	**C'è servizio camera?** *cheh sayr<u>veet</u>seeo <u>ka</u>mayra*

YOU MAY SEE

SOLO PER RASOI	shavers only
USCITA D'EMERGENZA	emergency exit
PORTA ANTINCENDIO	fire door
NON DISTURBARE	do not disturb
FARE … PER OTTENERE **LA LINEA ESTERNA**	dial … for an outside line

Personal needs

The key to my room, please.	**La chiave della camera, per piacere.** *la keeaavay daylla kamayra pehr peeaachayray*
I've lost my key.	**Ho perso la chiave.** *o pehrso la keeaavay*
I've locked myself out of my room.	**Mi sono chiuso(-a) fuori della camera.** *mee sono keeooso(-a) fworee daylla kamayra*
Could you wake me at …?	**Può svegliarmi alle …?** *pwo zvaylyaarmee allay*
I'd like breakfast in my room.	**Vorrei la colazione in camera.** *vorrehee la kolatseeonay een kamayra*
Can I leave this in the safe?	**Vorrei mettere questo in cassaforte.** *vorrehee mayttehray kwaysto een kassafortay*
Could I have my things from the safe?	**Vorrei ritirare le mie cose dalla cassaforte.** *vorrehee reeteeraaray lay meeay kosay daylla kassafortay*
Where is …?	**Dov'è …?** *doveh?*
a maid	**una cameriera** *oona kamareeehra*
a bellman [porter]	**un portiere** *oon porteeayray*
our tour representative	**il nostro rappresentante?** *eel nostro rappraysayntaantay*
Do you have a(n)/some …?	**Ha …?** *ah*
bath towel	**un asciugamano** *oon ashoogamaano*
blanket	**una coperta** *oona kopehrta*
hangers	**grucce portabiti** *grootchay portabeetee*
pillow	**un cuscino** *oon koosheeno*
soap	**del sapone** *dayl saponay*
Is there any mail for me?	**C'è posta per me?** *cheh posta pehr meh*
Are there any messages for me?	**Ci sono messaggi per me?** *chee sono mayssadjee pehr meh*

Renting

We've reserved an apartment/cottage in the name of …	**Abbiamo prenotato un appartamento/una villa a nome di …** *abbeeamo praynotato oon appartamaynto/oona veella ah nomay dee*
Where do we pick up the keys?	**Dove passiamo a prendere le chiavi?** *dovay passeeamo a prayndehray lay keeaavee*
Where is/are the …?	**Dov'è …?/Dove sono …?** *doveh/doveh sono*
electric meter	**il contatore dell'elettricità** *eel kontatoray dayll aylehttreecheeta*
fuses	**i fusibili** *ee foozeebeelee*
stopcock	**il rubinetto di arresto** *eel roobeenehtto dee arraysto*
water heater	**lo scaldaacqua** *low skalda-akwa*
Are there any spare …?	**Ci sono … di ricambio?** *chee sono … dee reekambeeo*
fuses	**fusibili** *foozeebeelee*
gas bottles	**bombole di gas** *bombolay dee gaz*
sheets	**lenzuola** *layntsoo-ola*
Which day does the maid come?	**Che giorno viene la cameriera?** *kay jorno veeaynay la kamareeayra*
Where/When do I put out the trash?	**Dove/Quando si mettono fuori i rifiuti?** *dovay/kwando see mehttono fworee ee reefeeootee*

Problems?

Where can I contact you?	**Dove posso contattarla?** *dovay posso kontattaarla*
How does the stove/water heater work?	**Come funziona la stufa/lo scaldaacqua?** *komay foontseeona la stoofa/lo skalda-akwa*
The … is dirty.	**Il … è sporco.** *eel … eh sporko*
The … has broken down.	**La … non funziona.** *la … non foontseeona*
We accidentally broke/lost …	**Abbiamo accidentalmente rotto/perso …** *abbeeamo acheedayntalmayntay rotto/pehrso*

USEFUL TERMS

dishes [crockery]	**le stoviglie**	*lay stoveelyay*
freezer	**il congelatore**	*eel konjaylatoray*
frying pan	**la padella**	*la padehlla*
kettle	**il bollitore**	*eel bolleetoray*
lamp	**la lampada**	*la lampada*
refrigerator	**il frigorifero**	*eel freegoreefayro*
saucepan	**la pentola**	*la payntola*
stove [cooker] (gas/electric)	**la cucina a gas/elettrica**	*la koocheena a gaz/aylehttreeka*
utensils [cutlery]	**le posate**	*lay posatay*
washing machine	**la lavatrice**	*la lavatreechay*
water heater	**lo scaldaacqua**	*lo skalda-akwa*

Rooms

balcony	**il balcone**	*eel balkonay*
bathroom	**il bagno**	*eel baanyo*
bedroom	**la camera da letto**	*la kamayra da lehtto*
dining room	**la sala da pranzo/il tinello**	*la saala da prandzo/eel teenehllo*
kitchen	**la cucina**	*la koocheena*
living room	**il soggiorno**	*eel sodjorno*
bathroom [toilet]	**la toilette**	*la toaylehteh*

YOUTH HOSTEL

Do you have any places left for tonight?	**Avete posti liberi per questa notte?** *postee leebayree pehr kwaysta nottay*
Do you rent bedding?	**Noleggiate la biancheria da letto?** *nolehdjatay la beeankayreea da lehtto*
What time are the doors locked?	**A che ora chiudete?** *a kay ora keeoodaytay*

CAMPING

Reservations

Is there a campsite near here?	**C'è un campeggio qui vicino?** *cheh oon kampaydjo kwee veecheeno*
Do you have space for a tent/trailer [caravan]?	**Avete un posto per una tenda/una roulotte?** *avaytay oon posto pehr oona tehnda/oona roolot*
What is the charge …?	**Quanto costa …?** *kwanto kosta*
per day/week	**al giorno/alla settimana** *al jorno/alla saytteemaana*
for a tent/a car	**per una tenda/un'auto(mobile)** *pehr oona tehnda/oonowto (oon owtomobeelay)*
for a trailer [caravan]	**per una roulotte** *pehr oona roolot*

Facilities

Are there cooking facilities on site?	**Ci sono attrezzature per cucinare?** *chee sono attraytsatooray pehr koocheenaaray*
Are there any electrical outlets [power points]?	**Ci sono delle prese di corrente?** *chee sono dayllay prayzay dee korrayntay*
Where is/are the …?	**Dov'è/Dove sono …?** *doveh/dovay sono*
drinking water	**l'acqua potabile** *lakwa potabeelay*
trash cans [dustbins]	**i bidoni dei rifiuti** *ee beedonee day reefeeootee*
laundry facilities	**la lavanderia (sing.)** *la lavandayreea*
showers	**le docce** *lay dotchay*
Where can I get some butane gas?	**Dove si compra il gas?** *dovay see kompra eel gas*

YOU MAY SEE

CAMPEGGIO VIETATO	no camping
ACQUA POTABILE	drinking water
VIETATO ACCENDERE FUOCHI/ CUCINARE ALL'APERTO	no fires/barbeques

Complaints

It's too sunny.	**È troppo esposto al sole.** *eh troppo aysposto al solay*
It's too shady/crowded.	**È troppo ombreggiato/affollato.** *eh troppo ombraydjaato/affollaato*
The ground's too hard/uneven.	**Il terreno è troppo duro/in dislivello.** *eel tayrrayno eh troppo dooro/een deesleevehllo*
Do you have a more level spot?	**C'è uno spazio su terreno più livellato?** *cheh oono spatseeo soo tayrrayno peeoo leevehllaato*
You can't camp here.	**Qui non può campeggiare.** *kwee non pwo kampaydjaaray*

Camping equipment

air mattress	**il materassino di gomma** *eel matayrassino dee gomma*
butane gas	**il campingaz** *eel campingaz*
campbed	**il lettino da campeggio** *eel lehtteeno da kampaydjo*
charcoal	**il carbone** *eel karbonay*
flashlight [torch]	**la torcia** *la torcheea*
groundcloth [groundsheet]	**il telone impermeabile** *eel taylonay eempehrmeeaabeelay*
hammer	**il martello** *eel martehllo*
kerosene [primus] stove	**il fornello da campeggio** *eel fornayllo da kampaydjo*
knapsack/backpack	**lo zaino** *lo dzaaeeno*
mallet	**il maglio** *eel malyo*
matches	**i fiammiferi** *ee feeammeefayree*
sleeping bag	**il sacco a pelo** *eel sakko a paylo*
tent	**la tenda** *la taynda*
tent pegs	**i picchetti** *ee peekkehttee*
tent pole	**il palo della tenda** *eel palo daylla.taynda*

Checking out

Customers are required by law to have a receipt (**ricevuta fiscale**) for any services or goods purchased in hotels, shops, and restaurants.

Tipping: a service charge is generally included in hotel and restaurant bills. However, if the service has been particularly good, you may want to leave an extra tip.

What time do we have to check out?	**A che ora dobbiamo lasciare libere le camere?** *a kay ora dobbeeaamo lashaaray leebayray lay kamayray*
Could we leave our baggagehere until …?	**Possiamo lasciare i bagagli fino alle …?** *posseeaamo lashaaray ee bagalyee feeno allay …*
I'm leaving now.	**Parto ora.** *parto ora*
Could you call me a taxi, please?	**Può chiamarmi un tassì, per piacere?** *pwo keeamaarmee oon tassee pehr peeachayray*
It's been a very enjoyable stay.	**È stato un soggiorno molto piacevole.** *eh staato oon sodjorno molto peeachayvolay*

PAYING

May I have my bill, please?	**Vorrei il conto, per favore.** *vorrehee eel konto pehr favoray*
I think there's a mistake.	**Penso che ci sia un erroreo.** *paynso kay chee seea oon ayrroray*
I've made … telephone calls.	**Ho fatto … telefonate.** *oh fatto … taylayfonatay*
I've taken … from the minibar.	**Ho preso … dal minibar.** *oh prayzo … dal minibar*
Can I have an itemized bill?	**Vorrei un conto dettagliato, per favore.** *vorrehee oon konto dayttalyaato pehr favoray*

TIPPING		
Bellman [Porter] €2–3	Hotel maid (per week) €5	Waiter 5–10%

EATING OUT

RESTAURANTS

Autogrill _owtogreel_
A large restaurant on an expressway [motorway]; usually table and cafeteria service available.

Bar _bar_
Bar; can be found on virtually every street corner; coffee and drinks served. In most of them you first have to pay and get a ticket from the cashier. Then you go to the counter and order what you want.

Caffè _kaffeh_
Coffee shop; generally food isn't served there except for breakfast. If it offers panini (sandwiches) or toast you'll be able to get a snack. Coffee shops always serve alcoholic beverages.

Gelateria _jaylatayreea_
Ice cream parlor; Italian ice cream is very tasty, rich and creamy, often reminiscent of old-fashioned, homemade ice cream. Ice cream and pastries can also be bought and consumed in a **sala da tè.**

Locanda _lokanda_
Simple restaurant serving local dishes.

Osteria _ostayreea_
Inn; wine and simple food are served.

Paninoteca _paneenotayka_
A sort of coffee shop where you can find a great variety of sandwiches (**panini**) served hot or cold.

Ristorante _reestorantay_
You'll encounter restaurants classified by stars or forks and knives and endorsed by everyone including travel agencies, automobile associations and gastronomic guilds. Bear in mind that any form of classification is relative. Some restaurants are judged according to their fancy décor while others – linen and chandeliers aside – are rated merely by the quality of their cooking.

Trattoria _trattoreea_
A medium-priced restaurant serving meals and drinks. The food is simple but can be surprisingly good if you happen to hit upon the right place. A more modest type of **trattoria** is the **taverna.** Bear in mind that some very expensive restaurants may call themselves **Osteria, Trattoria** or **Taverna.**

Most restaurants display a menu in the window. Many offer a tourist menu (**menù turistico**), a fixed-price three- or four-course meal with limited choice, or the specialty of the day (**piatto del giorno**).

All restaurants, no matter how modest, must issue a formal bill (**la ricevuta fiscale**) with VAT, or sales tax (**I.V.A.**). A customer may actually be stopped outside the premises and fined if he or she cannot produce this receipt. The bill usually includes cover (**il coperto**) and service (**il servizio**) charges as well.

You may have difficulty finding a restaurant with a non-smoking area.

MEAL TIMES

la colazione *la kolatseeonay*
Breakfast is usually served at the hotel from 7 to 10 a.m. Hotels usually offer coffee or tea, bread, butter and jam. Italians usually have just a cappuccino and a brioche for breakfast.

il pranzo *eel prandzo*
Lunch is served from 12.30 to 2 p.m.

la cena *la chayna*
Dinner begins at 8 p.m., but hotels tend to open their dining rooms earlier just for foreign tourists. The names of meals can be confusing. Lunch is sometimes called **colazione** and dinner **pranzo**, especially in towns. If you are invited out, make sure of the time, so you don't turn up at the wrong meal.

ITALIAN CUISINE

Italian cuisine consists of a lot more than just pasta. You will be amazed at the rich variety available: tasty hors d'œuvres, long-simmered soups, traditional meat dishes, fresh fish and shellfish, high-quality poultry, an incredible number of cheeses, not to mention the magnificent cakes and ice cream.

Each of Italy's 18 regions has its own specialty, never lacking in flavor or originality, inspired by sun-drenched fruit and vegetables. Italian cooking is like the country itself: colorful, happy, generous, exuberant.

wine cellar	**la cantina**	pizza parlor	**la pizzeria**
take-out/take-away	**da portar via**	self-service	**il self-service**
pub/public house	**il pub**	cafeteria	**il caffè**
stall	**la bancarella**	snack bar	**il bar**
canteen	**la mensa**		

A table for … 1/2/3/4	**Un tavolo per …** *oon tavolo pehr* **uno(-a)/due/tre/quattro** *oono(-a)/doo-ay/tray/kwattro*
Thank you.	**Grazie.** *graatseeay*
The bill, please.	**Il conto, per piacere.** *eel konto pehr peeachayray*

FINDING A PLACE TO EAT

Can you recommend a good restaurant?	**Può consigliare un buon ristorante?** *pwo konseelyaaray oon bwon reestorantay*
Is there a … near here?	**C'è … qui vicino?** *cheh … kwee veecheeno*
traditional local restaurant	**un ristorante con cucina tradizionale** *oon reestorantay kon koocheena tradeetseeonaalay*
Chinese/Greek restaurant	**un ristorante cinese/greco** *oon reestorantay cheenaysay/grayko*
inexpensive restaurant	**una trattoria** *oona trattoreea*
Turkish restaurant	**un ristorante turco** *oon reestorantay toorko*
vegetarian restaurant	**un ristorante vegetariano** *oon reestorantay vayjaytareeaano*
Where can I find a/an …?	**Dove si trova …?** *dovay see trova*
burger stand	**un chiosco dove vendono hamburger** *oon keeosko dovay vayndono hamburger*
café	**un bar** *oon bar*
café with terrace/garden	**un bar con terrazza/giardino** *oon bar kon tayrratsa/jardeeno*
fast-food restaurant	**una tavola calda (un self-service)** *oona tavola kalda (oon self-service)*
ice cream parlor [parlour]	**una gelateria** *oona jaylatayreea*
pizzeria	**una pizzeria** *oona peettsayreea*
steak house	**ristorante specializzato in bistecche** *reestorantay spaychaleedzato een beestaykkay*

RESERVATIONS

I'd like to reserve a table for 2.	**Vorrei prenotare un tavolo per due.** *vorrehee praynotaaray oon tavolo pehr dooay*
For this evening/ tomorrow at ...	**Per questa sera/domani alle ...** *pehr kwaysta sayra/domanee allay*
We'll come at 8:00.	**Arriveremo alle otto.** *arreevayraymo allay otto*
A table for 2, please.	**Un tavolo per due, per piacere.** *oon tavolo pehr dooay pehr peeachayray*
We have a reservation.	**Abbiamo una prenotazione.** *abbeeamo oona praynotatseeonay*

YOU MAY HEAR

A che nome, prego?	What's the name, please?
Mi dispiace. Siamo al completo.	I'm sorry. We're very busy/full.
Avremo un tavolo libero fra ... minuti.	We'll have a free table in ... minutes.
Dovrà ritornare fra ... minuti.	You'll have to come back in ... minutes.

Where to sit

Could we sit over there?	**Possiamo sederci là?** *posseeaamo saydayrchee la*
in a non-smoking area	**in una zona per non fumatori** *een oona dzona pehr non foomatoree*
by the window	**vicino alla finestra** *veecheeno alla feenaystra*

IN A RESTAURANT

Scusi! *scoosee* (Excuse me!)
Sì, Signora. *see sinyohrah* (Yes, m'am.)
Il menù, per favore. *eel maynoo pehr favoray* (The menu, please.)
Certamente. *cherta menteh* (Certainly.)

YOU MAY HEAR

E' pronto(-a) per ordinare?	Are you ready to order?
Che cosa prende/desidera?	What would you like?
Vuole ordinare prima le bibite?	Would you like to order drinks first?
Consiglio …	I recommend …
Non abbiamo …	We haven't got …
Ci vogliono … minuti.	That will take … minutes.
Buon appetito!	Enjoy your meal.

ORDERING

Excuse me! — **Scusi!** *scoosee*

May I see the wine list, please? — **Posso vedere la lista dei vini, per piacere?** *posso vedayray la leesta dehee veenee pehr peeachayray*

Do you have a set menu? — **Avete un menù fisso?** *avaytay oon maynoo feesso*

Can you recommend some typical local dishes? — **Può consigliare dei piatti tipici della regione?** *pwo konseelyaarmee dehee peeattee teepeechee daylla rayjonay*

Could you tell me what … is? — **Cos'è …?** *kozay*

I'd like … — **Vorrei …** *vorrehee*

a bottle/glass/carafe of … — **una bottiglia/un bicchiere/una caraffa di …** *oona botteelya/oon beekkeeehray/oona karaffa dee*

IN A RESTAURANT

Un tavolo per due, per piacere. *oon tavolo per dooay pehr peeachayray* (A table for two, please.)
Fumatori o non fumatori? *foomatoree o non foomatoree* (Smoking or non-smoking?)
Non fumatori. *non foomatoree* (Non-smoking.)

37

I prefer …	**Preferisco … senza …**
without the …	*prayfayreesko … sayntsa*
With a side order of …	**Con contorno di …**
	kon kontorno dee
Could I have salad instead of vegetables, please?	**Si può avere insalata al posto della verdura?**
	see pwo avayray eensalaata al posto daylla verdoora
Does the meal come with vegetables/potatoes?	**Il piatto include legumi/patate?**
	eel peeatto eenklooday laygoomee/patatay
Do you have any sauces?	**Ha delle salse?** *ah dayllay salsay*
Would you like … with your dish?	**Vuole … con il Suo piatto?**
	vwolay kon eel soo-o peeatto
vegetables	**verdura**
	vayrdoora
mixed salad	**insalata mista** *eensalaata meesta*
potatoes/French fries [chips]	**patate/patatine fritte**
	patatay/patateenay freettay
sauce	**la salsa** *la salsa*
ice	**il ghiaccio** *eel geeatcho*
May I have some …?	**Mi può portare …?**
	mee pwo portaaray
bread	**del pane** *dayl panay*
butter	**del burro** *dayl boorro*
lemon	**del limone** *dayl leemonay*
mustard	**della senape** *daylla saynapay*
pepper	**del pepe** *dayl paypay*
salt	**del sale** *dayl salay*
seasoning (oil/vinegar)	**dei condimenti (olio/aceto)**
	dehee kondeemayntee (olyo/achayto)
sugar	**dello zucchero**
	dayllo tsookkayro
(artificial) sweetener	**del dolcificante**
	dayl dolcheefeekantay

General requests

Could you bring a(n) (clean) …, please?	**Può portare … (pulito), per piacere?**
	pwo portaaray (pooleeto) pehr peeachayray
ashtray	**un portacenere**
	oon portachaynayray
cup/glass	**una tazza/un bicchiere**
	oona tattsa/oon beekkeeeehray
fork/knife	**una forchetta/un coltello**
	oona forkehtta/oon koltehllo
napkin	**un tovagliolo** *oon tovalyolo*
plate/spoon/little spoon	**un piatto/un cucchiaio/un cucchiaino**
	oon peeatto/oon kookkeeaeeo/oon kookkeeaeeno
I'd like some more …, please.	**Vorrei ancora un po' di …, per piacere.**
	vorrehee ankora oon poh dee … pehr peeachayray
Nothing more, thanks.	**Nient'altro, grazie.** *neeehntaltro gratseeay*
Where are the restrooms [toilets]?	**Dov'è la toilette?**
	dovay la toylayttay

Special requirements

I can't eat food containing …	**Non posso mangiare piatti che contengono …**
	non posso manjaaray peeattee kay kontayngono
salt/sugar	**sale/zucchero** *salay/tsookkayro*
Do you have meals/drinks for diabetics?	**Avete piatti/bevande per diabetici?** *avaytay peeattee/bayvanday pehr deeabayteechee*
Do you have vegetarian dishes?	**Avete piatti vegetariani?**
	avaytay peeattee vayjaytareeanee

For the children

Do you have children's portions?	**Fate porzioni per bambini?**
	fatay portseeonee pehr bambeenee
Could you bring a child's seat, please?	**Può portare un seggiolone per bambini, per piacere?** *pwo portaaray oon saydjolonay pehr bambeenee pehr peeachayray*

FAST FOOD

Bars and cafés play an important part in Italian life; there is one on almost every corner. They are an ideal place to meet people, revive weary feet, write postcards, study maps, or just watch the world go by while sipping a cappuccino or beer. Bar staff are usually friendly and a great source of local information.

Something to drink

I'd like …	**Vorrei …** _vorrehee_
a beer	**una birra** _oona beerra_
coffee	**un caffè** _oon kaffeh_
with milk	**con latte** _kon lattay_
tea	**un tè** _oon teh_
red/white wine	**del vino rosso/bianco** _dayl veeno rosso/beeanko_

And to eat …

A piece/slice of …, please.	**Un pezzo/una fetta di … , per piacere** _oon pehtso/oona fehtta dee … pehr peeachayray_
I'd like two of those.	**Vorrei due di quelli(e).** _vorrehee doo-ay dee kwehllee (ay)_
burger/French fries	**un hamburger/delle patatine fritte** _oon hamburger/dayllay patateenay freettay_
cake/sandwich	**una torta/un panino** _oona torta/oon paneeno_
bun/pastry	**una pasta** _oona pasta_
an ice cream	**un gelato** _oon jaylaato_

Ice cream; flavors include: **alla vaniglia** or **alla crema** (vanilla), **al cioccolato** (chocolate), **alla fragola** (strawberry), **al limone** (lemon), **misto** (mixed).

a sandwich	**un panino** _oon paneeno_

Sandwich; you may want yours **con il formaggio** (cheese), **con il prosciutto cotto** (ham), **con il prosciutto crudo** (Parma ham) or **con il al salame** (salami).

A … portion, please.	**Una porzione … , per piacere.** _oona portseeonay … pehr peeachayray_
small/medium/large	**piccola/media/grande** _peekkola/medeea/granday_

IN A CAFÉ

Due caffè, per piacere. _dooay kaffeh_ pehr peea_chay_ray
(Two coffees, please.)
Nient'altro? neeayn _taltro (Anything else?)_
No, grazie. no _graatseeay (No, thanks.)_

COMPLAINTS

I have no knife/ fork/spoon.	**Non ho il coltello/la forchetta/il cucchiaio.** non oh eel kol_tay_llo/la for_kay_tta/eel kookee_a_eeo
There must be some mistake.	**Deve esserci un errore.** _day_vay _ehs_sayrchee oon ehr_ro_ray
That's not what I ordered.	**Non ho ordinato questo.** non oh ordee_naa_to kwaysto
I ordered …	**Ho ordinato …** oh ordee_naa_to
The meat is …	**La carne è …** la _kar_nay eh
overdone	**troppo cotta** _troppo kotta_
underdone	**non abbastanza cotta** non abba_stant_sa _kotta_
too tough	**troppo dura** _troppo doora_
This is too …	**Questo è troppo …** kwaysto eh _troppo_
bitter/sour	**amaro/aspro** a_maaro/aspro_
This … is cold.	**Questo … è freddo.** kwaysto … eh _frehddo_
This isn't fresh.	**Questo non è fresco.** kwaysto non eh _fraysko_
How much longer will our food be?	**Quanto dobbiamo aspettare ancora?** _kwan_to dobbee_aa_mo aspayt_ta_ray an_kora_
We can't wait any longer. We're leaving.	**Non possiamo più aspettare. Andiamo** **via.** non possee_aa_mo pee_oo_ aspeht_taa_ray andee_aa_mo _veea_
This isn't clean.	**Questo non è pulito.** kwaysto non eh poo_lee_to
I'd like to speak to the head waiter/manager.	**Vorrei parlare con il capocameriere/** **il direttore.** Vor_reh_e par_laa_ray kon eel kapokamayree-_eh_ray/eel deerayt_to_ray

PAYING

A service charge (**il servizio**) is generally included in restaurant bills, but if the service has been especially good, an extra tip (**la mancia**) is appropriate and appreciated: 5–10%. You may also find the following items added to your bill: **coperto** (cover charge), **supplemento** (surcharge).

The check [bill], please.	**Il conto, per piacere.**
	eel konto pehr peeachayray
We'd like to pay separately.	**Vorremmo pagare separatamente.**
	vorrehmmo pagaaray sayparatamayntay
It's all together, please.	**Un conto unico, per piacere.**
	oon konto ooneeko pehr peeachayray
I think there's a mistake.	**Penso ci sia un errore.**
	paynso chee seea oon ehrroray
What is this amount for?	**Per cosa è questa cifra?**
	pehr kosa eh kwaysta cheefra
I didn't order that. I had …	**Non ho ordinato questo. Ho preso …**
	non oh ordeenaato kwaysto. oh prayzo
Is service included?	**Il servizio è compreso ?**
	eel sayrveetseeo eh komprayzo
I would like to pay with this credit card.	**Vorrei pagare con la carta di credito.**
	vorrehee pagaaray kon la karta dee kraydeeto
I haven't got enough cash.	**Non ho abbastanza contanti.**
	non oh abbastantsa kontantee
Could I have a receipt?	**Vorrei la ricevuta.**
	vorrehee la reechayvoota

IN A RESTAURANT

Il conto, per piacere. *eel konto pehr peeachayray*
(The bill please.)
Certamente. Ecco a Lei. *chertamenteh ekko a lay*
(Of course. Here you are.)
Grazie. *graatseeay (Thank you.)*

COURSE BY COURSE

Breakfast

I'd like …	**Vorrei …** *vorrehee*
bread	**del pane** *dayl paanay*
butter	**del burro** *dayl boorro*
eggs	**delle uova** *dayllay wova*
fried/scrambled	**fritte/strapazzate** *freettay/strapattsaatay*
fruit juice	**un succo di frutta** *oon sookko dee frootta*
grapefruit/orange	**un pompelmo/un'arancia** *oon pompaylmo/oon arancheea*
milk	**del latte** *dayl lattay*
jam	**della marmellata** *daylla marmayllaata*
marmalade	**della marmellata d'arance** *daylla marmayllaata daranchay*
honey	**del miele** *dayl mee-aylay*
rolls	**dei panini** *dehee paneenee*
toast	**del pane tostato** *dayl paanay tostaato*

Appetizers/Starters

anchovies	**acciughe** *achoogay*
assorted appetizer	**antipasto assortito** *anteepasto assorteeto*
artichoke hearts in olive oil	**carciofini sott'olio** *karchofeenee sottolyo*
cured pork shoulder	**coppa** *koppa*
Bologna sausage	**mortadella** *mortadehlla*
cured ham from Parma	**prosciutto crudo di Parma** *proshootto kroodo dee parma*
pickled vegetables	**sottaceti** *sottachaytee*

bagna cauda *baanya kaooda*
raw vegetables accompanied by a hot sauce made from anchovies, garlic, oil, butter and sometimes truffles (Northern Italy)

Pizza (plural **pizze**) is one of Italy's best-known culinary exports. The variety of toppings is endless. A **calzone** has basically the same ingredients, but the pastry forms a sealed sandwich, with the filling inside.

con i funghi	*kon ee foonggee*	with mushrooms
capricciosa	*kapreetchosa*	the cook's specialty
siciliana	*seecheeleeaana*	with black olives, capers and cheese

margherita *margayreeta*
named after Italy's first queen, the pizza ingredients (tomato, cheese and basil or oregano) reflect the national colors

napoletana *napolaytaana*
the classic pizza with anchovies, tomatoes, and cheese

quattro formaggi *kwattro formadjee*
pizza with four types of cheese, usually including **gorgonzola** and **caciotta**

quattro stagioni *kwattro stajonee*
"four seasons", containing a variety of vegetables: tomatoes, artichokes, mushrooms, olives; plus cheese, and ham

Soups

An Italian meal always includes a **pastasciutta** or a soup; some of them are sufficient for a main course.

brodo di manzo	*brodo dee manzo*	beef broth
busecca	*boozaykka*	thick tripe, vegetable and bean soup
cacciucco	*kachookko*	spicy seafood chowder/stew
crema di legumi	*krehma dee laygoomee*	legumes cream soup
minestrone	*meenehstronay*	vegetable soup (sometimes with noodles) sprinkled with parmesan cheese
passato di verdura	*passaato dee vehrdoora*	mashed vegetable soup, generally with croutons
zuppa alla pavese	*tsooppa alla pavayzay*	consommé with poached egg, croutons and cheese
zuppa di vongole	*tsooppa dee vonggolay*	clams and white wine soup

Pasta

Pasta (or **pastasciutta**) constitutes the traditional Italian first course. In addition to the well-known **spaghetti**, pasta comes in a bewildering variety of sizes and shapes– **penne** (quills), **tagliatelle** (flat noodles), and the following examples:

cannelloni *kanaylonee*
tubular dough stuffed with meat, cheese or vegetables, covered with a white sauce and baked

cappelletti *kapaylayttee*
small ravioli filled with meat, ham, cheese and eggs

fettuccine *faytoocheenay*
narrow flat noodles made with eggs

lasagne *lazaanyay*
thin layers of white or green (**lasagne verdi**) dough alternating with tomato sauce and sausage meat, white sauce and grated cheese; baked in the oven

tortellini *tortehlleenee*
rings of dough filled with ground meat in broth or with a sauce

Fish and seafood

acciughe	*atchoogay*	anchovies
anguilla	*anggooeella*	eel
bianchetti	*beeangkayttee*	herring/whitebait
gamberi	*gambayree*	prawns
granchi	*grangkee*	crabs
merluzzo	*mayrloottso*	cod
polipo	*poleepo*	octopus
sogliola	*solyola*	sole

Fish specialties Specialità di pesce

anguilla alla veneziana *anggooeella alla vaynaytseeaana*
eel cooked in sauce made from tuna and lemon

fritto misto *freetto meesto*
fry of small fish and shellfish

lumache alle milanese *loomaakay allay meelanaysay*
snails with anchovy, fennel and wine sauce

stoccafisso *stokkafeesso*
dried cod cooked with tomatoes, olives and artichokes

Among small fowl considered gourmet dishes in Italy are lark (**allodola**), thrush (**tordo**) and ortolan (**ortolano**). They are usually grilled or roasted.

Vorrei ...	*vorrehee*	I'd like some ...
del manzo	*dayl mandzo*	beef
del pollo	*dayl pollo*	chicken
dell'anatra	*dayllaanatra*	duck
dell'oca	*daylloka*	goose
del prosciutto	*dayl proshootto*	ham
dell'agnello	*dayllanyehllo*	lamb
del maiale	*dayl maeeaalay*	pork
delle salsicce	*dayllay salseetchay*	sausages
del vitello	*dayl veetehllo*	veal

Meat dishes

bistecca alla fiorentina *beestaykka alla feeoraynteena*
grilled steak flavored with pepper, lemon juice and parsley

cima alla genovese *cheema alla jaynovaysay*
rolled veal stuffed with eggs, sausage and mushrooms

cotoletta alla milanese *kostolaytta alla meelanaysay*
breaded veal cutlet

fegato alla veneziana *faygato alla vaynaytseeaana*
thin slices of calf's liver fried with onions

filetto al pepe verde *feelaytto al paypay vehrday*
filet steak in a creamy sauce with green peppercorns

galletto amburghese *gallaytto amboorgaysay*
young tender chicken, oven-roasted

involtini *eenvolteenee*
thin slices of meat rolled and stuffed with ham

polenta e coniglio *polehnta ay koneelyo*
rabbit stew with cornmeal mush

pollo alla romana *pollo alla romaana*
diced chicken with tomato sauce and sweet peppers

saltimbocca alla romana *salteembokah alla romaana*
veal escalope braised in marsala wine with ham and sage

Vegetables/Salads

You'll recognize: **asparagi**, **broccoli**, **carote**, **patate**, **spinaci**, **zucchini**.

cavolo	_kaavolo_	cabbage
cipolle	_cheepollay_	onions
funghi	_foonggee_	mushrooms
insalata mista	_eensalaata meesta_	mixed salad
lattuga	_lattooga_	lettuce
piselli	_peesehllee_	peas
pomodoro	_pomodoro_	tomato
verdura mista	_vehrdoora meesta_	mixed vegetables

carciofi alla giudea _karchofee alla jeeoodeea_
deep-fried artichoke, originally a specialty of the old Jewish quarter in Rome

carciofi alla romana _karchofee alla romaana_
whole lightly stewed artichokes stuffed with garlic, salt, olive oil, wild mint (**mentuccia**) and parsley

fagioli alla toscana _fajolee alla toskana_
Tuscan-style beans, seasoned with salt, black pepper and crude olive oil

fagioli in umido _fajolee een oomeedo_
all types of haricot beans cooked in tomato sauce and spices

funghi porcini arrosto _foonggee porcheenee arrosto_
boletus mushrooms roasted or grilled with garlic, parsley and chili peppers

peperoni ripieni _paypayronee reepeeaynee_
stuffed sweet peppers (usually containing ground meat); similarly, zucchini is also served this way (**zucchini ripieni**)

Sauces

Italian cooks are masters at making the sauces that make spaghetti and macaroni taste so delicious.

al burro	_al boorro_	butter, grated parmesan
bolognese	_bolonyayzay_	tomatoes, ground meat, onions, herbs
carbonara	_karbonaara_	bacon, cheese, eggs, olive oil
pesto	_paysto_	basil leaves, garlic, cheese
al pomodoro	_al pommodoro_	tomatoes, garlic, basil

Cheese

bel paese	smooth cheese with delicate taste
caciotta	firm, usually mild cheese; some sharper varieties can be found
caciocavallo	firm, slightly sweet cheese from cow's or sheep's milk
gorgonzola	blue-veined cheese, rich with a tangy flavor
grana	a grained cheese similar to parmesan originating from Padova usually grated on pasta dishes
mascarpone	a thick, full-fat creamy cheese mostly used for desserts; similar to clotted cream
mozzarella	soft, unripened cheese with a bland, flavor, made from buffalo's milk in the south, elsewhere with cow's milk
parmigiano (-reggiano)	parmesan, a hard cheese generally grated for use in hot dishes and pasta but also eaten alone
pecorino	a hard cheese with a strong flavor made from sheep's milk usually grated on certain pasta dishes
provolone	a firm, tasty cheese
ricotta	soft cow's or sheep's milk cheese

Fruit

You'll recognize: **banane**, **dattero**, **limone**, **melone**, **pera**.

ciliege	_cheelee-ehjay_	cherries
uva	_oova_	grapes
arancia	_arancha_	orange
pesca	_pehska_	peach
prugna	_proonya_	plum
lamponi	_lamponee_	raspberries
fragole	_fraagolay_	strawberries
anguria	_angoorreea_	watermelon (northern Italy)
cocomero	_kokomayro_	watermelon (southern Italy)

Dessert

cassata siciliana _kassaata seecheeleeaana_
sponge cake garnished with sweet cream cheese, chocolate and candied fruit

tiramisù _teerameesoo_
mascarpone, eggs and sponge cake chocolate dessert

DRINKS

Aperitifs

Often bittersweet, some aperitifs have a wine and brandy base with herbs and bitters, while others may have a vegetable base.

americano *amayreekaano*: vermouth with bitters, brandy and lemon peel

aperol *apayrol*: a non-alcoholic bitters

bitter analcolico *beettehr analkoleeko*: a non-alcoholic aperitif

Campari *kampaaree*: reddish-brown bitters with orange peel and herbs

Campari soda *kampaaree soda*: Campari diluted with soda

Cynar *cheenaar*: produced from artichoke

gingerino *jeenjehreeno*: ginger-flavored aperitif

Martini *marhteenee*: brand-name vermouth, sweet or dry

neat/straight	**liscio** *leesho*
on the rocks	**con ghiaccio** *kon geeacho*
with (seltzer or soda) water	**con acqua (di seltz)** *kon akwa (dee sehltz)*

Beer

Do you have … beer?	**Avete della birra …?** *avayta daylla beerra*
bottled/draft/draught	**in bottiglia/alla spina** *een botteelya/alla speena*

Wine

Italy is one of the most important wine producers in Europe. Some of the country's best come from northwestern Italy (like *Barbaresco*, *Barbera* and *Barolo*). Italy's best-known wine abroad is Chianti, particularly **classico** and **riserva** (superior quality); the best is produced between Florence and Siena.

Quality bottled wine from the various regions is now easily available all over Italy in restaurants and specialized wine shops (*enoteche*).

Don't expect a trattoria to offer more than a few types of wine. In smaller places you may find **vino sfuso** (unbottled wine usually served as house wine) at a moderate price, served in one-quarter, one-half or one-liter carafes.

I'd like a bottle of white/ red wine.	**Vorrei una bottiglia di vino bianco/ rosso.** *vorrehee oona botteelya dee veeno beeanko/rosso*
I'd like the house wine, please.	**Desidero il vino della casa, per favore.** *dayzeedayro eel veeno dayllya kassa pehr favoray*

Italian wines may be named by place (e.g. *Chianti*, *Frascati*, *Asti*), descriptive term (e.g. **classico**, **dolce**, **riserva**, **superiore**), grape (e.g. **Barbera**, **Moscato**, **Pinot nero**), proprietary name or a combination of these elements.

Type of wine	*Examples*
sweet white wine	**Aleatico, Vino Santo (Tuscany); Marsala and Malvasia (Sicily), Moscato, Passito di Pantelleria**
dry white wine	**Frascati (Latium), Verdicchio dei Castelli di Jesi (Adriatic Marches), Orvieto (Umbria), Vermentino (Sardinia), Corvo bianco, Colombo Platino (Sicily); Cortese di Gavi (Liguria) Gavi dei Gavi (Piedmont) Chardonnay, Pinot bianco, Pinot grigio (Friuli); local white wine generally falls into this category**
rosé	**Lagrein (Trentino-Alto Adige)**
light-bodied red wine	**Bardolino, Valpolicella (Lake Garda); Vino Novello (in the Autumn); local red wine, including Italian-Swiss Merlot, usually fits into this category**
full-bodied red wine	**Barolo, Barbera, Barbaresco, Dolcetto, Gattinara, Nebbiolo (Piedmont); Amarone (Veneto); Brunello di Montalcino (one of the most famous wines in Italy), Chianti Classico, Vino Nobile di Montepulciano (Tuscany); Corvo Rosso (Sicily).**
sparkling wine	**Asti Spumante**
sparkling dry white wine	**Prosecco, Ferrari Brut Spumante; metodo champenoise in general**
sparkling sweet red wine	**Braghetto d'Acqui (Piedmont); Fragolino (made from "uva fragola" with a distinct strawberry flavour, Veneto region)**

Reading the label

abboccato semi-dry"	**leggero** light
amabile slightly sweet	**pieno** full-bodied
bianco white	**rosato/rosatello** rosé
DOC guarantee of origin	**rosso** red
DOCG highest quality wine	**secco** dry
dolce sweet	**spumante** sparkling
imbottigliato dal produttore	**vino del paese** local wine
all'origine bottled by producers	**vino tipico** basic table wine

50

Other drinks

You'll certainly want to take the opportunity to sip an after-dinner drink. If you'd like something that approaches French cognac try **Vecchia Romagna etichetta nera** or **Carpenet Malvolta Stravecchio**.

If you feel like an after-dinner drink (**un digestivo**), why not try the following:

amaro *amaaro*

Bitter; three of the most popular being *Amaro Averna*, *Amaro Lucano* or *Amaro Montenegro* (bittersweet), or a glass of *Fernet-Branca* (very bitter) should fit the bill.

liquore *leekworay*

Popular liqueurs include *Strega* (sweet herb), *Sambuca* (aniseed-flavored), *Amaretto* (almond), *Millefiori* (herb and alpine flower), *Silvestro* (herb and nut).

You'll recognize: **un brandy**, **un cognac**, **un gin e tonic**, **un porto**, **un rum**, **una vodka**.

Non-alcoholic drinks

I'd like …	**Vorrei …** *vorrehee*
hot chocolate	**una cioccolata calda** *oona chokkolaata kalda*
lemonade	**una limonata** *oona leemonaata*
milk shake	**un frullato** *oon froollaato*
mineral water	**dell'acqua minerale** *dayllakwa meenayraalay*
carbonated/non-carbonated	**gassata/naturale** *gassaata/natooraalay*
tonic water	**dell'acqua tonica** *dayllakwa toneeka*

un caffè *oon kaffeh*

Any coffee drinker will be spoiled in Italy; try un **caffè** (**espresso**), strong and dark with a rich aroma, served in demi-tasses, or **un ristretto** (concentrated espresso); alternatively, ask for **un caffè lungo** (weaker coffee), which can be **con panna** (with cream), or **con latte** (with milk). **Un cappuccino** (coffee and hot milk, sometimes dusted with cocoa) is also a must; while in summer, **un caffè freddo** (iced coffee) is popular.

un succo di frutta *oon sookko dee frootta*

Common juices include: **un succo di limone** (lemon), **di pompelmo** (grapefruit), **di pomodoro** (tomato) and **d'arancia** (orange); for a freshly squeezed fruit juice ask for **una spremuta**.

MENU READER

Italian cooking is essentially regional. Although there are many well-known dishes that are common to the whole of Italy, the terminology may vary from place to place. (There are at least half a dozen names for octopus or squid!) So, be prepared for regional variations to the terms appearing in this Menu Reader.

HOW IT IS COOKED

baked	al forno	al *forno*
breaded	impanato(-a)	eempanaato(-a)
boiled	bollito(-a)	bolleeto(-a)
braised	stufato(-a)	stoofaato(-a)
diced	tagliato(-a) a cubetti	talyaato(-a) a koobayttee
fried	fritto(-a)	freetto(-a)
grilled	alla griglia	alla greelya
roasted	arrosto(-a)	arrosto(-a)
poached	in camicia	een kameecha
marinated	marinato(-a)	mareenaato(-a)
sautéed	saltato(-a)	saltaato(-a)
smoked	affumicato(-a)	affoomeekaato(-a)
spicy	speziato(-a)/piccante	spaytsaato(-a)/peekkantay
steamed	al vapore	al vaporay
stewed	in umido	een oomeedo
stuffed	ripieno(-a)	reepeeayno(-a)
creamed	in purè	een pooreh
very rare	quasi crudo(-a)	kwasee kroodo(-a)
rare/underdone	al sangue	al sanway
medium	a puntino	a poonteeno
well-done	ben cotto(-a)	behn kotto (a)

A

a puntino medium
a scelta choice
abbacchio roast lamb; ~ al forno
con patate with potatoes; ~ alla

cacciatora "hunting style": diced and cooked with white wine, garlic, rosemary, anchovy paste and peppers
abbacchio alla scottadito tender grilled lamb cutlets

(all')abruzzese Abruzzi style; with red peppers and sometimes ham
acciughe anchovies
aceto vinegar
acetosella sorrel
acqua water; **~ calda** hot water; **~ minerale** mineral water; **~ tonica** tonic water
acquacotta soup of bread and vegetables, sometimes with egg and cheese
affettati cold cuts; **~ misti** mixed cuts of pork
affogato poached
affumicato smoked
aglio garlic; **~ olio, peperoncino** sauce of garlic, olive oil, sweet peppers, anchovies and parmesan
agnello lamb; **~ abbacchio** very young lamb
agnolotti round-filled pasta
(all')agro dressing of lemon juice and oil
agrodolce sweet-sour dressing of caramelized sugar, vinegar and flour
aguglie garfish
ai ferri grilled
ai funghi (pizza) with mushrooms
ai funghi porcini sauce of boletus mushrooms
al burro with butter and grated parmesan
al forno baked
al sangue rare/underdone
al sugo with tomato sauce and grated parmesan
al tartufo sauce of grated truffle
al, all', alla in the style of; with
ala wing
albicocca apricot
alfredo dairy sauce
alice anchovy

alici al limone baked anchovies with lemon juice
alla boscaiola with eggplant, mushrooms and tomato sauce
alla carrettiera "cart driver style"; with hot peppers and pork
alla graticola barbequed
alla griglia grilled
alla milanese with marrow, white wine, saffron and parmesan (risotto)
alla Norma with spices and tomato sauce *(Sicily)*
alla pescatora with tomatoes and seafood
alla rustica with garlic, anchovies and oregano
alla spina draft/draught (beer)
alle vongole sauce of clams, garlic, parsley, pepper, olive oil, sometimes tomatoes
allo spiedo broiled; spit-roasted
allodola lark
alloro bay leaf
amaro after-dinner drink/digestive
amatriciana sauce of tomatoes, pancetta, onions, garlic and hot pepper
americano a vermouth
ananas pineapple
anelli small egg-pasta rings
anguilla eel; **~ alla veneziana** cooked in sauce made from tuna and lemon
anguria watermelon *(northern Italy)*
animelle di vitello calf's sweet-breads fried in butter and Marsala
anitra duck; **~ selvatica** wild duck
annegati slices of meat in white wine or Marsala

antipasti appetizers, hors d'oeuvres; **~ a scelta** of one's choice; **~ assortiti** assorted; **~ di mare** seafood

aperitivi aperitifs

Aperol a non-alcoholic bitters

arachidi peanuts

aragosta lobster

arancia orange

aranciata orangeade

arancini popular and tasty southern Italian rice snack specialties

aringa herring

arista loin of pork; **~ alla fiorentina** roast with garlic, cloves and rosemary

arrosto roast(ed)

arselle scallops

asparagi asparagus; **~ alla Fiorentina** with fried eggs and cheese

assortito assorted

astice lobster

attesa: 15 minuti waiting time: 15 minutes

baccalà dried salt cod; **~ alla romana** cooked with tomato sauce, garlic and parsley; **~ alla vicentina** cooked in milk

bagna cauda raw vegetables served with a hot sauce (*a specialty in northern Italy*)

barbabietola beet

basilico basil

bavette type of flat spaghetti

beccaccia woodcock

beccaccino snipe

bel paese smooth cheese with delicate taste

ben cotto well-done

bevande drinks; **~ analcoliche** non-alcoholic drinks

bianchetti herring/whitebait

bianco white (wine)

bibita soft drink

bicchiere glass

bieta swiss chard

bionda light (beer)

birra beer; **~ rossa** stout (dark beer)

biscotti cookies/biscuits

bistecca steak; **~ di cinghiale** wild boar in a sweet-sour sauce; **~ alla fiorentina** grilled and flavored with pepper, lemon juice and parsley; **~ di filetto** rib steak

bitter analcolico a non-alcoholic aperitif

bollito boiled

bollito misto mixed boiled meats

bologna smooth, mild, slightly smoked sausage, usually of pork or beef, occasionally of veal or chicken

bolognese sauce of tomatoes, ground meat, onions and herbs

bottiglia bottle

braciola chop or cutlet

branzino (sea) bass

brasato braised

briciolata olive oil, black pepper and crisp breadcrumb sauce

broccoli broccoli; **~ al burro e formaggio** with butter and cheese; **~ alla romana** sauteed in olice oil and braised in wine

brodo bouillon, broth, soup

bruidda fish soup

bucatini thick spaghetti; **~ con le sarde alla palermitana** with fresh sardines

budino pudding; **~ di ricotta** souffle with ricotta cheese and candied fruits

burrida fish stew with dogfish and skate *(Sardinia)*

burro butter; **~ e salvia** butter and sage sauce

busecca thick tripe, vegetable and bean soup

C

cacciagione game

cacciucco spicy seafood chowder/stew

cachi persimmon

caciocavallo firm, slightly sweet cheese

caciotta firm, mild cheese

caffè coffee

caffè freddo iced coffee

calamaretti baby squid

calamari squid

caldo hot

camoscio chamois

Campari reddish-brown bitters, flavored with orange peel and herbs; has a quinine taste; **~ soda** *campari* diluted with soda, one of the most common Italian apertifis

canederli bread, ham and salami dumplings

cannariculi fried honey biscuits

cannella cinnamon

cannelloni stuffed tubular pasta baked with a white sauce; **~ alla partenopea** with ricotta, mozzarella and ham

cannoli sweetened ricotta cheese stuffed in deep-fried pastry shells

canoe di mele canoe-shaped pastry boats with rum pastry cream and glazed apples

canoe salate savory canoes

capellini thin type of spaghetti

caponata olives, eggplants and anchovies *(Sicily)*

capone apparecchiate mahi mahi fish fried with tomatoes, capers, olives *(Sicily)*

cappelletti "little hats" filled pasta

capperi capers

cappone capon

capretto kid goat; **~ ripieno al forno** stuffed with herbs and oven-roasted

capricciosa the cook's specialty (pizza)

capriolo roebuck

carbonara sauce of bacon, pepper, pecorino, cheese, eggs and olive oil

carciofi artichokes; **~ alla giudea** deep-fried; **~ alla romana** lightly stewed and stuffed

carciofini sott'olio artichoke hearts in olive oil

carne meat; **~ ai ferri** grilled

carota carrot; **~ rossa** beet

carpa carp

carrettiera sauce of tuna, mushrooms, tomato purée, freshly ground pepper

cassata ice cream with candied fruit (spumone); **~ siciliana** garnished sponge cake

castagna chestnut

castagnaccio chestnut cake with sultanas and pine nuts *(Tuscany)*

caviale caviar

cavolfiore cauliflower; **~ stracciato** boiled and fried in olive oil and garlic

cavolini di Bruxelles Brussels sprouts

cavolo cabbage
ceci chickpeas
cedro citron
cereali cereal
cervello brains
cervo deer
cetriolini pickles/gherkins
cetriolo cucumber
chiodi di garofano cloves
cicoria chicory
ciliege cherries
cima alla genovese rolled veal stuffed with eggs, sausage and mushrooms
cima genovese cold veal stuffed with onions, herbs and calf's brains
cinghiale wild boar
cioccolata (calda) (hot) chocolate
cipolle onions
cipollina spring onion
clementino seedless mandarin orange
cocomero watermelon (*Rome, southern Italy*)
colazione breakfast
con with
con acqua (di seltz) with (seltzer or soda) water
con briciolata with toasted breadcrumbs
con i funghi with mushrooms
con ghiaccio on the rocks (with ice)
con il sugo di melanze e peperoni sauce with pepper and eggplant
con il latte with milk
con le lumache with snails and parsley
con il limone with lemon
con la panna with cream
con le polpettine with tiny meatballs

con la porchetta with tasty cold pork (sandwich)
con la salsa di noci with walnut sauce
conchiglie conch shell-shaped pasta
coniglio rabbit; **~ ai capperi** cooked with capers
contorno a scelta choice of vegetables
coppa cured pork shoulder
cosciotto leg
costata al prosciutto filled chop
costola rib
costolette di maiale al finocchio braised pork chops with white wine and fennel seed
cotechino con lenticchie sausage-like spicy pork mix
cotogna quince
cotoletta cutlet; **~ alla milanese** breaded veal cutlet
cotto cooked; **~ a vapore** steamed
cozze mussels
crema custard; **~ di legumi** legumes cream soup; **~ di pomodori** tomato cream soup
crespelle di farina dolce chestnut-flour crepes with ricotta and rum
crostacei shellfish
crostata pie; **~ di mele** apple pie; **~ di ricotta** cheesecake with raisins and Marsala
crudo di Parma cured ham from Parma
cumino cumin
cuscus couscous
Cynar aperitif produced from artichoke

d', di of
datteri dates

decaffeinato decaffeinated
dentice type of sea bream
digestivo after-dinner drink
ditali pasta thimbles
dolce cake; dessert; mild (cheese); sweet (wine)
doppio double (a double shot)

E

elicoidali short, twisted pasta tubes
eperlano smelt

F

fagiano pheasant; **~ al tartufo** stuffed with truffles
fagioli (haricot) beans; **~ all'uccelletto** cooked in tomatoes and black olives; **~ in umido** cooked in tomato sauce
fagioli alla toscana Tuscan-style beans, simmered for hours and garnished with salt, black pepper and crude olive oil
fagiolini French (green) beans
faraona guinea fowl
farcito stuffed
farfalle butterfly-shaped pasta
farfallini small bow-shaped egg-pasta
favata beans and port stew *(Sardinia)*
fave broad beans
fazzoletti salati savory turnovers
fegato liver; **~ alla veneziana** thin slices fried with onions; **~ alla salvia** with tomatoes, garlic and sage
fesa round cut from the rump
fetta di pizza slice of pizza
fettuccine egg-pasta ribbons; **~ Alfredo** with parmesan and cream
fico fig

filetto fillet; **~ al pepe verde** fillet steak served in a creamy sauce with green peppercorns
finocchio fennel
focaccia savory flatbread; **~ alla salvia** sage bread; **~ alla salsiccia** sausage bread; **~ alle noci** walnut bread; **~ genovese** savory bread with sage and olive oil
focaccia al gorgonzola warm yeast flatbread topped with cheese
fonduta hot dip of Fontina cheese, egg yolks and truffles
formaggio cheese
fragole strawberries
fragoline di bosco wild strawberries
freddo cold
frittata omelet; **~ campagnola** with onion, grated cheese, milk and cream; **~ primaverile** with vegetables
fritte al buro nero brains with black butter
fritte alla fiorentina marinated, breadcrumbed, fried brains served with spinach
fritto fried
fritto misto a fry of various small fish and shellfish or meat and vegetables
frullato milk-shake
frustenga cornmeal fruit cake
frutta fruit
frutti di mare seafood
funghi mushrooms; **~ alla parmigiana** stuffed with breadcrumbs, Parmesan, garlic, herbs; **~ porcini arrosto** roasted or grilled with chili peppers
fusilli pasta twists

G

galletto amburghese young tender chicken, oven-roasted

gallina stewing fowl
gallo cedrone grouse
gamberetti shrimps
gamberi prawns
gassata carbonated/fizzy (water)
gelato ice cream
gianduia cold chocolate pudding
gin e tonic gin and tonic
gingerino ginger-flavored aperitif (also sold in small bottles)
gnocchi alla genovese dumplings with pesto sauce
gnocchi di patate potato dumplings
gorgonzola blue-veined cheese
granchi crabs
granita coarse sorbet ice cream
gronghi conger eel

i nostri piatti di carne sono serviti con contorno our meat dishes are accompanied by vegetables
in bianco without tomato sauce
in bottiglia bottled (beer)
in casseruola in casserole
in umido stewed
indivia endive
insalata salad
insalata di frutti di mare prawns and squid with lemon, pickles and olives
insalata di pollo chicken salad with green salad, lemon and cream
insalata mista mixed salad
insalata russa diced boiled vegetables in mayonnaise
involtini thin slices of meat (beef, veal or pork) rolled and stuffed

lamponi raspberries

lamprede lampreys
lasagne thin layers of pasta lined with meat and tomato sauce with Bel Paese and Mozzarella cheeses; ~ **al forno** oven baked lasagna; ~ **con l'anitra** with duck; ~ **con le verdure** vegetable lasagna
lasagnette del lucchese lasagna with sauce of spinach, ricotta, chicken livers
lattaiolo cinnamon custard
latte milk
lattuga lettuce
lauro bay
leggero light (wine)
lenticchie lentils
lepre hare; ~ **in agrodolce** with pine kernels, sultanas and chocolate; ~ **piemontese** cooked in Barbera wine, sprinkled with herbs and bitter chocolate
lesso boiled
limonata lemonade
limone lemon
lingua tongue
linguine type of flat spaghetti
liquore liqueur
liscio straight/neat
lo chef consiglia the chef recommends ...
lombata/lombo loin
lombo di maiale al forno garlic-roasted pork loin
lombo di maiale al prosciutto grilled pork loin with prosciutto
luccio pike
luganeghe fresh pork sausages sold by the length
lumache snails; snail shell-shaped pasta
lumache alle milanese snails with anchovy, fennel and wine sauce

lumache di mare sea snails
lunette half-moon-shaped stuffed pasta

M

maccheroni alla chitarra handmade pasta cut into strips
macchiato with milk (coffee)
maggiorana marjoram
maiale pork
malfatti thin pasta strips
mandarino tangerine
mandorle almonds
manzo beef
margherita tomato, cheese and basil pizza
marinara sauce of tomatoes, olives, garlic, clams and mussels
marinato marinated
marmellata jam; **~ d'arance** marmalade
mascarpone a thick, full-fat creamy cheese mostly used for desserts, similar to clotted cream
Martini a brand-name vermouth, sweet or dry; not to be confused with a martini cocktail
medaglioni round fillet
mela apple
melanzane eggplant/aubergine
mele apples
melone melon
menta mint
menù a prezzo fisso set menu
merlano whiting
merluzzo cod
mezzo pollo arrosto half a roasted chicken
midollo marrow
miele honey
minestra soup; **~ di funghi** cream of mushroom soup; **~ di sedano e**

riso celery and rice; **~ in brodo** with noodles or rice
minestrone a thick vegetable soup (sometimes with noodles) sprinkled with parmesan cheese
mirtilli blueberries
misto mixed
molle soft (egg)
montone mutton
more blackberries
mortadella Bologna sausage
mostaccioli chocolate biscuits
mozzarella soft, unripened cheese; **~ con i pomodori** with tomatoes

N

napoletana anchovies, tomatoes, cheese (pizza topping)
nasello coal-fish
naturale still (water)
nero black (coffee)
nocciole hazelnuts
noce di cocco coconut
noce moscata nutmeg
noci walnuts
nodini veal chops

O

oca goose
odori herbs
olio (d'oliva) (olive) oil
olive olives
orata type of sea bream
orecchiette ear-shaped pasta
origano oregano
ortolano ortolan
osso buco braised veal knuckles and shins
ostriche oysters

P

palombacce allo spiedo wood pigeon, spit-roasted

pan di Spagna sponge cake
pancetta affumicata smoked bacon
pandorato alla crema di formaggio fried bread with cream cheese
pandoro large, Cristmas sponge cake served with powdered vanilla on top
pane bread; **~ al latte** milk bread; **~ all'olio** olive oil white bread; **~ tostato** toast
pane, grissini e coperto bread, breadsticks (**grissini**) and table cover charge
panettone butter-enriched Christmas bread with candied fruit, sultanas and raisins
panforte similar to **pangiallo**
pangiallo fairly hard nut and honey cake
panini rolls
panino imbottito sandwich
panna cotta delicious Italian adaptation of blancmange and creme brulé
panpepato very spicy nut cake
pansotti con salsa di noci alla ligure triangles stuffed with greens in walnut sauce
pappardelle fat ribbons of egg-pasta; **~ alla lepre** with hare sauce
papriot thick spinach soup
parmigiana breaded aubergine slices with tomato sauce and mozzarella
parmigiano (-reggiano) parmesan cheese
passato di verdura mashed vegetable soup, generally with croutons
pasta pasta, noodles; **~ e ceci** with chickpeas; **~ e fagioli** with beans

pasta Maddalena plain génoise cake
pastasciutta pasta
pasticcini pastries
pasticcio macaroni, white sauce, meat and tomato
pastiera ricotta cake with wheat berries
pastina small pasta pieces; **~ in brodo** in broth
patate potatoes
patatine fritte French fries, chips
pecorino hard sheep's cheese
penne pasta quills
peperonata peppers sauteed with tomato and onion
peperoni peppers; **~ ripieni** stuffed
pera pear
pernice partridge
pesca peach
pescanoce nectarine
pesce all'acqua pazza fish cooked in seawater
pesce persico perch
pesce spada swordfish
pesche peaches
pesce fish; **~ al cartoccio** baked in a parchment envelope; **~ in carpione** boiled and cooked in vinegar, served cold with lemon
pestingolo rich fruit cake with figs and honey
pesto sauce of basil leaves, garlic, cheese and sometimes pine kernels *(Liguria)* and marjoram
piatti di carne meat dishes
piatti freddi cold dishes
piatto del giorno dish of the day
piccante sharp (cheese)
piccata al marsala thin

\veal escalope braised in marsala sauce

piccione pigeon

pieno full-bodied (wine)

pinoli pine nuts

piselli peas; **~ al prosciutto** cooked slowly with Parma ham and bacon

piviere plover

pizelle fried bread with tomato sauce

pizza pizza

polenta mush made from cornmeal; **~ alla piemontese** layered with meat; **~ e coniglio** with rabbit stew; **~ e uccelli** with roasted small birds *(northern Italy)*

pollame poultry

pollo chicken; **~ all'abruzzese** with sweet peppers; **~ alla romana** diced and served with tomato sauce and sweet peppers; **~ alla diavola** highly spiced and grilled chicken; **~ novello** spring chicken

polpette meatballs

polpettone meat loaf of seasoned beef or veal

polpo octopus

pomodori tomatoes

pomodori e capperi salad with capers

pompelmo grapefruit

porcellino da latte suckling pig

porcetto arrosto suckling spit-roasted pig *(Sardinia)*

porchetta roasted whole pig with fennels and sausages

porcini boletus mushrooms

porrata bacon and leeks in yeast dough crust

porro leek

porto port

prezzemolo parsley

primo piatto first course

prosciutto ham

prosciutto crudo con melone/ con fichi sliced melon or figs with cured ham from Parma

provolone firm cheese

prugna plum

prugna secca prune

puttanesca sauce of capers, black olives, parsley, garlic, olive oil, black pepper

Q

quaglia quail

quattro formaggi four types of cheese (pizza topping) or sauce

quattro stagioni vegetables, cheese, ham and bacon (pizza topping)

R

radicchio a kind of bitter red and white lettuce

ragù sauce like bolognese

ravanelli radishes

ravioli alla piemontese ravioli with beef and vegetable stuffing

razza ray

ribes red currants

ribes nero black currants

ricci sea urchins

ricciarelli delicate honey and almond biscuit *(Tuscany)*

ricotta soft cow's or sheep's milk cheese

rigatoni short, wide pasta tubes; **~ alla pagliata** with veal guts

risi e bisi rice with peas and bacon

riso rice

riso con le seppie rice cooked with the ink from squid

riso in bianco boiled rice with butter and grated parmesan

risotto rice casserole;

~ con fegatini with chicken livers;

~ con gamberetti in bianco with prawns and wine

rognoncini trifolatti kidneys sauteed with Marsala

rognoni kidneys

rombo turbot

rosato rosé (wine)

rosbif roast beef

rosmarino rosemary

rosso red (wine)

ruote wheel-shaped pasta

salame spicy sausages made with uncooked beef or pork, often flavored with pepper and garlic

salciccia small sausage, country-style pork mixture

sale salt

salmone salmon

salse sauces

saltimbocca veal escalopes with prosciutto ham; **~ alla romana** braised in marsala wine with sage

salumi assorted pork products

salvia sage

sardine sardines; **~ all'olio** in oil

sauersuppe sour tripe soup marinated in white wine vinegar

scalogno shallot

scaloppina veal escalope;

~ alla valdostana filled with cheese and ham; **~ al marsala** with Marsala wine

scampi prawns

sciule pieuno onions stuffed with macaroons, breadcrumbs, cheese, spices and sultanas

scorfano sea-scorpion, sculpin

scura dark (beer)

secco dry (wine)

secondo piatto second (main) course

sedano celery

selvaggina venison

semifreddo ice cream cake

senape mustard

seppia cuttlefish

seppie con piselli baby squid and peas

sfogliatelle sweet Ricotta cheese turnovers

sgombri in umido stewed mackerel in white wine with green peas

sgombro mackerel

siciliana with black olives, capers and cheese (pizza)

sodo hard (egg)

sogliola sole

sogliole alla mugnaia sole sautéed in butter, garnished with parsley and lemon

solubile instant (coffee)

sottaceti pickled vegetables

spaghetti all'amatriciana spaghetti with tomato, bacon and Pecorino cheese sauce

spalla shoulder

specialità della casa specialties of the house

specialità di pesce fish specialties

specialità locali local specialties

spezie spices

spezzatino meat or poultry stew

spezzatino di cinghiale alla cacciatora diced wild boar stewed in white wine with garlic and bay leaves

spezzato di tacchino turkey casserole with olives *(Umbria)*

spiedino pieces of meat grilled or roasted on a skewer

spigola sea bass

spinaci spinach

spremuta di ... freshly squeezed (juice)

spumante sparkling (wine)

stecca di cioccolato chocolate bar

stelline small pasta stars

stoccafisso dried cod

storione sturgeon

stracciatella clear egg and cheese soup

stracotto meat stew with sausages, beef and vegetables in white wine, slowly cooked for several hours *(Tuscany)*

strangola preti bread and spinach dumpling

straniera foreign (beer)

su ordinazione made to order

succo di frutta fruit juice

supplemento extra charge

supplì very popular and tasty Italian rice croquettes with Mozzarella cheese and minced meat, breadcrumbed and fried

susina plum (yellow) or greengage

T

tacchino turkey

tagliatelle egg-pasta ribbons

tartufi truffles

tartufi di cioccolata chocolate truffles

timballo con le sarde macaroni, sardines, pine nuts, fennel, raisins

timo thyme

tiramisù sponge cake, mascarpone, eggs and chocolate dessert

tisana herb tea

tonno tuna

tonno alla livornese fried tuna in slices, stewed in garlic and tomato

tordo thrush

torrone delicious Italian nougat which can be found hard and crispy or soft, also chocolate flavored.

torta cake; pie

torta di cioccolata chocolate cake

torta di frutta fruit cake

torta di mandorle almond pie

torta di mele apple pie

torta di ricotta delicious pie made with ricotta cheese (roughly similar to cheese cake)

torta manfreda liver pate with Marsala and Parmesan

torta margherita layered cake with meringue, fresh fruit and whipped cream

tortelli di zucca big tortellini with pumpkin stuffing

tortellini stuffed egg-pasta rings; ~ **alla panna con tartufi** with cream and truffles; ~ **di piccioncello** with pigeon stuffing

tortino di zucchine zucchini with white sauce

triglie red mullet; ~ **alla livornese** baked; ~ **alla siciliana** grilled with orange peel and white wine

trippa tripe; ~ **alla fiorentina** and beef braised in a tomato sauce and served with cheese *(Tuscany)*; ~ **verde** in green sauce

trota trout: ~ **alla brace** grilled

tutto mare seafood sauce

tè tea; ~ **freddo** iced tea

uova eggs
uova alla romana omelet with beans, onions and herbs
uova e pancetta bacon and eggs
uova e prosciutto ham and eggs
uova fritte fried eggs
uova strapazzate scrambled eggs
uovo alla coque boiled egg
uva bianca/nera white/black grapes
uva passa raisins
uva spina gooseberries

vaniglia vanilla
veneziana sweet bread with whole almonds
verde with creamed green vegetables
verdura mista mixed vegetables
verdure vegetables; **~ di stagione** vegetables in season
vermicelli thin spaghetti
verza green cabbage
vincisgrassi cooked pasta with cream sauce and gravy
vino wine
vitello veal; **~ alla bolognese** cutlet cooked with Parma ham and cheese; **~ tonnato** cold with tuna fish sauce; **~ valdostana** stuffed with soft cheese
vongole clams

whisky (e soda/con seltz) whisky (and soda)
würstel frankfurters

zabaglione egg yolks, sugar and Marsala wine
zafferano saffron
zampone pig's foot/trotter filled with seasoned pork, boiled and served in slices
zenzero ginger
ziti long, solid eggless-pasta tubes
zucca pumpkin, gourd; **~ gialla al forno** baked and served with parmesan cheese (winter only)
zucchero sugar
zucchini ripieni stuffed zucchini (usually containing mince meat)
zuppa soup; **~ alla cacciatora** meat soup with mushrooms; **~ alla marinara** spicy fish chowder/stew; **~ alla pavese** consommé with poached egg, croutons and grated cheese; **~ alla senese** sausages with lentils; **~ alla veneta** vegetable soup with white wine and noodles; **~ di bue con spaghettini** spaghetti in beef soup; **~ di cipolle** onion soup with brandy; **~ di cozze** mussels soup; **~ di datteri di mare** sea dates (kind of mussel) soup; **~ di frutti di mare** seafood soup; **~ di pesce** spicy fish chowder/stew; **~ di vongole** clams and white wine soup
zuppa inglese sponge cake steeped in rum with custard or whipped cream

TRAVEL

ESSENTIAL

1/2/3 for ...	**Uno/due/tre per ...** *oono/doo-ay/tray pehr*
A ticket to ...	**Un biglietto per ...** *oon beelyaytto pehr*
one-way [single]	**solo andata** *solo andaata*
round-trip [return]	**andata e ritorno** *andaata ay reetorno*
How much ...?	**Quanto ... ?** *kwanto*

SAFETY

Would you accompany me ...?	**Le dispiace accompagnarmi?** *lay disspeeachay akkompanyaarmee*
to the bus stop	**alla fermata dell'autobus** *alla fayrmaata dayllowtobooss*
to my hotel	**al mio albergo** *al meeo albayrgo*
I don't want to ... on my own.	**Non voglio ... da solo(-a).** *non volyo ... da solo(-a)*
stay here	**rimanere qui** *reemanayray kwee*
walk home	**rientrare a piedi** *reeayntraaray ah peeaydee*
I don't feel safe here.	**Non mi sento sicuro(-a) qui.** *non me saynto seekooro(-a) kwee*

IN A TRAIN STATION

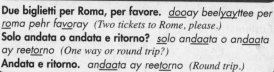

Due biglietti per Roma, per favore. *dooay beelyayttee per roma pehr favoray (Two tickets to Rome, please.)*
Solo andata o andata e ritorno? *solo andaata o andaata ay reetorno (One way or round trip?)*
Andata e ritorno. *andaata ay reetorno (Round trip.)*

ARRIVAL

Most visitors, including citizens of all EU{European Union} countries, the US, Canada, Eire, Australia and New Zealand, require only a valid passport for entry to Italy.

Import restrictions between EU countries have been relaxed on items for personal use or consumption which are bought duty-paid within the EU. Suggested maximum: 90L. wine or 60L. sparkling wine, 20L. fortified wine, 10L. spirits and 110L. beer.

There are duty-free shops at the following airports: Bologna, Genova, Milan, Naples, Pisa, Rimini, Rome Ciampino, Rome Fiumicino, Turin, and Venice.

Passport control

We have a joint passport.	**Abbiamo un passaporto comune.** *abbeeamo oon passaporto komoonay*
The children are on this passport.	**I bambini sono su questo passaporto.** *ee bambeenee sono soo kwaysto passaporto*
I'm here on vacation [holiday]/business.	**Sono qui in vacanza/per lavoro.** *sono kwee in vakantsa/ pehr lavoro*
I'm just passing through.	**Sono solo di passaggio.** *sono solo dee passadjo*
I'm going to …	**Vado a …** *vado a*
I'm …	**Sono …** *sono*
on my own	**da solo(-a)** *da solo(-a)*
with my family	**con la mia famiglia** *kon la meea fameelya*
with a group	**con un gruppo** *kon oon groopo*

Customs

I have only the normal allowances.	**Ho solo beni in esenzione fiscale.** *oh solo baynee een ayzentseeonay feeskalay*

It's a gift.	**È un regalo.**
	eh oon raygaalo
It's for my personal use.	**È per uso personale.**
	eh pehr oozo pehrsonaalay
I would like to declare …	**Vorrei dichiarare …**
	vorrehee deekeeaaraaray
I don't understand.	**Non capisco.**
	non kapeesko
Does anyone here speak English?	**C'è qualcuno che parla inglese?**
	cheh kwalkoono kay parla eengglaysay

Duty-free shopping

What currency is this in?	**In che valuta è?**
	een kay valoota eh
Can I pay in …	**Posso pagare in …**
	posso pagaaray een
dollars	**dollari** *dollaree*
euros	**euro** *ayooro*
pounds	**sterline** *stayrleenay*

YOU MAY SEE

IL CONTROLLO PASSAPORTI	passport control
LA FRONTIERA	border crossing
LA DOGANA	customs
NIENTE DA DICHIARARE	nothing to declare
MERCI DA DICHIARARE	goods to declare
ESENTE DA DAZIO	duty-free

YOU MAY HEAR

Ha qualcosa da dichiarare?	Do you have anything to declare?
Per questo deve pagare la dogana.	You must pay duty on this.
Dove l'ha comprato?	Where did you buy this?
Apra questa borsa, per favore.	Please open this bag.
Ha altri bagagli?	Do you have any more luggage?

67

PLANE

Italian cities and major islands are well connected by air. This includes a shuttle service (**Arcobaleno**) between Rome and Milan every 20 minutes. Domestic flights can be expensive. However, cheaper rates can be obtained off-peak, and special fares are generally available for family groups, young people/students and senior citizens.

Tickets and reservations

When is the ... flight to ...?	**Quando parte il volo ... per ...?** _kwando partay eel volo ... pehr_
first/next/last	**il primo/il prossimo/l'ultimo** _eel preemo/eel prosseemo/loolteemo_
I'd like 2 tickets to ...	**Vorrei due biglietti per ...** _vorrehee doo-ay beelyayttee ... pehr_
one-way [single]	**di andata** _dee andaata_
round-trip [return]	**di andata e ritorno** _dee andaata ay reetorno_
first class	**prima classe** _preema klassay_
economy class	**classe turistica** _klassay tooreesteeka_
business class	**business class** _business klass_
How much is a flight to ...?	**Quanto costa il volo per ...?** _kwanto kosta eel volo pehr_
I'd like to ... my reservation for flight number ...	**Vorrei ... la mia prenotazione per il volo numero ...** _vorrehee ... la meea praynotatseeonay pehr eel volo noomayro_
cancel	**annullare** _annoollaaray_
change	**cambiare** _kambeeaaray_
confirm	**confermare** _konfayrmaaray_

Enquiries about the flight

How long is the flight?	**Quanto dura il volo?** _kwanto doora eel volo_
What time does the plane leave?	**A che ora decolla l'aereo?** _ah kay ora daykolla la-ayrayo_
What time will we arrive?	**A che ora arriveremo?** _ah kay ora arreevayraymo_

68

| What time do I have to check in? | **A che ora devo registrare i bagagli?** *ah kay <u>ora day</u>vo rayjees<u>traa</u>ray ee ba<u>gaa</u>lyee* |

Checking in

Where is the check-in counter for flight …?	**Dov'è il banco accettazione per il volo …?** *<u>dovay ell banko</u> achaytatsee<u>o</u>nay pehr eel <u>vo</u>lo*
I have …	**Ho …** *oh*
3 suitcases to check in	**tre valige da registrare** *treh va<u>lee</u>jay da rayjees<u>traa</u>ray*
2 pieces of hand luggage	**due borse a mano** *<u>doo</u>-ay <u>bor</u>say ah <u>ma</u>no*

YOU MAY HEAR

Il suo biglietto/passaporto/ la sua carta d'imbarco.	Your ticket/passport/ boarding card.
Preferisce un posto vicino al finestrino o al corridoio?	Would you like a window or an aisle seat?
Fumatori o non fumatori?	Smoking or non-smoking?
Si accomodi nella sala partenze.	Please go through to the departure lounge.
Quanti pezzi/quante valige ha?	How many pieces of luggage do you have?
Ha un eccesso di bagaglio.	You have excess luggage.
Deve pagare un supplemento di … euro per ogni chilo in più.	You'll have to pay a supplement of euros per kilo of excess luggage.
Questo bagaglio a mano è troppo pesante/grande.	That's too heavy/ large for hand luggage.
Ha fatto i bagagli personalmente?	Did you pack these bags yourself?
Ci sono articoli elettrici o taglienti?	Do they contain any sharp or electrical items?

YOU MAY SEE

ARRIVI	arrivals
PARTENZE	departures
I CONTROLLI DI SICUREZZA	security check
TENERE CON SÉ I BAGAGLI	do not leave luggage unattended

Information

Is there any delay
on flight …?

C'è un ritardo sul volo …?
cheh oon reetardo sool volo

How late will it be?

Di quanto ritarderà?
dee kwanto reetardayra

Has the flight
from … landed?

È atterrato il volo da …?
eh attayrraato eel volo da

Which gate does flight …
leave from?

Da quale uscita parte il volo …? *da
kwalay oosheeta partay eel volo*

Boarding/In-flight

Your boarding pass,
please.

La sua carta d'imbarco, per favore. *la
sooa karta deembarko pehr favoray*

Could I have a drink/
something to eat, please?

**Può portarmi qualcosa da bere/da
mangiare, per favore?** *pwo portaarmee
kwalkosa da bayray/da manjaaray
pehr favoray*

Please wake me for
the meal.

Mi svegli per il pasto, per favore. *mee
svaylyee pehr eel pasto pehr favoray*

What time will we arrive?

A che ora arriveremo?
ah kay ora arreevayraymo

An airsick bag, quick,
please.

Presto un sacchetto di carta, per favore.
praysto oon sakkaytto dee karta pehr favoray

Arrival

Where is/are the …?

Dov'è/Dove sono …? *doveh/dovay sono*

currency exchange

l'ufficio cambio *looffeecho kambeeo*

buses

gli autobus *lyee owtobooss*

car rental

il noleggio auto *eel nolaydjo owto*

exit

l'uscita *loosheeta*

taxis

i tassì *ee tassee*

Is there a bus into town?

C'è un autobus per il centro?
cheh oon owtobooss pehr eel chayntro

How do I get to
the … Hotel?

Come si arriva all' albergo …?
komay see arreeva allalbayrgo

Luggage/Baggage

Tipping: The suggested rate for the porter is €1–2 per bag; in railway stations, tariffs are generally displayed.

Porter! Excuse me!	**Facchino! Scusi!** *fakkeeno. skoozee*
Could you take my luggage to …?	**Può portarmi i bagagli fino …?** *pwo portaarmee ee bagalyee feeno*
a taxi/bus	**al tassì/alla fermata dell'autobus** *al tassee/ alla faymaata daylowtobooss*
Where is/are …?	**Dov'è/Dove sono …?** *doveh /dovay sono*
luggage carts [trolleys]	**i carrelli** *ee karrayllee*
baggage lockers	**il deposito bagagli automatico** *eel dayposeeto bagalyee owtomateeko*
baggage check [left-luggage office]	**il deposito bagagli** *eel dayposeeto bagalyee*
Where is the luggage from flight …?	**Dove sono i bagagli del volo …?** *dovay sono ee bagalyee dayl volo*

Loss, damage and theft

My luggage has been lost.	**Ho smarrito i bagagli.** *oh smarreeto ee bagalyee*
My luggage has been stolen.	**Il mio bagaglio è stato rubato.** *eel meeo bagaalyo eh staato roobaato*
My suitcase was damaged.	**La mia valigia è stata danneggiata.** *la meea valeeja eh staata dannaydjaata*

YOU MAY HEAR

Può descrivere i suoi bagagli?	What does your luggage look like?
Ha l'etichetta di ricupero bagagli?	Do you have the claim check/ reclaim tag?
I suoi bagagli …	Your luggage …
potrebbero essere stati mandati a …	may have been sent to …
potrebbero arrivare più tardi	may arrive later
Ritorni domani, per favore.	Please come back tomorrow.
Chiami questo numero per controllare se i suoi bagagli sono arrivati.	Call this number to check if your luggage has arrived.

TRAIN

EuroCity (EC) *ayoorosseetee*
International express connecting main European cities; first and second class. A supplement is payable and reservations are obligatory.

Pendolino-ETR 450 (P) *pehndoleeno*
High-speed train connecting major Italian cities. Luxury first class and second class; tickets include hostess service and a meal. Reservations are obligatory.

Rapido *raapeedo*
Long-distance express train stopping at major cities only; first and second class.

Intercity (IC) *"intercity"*
Intercity express with very few stops; luxury, international service with first and second class. Seat reservations are essential and a special supplement is charged.

Espresso (EXP) *aysprehsso*
Long-distance express train, stopping at major stations.

Diretto (D) *deerehtto*
Slower than the Espresso, it stops at most stations.

Interregionale (IR) *eentehrrayjeeonalay*
Train stopping at main stations within a region.

Regionale (R) *rayjeeonalay*
Local train stopping at many smaller locations. Not very fast, but an excellent means of visiting small hilltop towns that abound in Italy. Marked by a white "R" on a black background (to distinguish it from the **Rapido**).

carrozza ristorante *karrottsa reestorantay*
Dining car. Some services include self-service restaurant cars. In addition, most trains have snacks and refreshments available.

vagone letto *vagonay lehtto*
Sleeping car with individual compartment and washing facilities. Sleeping cars containing berths with blankets and pillows (**carrozza cuccette**) are also available on some lines.

The National Railways (**Ferrovie dello Stato – FS**) publishes a free, easy-to-consult pocket timetable of the major trains running throughout Italy. Italy's trains can be crowded; if you haven't booked, it's wise to arrive at the station at least 30 minutes before departure to be sure of a seat.

Check out the various reductions and travel cards available. These include: **Biglietto turistico di libera circolazione** (for extensive "travel-at-will," only available outside Italy).

To the station

How do I get to the (main) rail station?	**Come si arriva alla stazione ferroviaria (principale)?** _komay see arreeva alla statseeonay fayrroveeaareea (preencheepaalay)_
Do trains to … leave from … Station?	**I treni per … partono dalla stazione di …?** _ee traynee pehr … partono dalla statseeonay dee_
Is it far?	**È lontano?** _ay lontano_
Can I leave my car there?	**Posso lasciare la macchina alla stazione?** _posso lashaaray la makkeena alla statseeonay_

At the station

Where is/are …?	**Dov'è/Dove sono …?** _doveh /dovay sono_
currency exchange office	**l'ufficio cambio** _looffeecho kambeeo_
information desk	**lo sportello informazioni** _lo sportayllo eenformatseeonay_
baggage check [left-luggage office]	**il deposito bagagli** _eel dayposeeto bagaalyee_
lost-and-found [lost property office]	**l'ufficio oggetti smarriti** _looffeecho odjayttee smarreetee_
luggage lockers	**il deposito bagagli automatico** _eel dayposeeto bagaalyee owtomaateeko_
platforms	**i binari** _ee beenaaree_
snack bar	**il bar** _eel bar_
ticket office	**la biglietteria** _la beelyayttayreea_
waiting room	**la sala d'aspetto** _la sala daspaytto_

YOU MAY SEE

ENTRATA	entrance
USCITA	exit
AI BINARI	to the platforms
INFORMAZIONI	information
PRENOTAZIONI	reservations
ARRIVI	arrivals
PARTENZE	departures

Tickets

It is very important to validate tickets before commencing your journey by inserting them in machines (generally yellow) positioned on platforms; otherwise you will be liable for a fine.

I'd like a ticket to …	**Vorrei un biglietto per …** *vorrehee oon beelyayto pehr*
one-way [single]	**andata** *andaata*
round-trip [return]	**andata e ritorno** *andaata ay reetorno*
first/second class	**prima/seconda classe** *preema/saykonda klassay*
I'd like to reserve a …	**Vorrei prenotare …** *vorrehee praynotaaray*
window/aisle seat	**un posto vicino al finestrino/ al corridoio** *oon posto veecheeno al feenaystreeno/al korreedoyo*
Is there a sleeping car [sleeper]?	**C'è un vagone letto?** *cheh oon vagonay laytto*
I'd like a … berth.	**Vorrei una cuccetta …** *vorrehee oona koochaytta*
upper/lower	**in alto/in basso** *in altoh/in bassoh*

Price

How much is that?	**Quant'è?** *kwanteh*
Do you offer a cheap same-day round-trip ticket?	**C'è una tariffa economica per andata e ritorno in giornata?** *che oona tareeffa aykonomeeka pehr andaata ay reetorno een jornaata*
Is there a discount for …?	**C'è una riduzione per …?** *cheh oon reedootseeonay pehr*

children/families	**bambini/famiglie**
	bam<u>bee</u>nee/fa<u>mee</u>lyay
senior citizens	**anziani** *antsee<u>a</u>nee*
students	**studenti** *stoo<u>dayn</u>tee*

Queries

Do I have to change trains?	**Devo cambiare treno?** *<u>day</u>vo kambee<u>aa</u>ray <u>tray</u>no*
You have to change at …	**Deve cambiare a …** *<u>day</u>vay kambee<u>aa</u>ray ah*
How long is this ticket valid for?	**Per quanto tempo è valido questo biglietto?** *pehr <u>kwan</u>to <u>taym</u>po eh <u>va</u>leedo <u>kway</u>sto beel<u>yay</u>to*
Can I return on the same ticket?	**Posso ritornare con lo stesso biglietto?** *<u>pos</u>so reetor<u>naa</u>ray kon lo <u>stay</u>sso beel<u>yay</u>tto*
Which car [coach] is my seat in?	**In quale carrozza è il mio posto?** *een <u>kwa</u>lay kar<u>rot</u>sa eh eel <u>mee</u>o <u>pos</u>to*
Is there a dining car on the train?	**C'è il vagone ristorante sul treno?** *cheh eel va<u>go</u>nay reesto<u>ran</u>tay sool <u>tray</u>no*

Train times

Could I have a timetable, please?	**Ha l'orario, per favore?** *ah lo<u>ra</u>reeo pehr fa<u>vo</u>ray*
When is the … train to … ?	**Quando parte … treno per …** *<u>kwan</u>do <u>paar</u>tay … <u>tray</u>no pehr*
first/next/last	**il primo/il prossimo/l'ultimo** *eel <u>pree</u>mo /eel <u>pros</u>seemo/ <u>lool</u>teemo*
How frequent are the trains to …?	**Che frequenza hanno i treni per …?** *kay fray<u>kwayn</u>tsa <u>an</u>no ee <u>tray</u>nee pehr*
once/twice a day	**una volta/due volte al giorno** *<u>oo</u>na <u>vol</u>ta/<u>doo</u>ay <u>vol</u>tay al <u>jor</u>no*

5 times a day	**cinque volte al giorno**
	cheenkweh voltay al jorno
every hour	**ogni ora**
	onyee ora
What time do they leave?	**A che ora partono?**
	ah kay ora partono
on the hour	**ad ogni ora precisa**
	ad onyee ora praycheesa
What time does the train stop at …?	**A che ora ferma il treno a …?**
	ah kay ora fayrma eel trayno ah
What time does the train arrive in …?	**A che ora arriva il treno a …?**
	ah kay ora arreeva eel trayno ah
How long is the trip [journey]?	**Quanto dura il viaggio?**
	kwanto doora eel veeadjo
Is the train on time?	**Il treno è in orario?**
	eel trayno eh een orareeo

Departures

Which platform does the train to … leave from?	**Da quale binario parte il treno per …?**
	da kwalay beenaareeo partay eel trayno pehr
Where is platform 4?	**Dov'è il binario quattro?**
	doveh eel beenaareeo kwattro
over there	**laggiù** *ladjoo*
on the left/right	**a sinistra/a destra**
	ah seeneestra/ah daystra
Where do I change for …?	**dove cambio per …?**
	dovay kambeeo pehr
How long will I have to wait for a connection?	**Quanto devo aspettare per la coincidenza?**
	kwanto dayvo aspayttaaray pehr la koeencheedayntsa

YOU MAY SEE	
FRENI D'EMERGENZA	emergency brake
PORTE AUTOMATICHE	automatic doors
SEGNALE D'ALLARME	alarm signal

Boarding

Is this the right platform for the train to …?	**È questo il binario del treno per …?** *eh kwaysto eel beenaareeo dayl trayno pehr*
Is this the train to …?	**È questo il treno per …?** *eh kwaysto eel trayno pehr*
Is this seat taken?	**Questo posto è occupato?** *kwaysto posto eh okoopaato*
I think that's my seat.	**Questo è il mio posto, credo.** *kwaysto eh eel meeo posto kraydo*
Are there any seats/berths available?	**Ci sono posti liberi/cuccette libere?** *chee sono postee leebayree/ koochayttay leebayray*
Do you mind …?	**Le dispiace …?** *lay dispeeachay*
if I sit here	**se mi siedo qui** *say mee seeaydo kwee*
if I open the window	**se apro la finestra** *say apro la feenaystra*

During the trip

How long are we stopping here?	**Per quanto tempo ci fermiamo a …?** *pehr kwanto taympo che fayrmeeaamo ah*
When do we get to …?	**Quando arriviamo a …?** *kwando arreeveeaamo ah*
Have we passed …?	**Abbiamo passato …?** *abbeeaamo passaato*
Where is the dining/ sleeping car?	**Dov'è la carrozza ristorante/il vagone letto?** *doveh la karrotsa reestorantay/eel vagonay lehtto*
Where is my berth?	**Dov'è la mia cuccetta?** *doveh la meea koo\chaytta*
I've lost my ticket.	**Ho perso il biglietto.** *oh payrso eel beelyaytto*

LONG-DISTANCE BUS

Bus travel can be a convenient way of traveling to smaller towns and a cheaper way to reach major cities. You'll find information on destinations and timetables at bus terminals, usually situated near railway stations. Main companies include *A.M.T.* (Genoa), *Appian Line* (Rome), *Autostradale*, *Lazzi*, *Pesci*, *Sadem*, *Sita*.

Where is the bus [coach] station?	**Dov'è la stazione delle corriere/ dei pullman?** *dov<u>eh</u> la statsee<u>o</u>nay d<u>ay</u>llay korree<u>eh</u>ray/d<u>a</u>yee p<u>u</u>llman*
When's the next bus [coach] to …?	**Quando parte il prossimo pullman per …?** *kw<u>a</u>ndo p<u>a</u>rtay eel pr<u>o</u>sseemo p<u>u</u>llman pehr*
Which terminal does it leave from?	**Da quale piazzola parte?** *da kw<u>a</u>lay piats<u>o</u>la p<u>a</u>rtay*
Where are the bus [coach] stops?	**Dove sono le piazzole di sosta?** *d<u>o</u>vay s<u>o</u>no ley piats<u>o</u>lay dee s<u>o</u>sta*
Does this bus [coach] stop at …?	**Questo pullman ferma a …?** *kw<u>a</u>ysto p<u>u</u>llman f<u>ay</u>rma ah*
How long does the trip [journey] take?	**Quanto dura il viaggio?** *kw<u>a</u>nto d<u>oo</u>ra eel veeadjo*

YOU MAY HEAR

Deve andare a quella fermata lì	You need that stop over there.
Deve prendere quella strada.	You need to go down that road.
Deve prendere l'autobus numero …	You need bus number …
Deve cambiare autobus a …	You must change buses at …

YOU MAY SEE

LA FERMATA DELL'AUTOBUS	bus stop
LA FERMATA A RICHIESTA	request stop
VIETATO FUMARE	no smoking
USCITA (D'EMERGENZA)	(emergency) exit

BUS

Many cities have introduced an automatic system of fare-paying. Instructions are usually also given in English. Most machines now give change, though usually limited to €1–2.

Bus or subway tickets are valid for 75 minutes and the fare is standard, irrespective of distance. If you're planning to travel extensively in one city, enquire about special runabout tickets, such as **biglietto giornaliero** (one-day ticket).

Buying tickets

Where can I buy tickets?	**Dove si comprano i biglietti?** _dovay see komprano ee beelyaytee_
A ... ticket to ..., please.	**Un bigletto per ..., per favore.** _oon beelyaytto pehr ... pehr favoray_
one-way/round-trip [single/return]	**di corsa semplice/circolare** _dee korsa saympleechay/cheerkolaaray_
bus pass	**per corse multiple** _pehr korsay moolteeplay_
day/weekly/monthly	**giornaliero/settimanale/mensile** _jornaleeehro/saytteemanaalay/maynseelay_
A book of tickets, please.	**Un blocchetto di biglietti, per favore.** _oon blokkaytto dee beelyaytee pehr favoray_
How much is the fare to ...?	**Quant'è il biglietto per ...?** _kwanteh eel beelyaytto pehr_

Traveling

Is this the right bus/tram to ...?	**È questo l'autobus/il tram per ...?** _eh kwaysto lowtobooss/eel tram pehr_
Could you tell me when to get off?	**Può dirmi quando devo scendere?** _pwo deermee kwando dayvo shayndayray_
Do I have to change buses?	**Devo cambiare autobus?** _dayvo kambeeaaray owtobooss_
How many stops are there to ...?	**Quante fermate ci sono per ...?** _kwantay fayrmaatay chee sono pehr_
Next stop, please!	**La prossima fermata, per favore!** _lah prosseema fayrmaata pehr favoray_

AT A BUS STATION

E' questo l'autobus per il centro? _eh kwaysto lowtobooss pehr eel chentro_ (Is this the bus to downtown?)

Sì, il numero otto. _see eel noomero otto_ (Yes, bus number 8.)

Grazie. _graatseeay_ (Thank you.)

Subway

The **metropolitana** in Rome and Milan provide big maps in every station to make the system easy to use. The fare is standard, irrespective of the distance traveled.

General Inquiries

Where's the nearest subway [metro] station?	**Dov'è la fermata della metropolitana più vicina?** _doveh la fayrmaata daylla maytropoleetaana peeoo veecheena_
Where can I buy a ticket?	**Dove si comprano i biglietti?** _dovay see komprano ee beelyayttee_
Could I have a map of the subway [metro]?	**Ha una carta/mappa della metropolitana?** _ah oona karta/mappa daylla maytropoleetaana_

Traveling

Which line should I take for …?	**Che linea devo prendere per …?** _kay leeneea dayvo prayndayray pehr_
Is this the right line for …?	**È questa la linea per …?** _eh kwaysta la leeneea pehr_
Which stop is it for …?	**Che fermata è per …?** _kay fayrmaata eh pehr_
How many stops is it to …?	**Quante fermate ci sono per arrivare a …?** _kwantay fayrmaatay chee sono pehr arreevaaray ah_
Is the next stop …?	**La prossima/fermata è …?** _la prosseema (fayrmaata) eh_
Where are we?	**Dove siamo?** _dovay seeaamo_
Where do I change for …?	**Dove devo cambiare per …?** _dovay dayvo kambeeaaray pehr_
What time is the last train to …?	**A che ora è l'ultimo treno per …?** _ah kay ora eh loolteemo trayno pehr_

Ferry

Regular boat, ferry and hydrofoil services run to the Italian islands. In addition to the large state-owned services such as _Tirrenia_ (esp. services to

Sicily and Sardinia), there are many other operators that access islands such as Capri, Ischia, Ponza, Ventotene, the Tremiti Islands, Elba and Giglio.

When is the … car ferry to …?	**Quando c'è … traghetto auto per …?**
	kwando cheh tragaytto owto pehr
first/next/last	**il primo/il prossimo/l'ultimo**
	eel preemo/ eel prosseemo/ loolteemo
hovercraft	**l'aliscafo** *laleeskaafo*
ship	**la nave** *la navay*
A round-trip [return] ticket for …	**Un biglietto di andata e ritorno per …**
	oon beelyaytto andaata ay r eetorno pehr
1 car and 1 trailer [caravan]	**un'auto e una roulotte**
	oonowto ay oona roolot
2 adults and 3 children	**due adulti e tre bambini**
	doo-ay adooltee ay tray bambeenee
I want to reserve a … cabin.	**Vorrei prenotare una cabina …** *vorrehee*
	praynotaaray oona kabeena
single/double	**singola/doppia** *seenggola/ doppeea*

BOAT TRIPS

Travelers to Venice can take tours on a myriad of canals, organized by the *Gondola Cooperative Service*. The price is usually quoted per gondola, which can seat 6 to 8 people, per 45 minutes, but you may be able to bargain. A cheaper, but less romantic, way of getting around are the water bus services: **vaporetti** (slow) and **diretti** (express).

Is there a …?	**C'è …?** *cheh*
boat trip	**una gita in barca**
	oona jeeta een baarka
Where can we buy tickets?	**Dove si comprano i biglietti?**
	dovay see komprano

YOU MAY SEE	
VIETATO L'ACCESSO AL PONTE AUTO	no access to car decks
LA SCIALUPPA DI SALVATAGGIO	life boat
LA CINTURA DI SALVATAGGIO	life preserver [life belt]
PUNTO DI RACCOLTA	meeting point

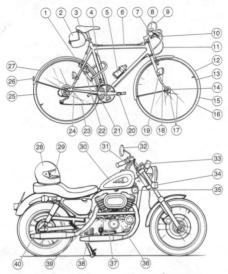

1 brake pad **il pattino/la pastiglia**	21 lock **la serratura**
2 bicycle bag **il borsello**	22 generator [dynamo] **la dinamo**
3 seat [saddle] **il sellino**	23 chain **la catena**
4 pump **la pompa**	24 rear light **il fanalino posteriore**
5 water bottle **la bottiglia dell'acqua**	25 rim **il cerchione**
6 frame **il telaio**	26 reflectors **il catarinfrangente**
7 handlebars **il manubrio**	27 fender [mudguard] **il parafango**
8 bell **il campanello**	28 helmet **il casco**
9 brake cable **il cavo dei freni**	29 visor **l'antiabbagliante**
10 gear shift [lever] **la leva del cambio**	30 fuel tank **il serbatoio**
11 gear [control] cable **il cambio**	31 clutch **la leva della frizione**
12 inner tube **la camera d'aria**	32 mirror **lo specchietto**
13 front/back wheel **la ruota anteriore/posteriore**	33 ignition switch **la leva dell'avviamento**
14 axle **l'asse**	34 turn signal [indicator] **l'indicatore di posizione**
15 tire **il pneumatico**	35 horn **il claxon**
16 wheel **la ruota**	36 engine **il motore**
17 spokes **i raggi**	37 gear shift **la leva del cambio**
18 bulb **la lampadina**	38 kick stand **il cavalletto**
19 headlamp **il fanalino anteriore**	39 exhaust pipe **la marmitta**
20 pedal **il pedale**	40 chain guard **il paracatena**

BICYCLE/MOTORBIKE

I'd like to rent a …	**Vorrei noleggiare …** *nolaydjaaray*
3-/10-gear bicycle	**una bici(cletta) a tre/dieci marce** *oona beechee(beecheeklaytta) ah tray/deeaychee marchay*
moped	**un motorino** *oon motoreeno*
mountain bike	**una mountain bike** *oona mountain bike*
motorbike	**una moto(cicletta)** *oona moto (motocheeklaytta)*
How much does it cost per day/week?	**Quanto costa al giorno/alla settimana?** *kwanto kosta al jorno/alla saytteemaana*
Do you require a deposit?	**Vuole una caparra?** *vwolay oona kaparra*
The brakes don't work.	**I freni non funzionano.** *ee fraynee non foontseeonano*
There are no lights.	**Non ci sono i fanalini.** *non chee sono ee fanaleenee*
The front/rear tire has a flat [puncture].	**il pneumatico anteriore/posteriore è bucato.** *eel pnayoomateeko antayreeoray/postayreeoray ay bookato*

HITCHHIKING

Where are you heading?	**In che direzione va?** *een kay deeraytseeonay va*
I'm heading for …	**Vado verso …** *vado vayrsoh*
Is that on the way to …?	**È sulla strada per …?** *eh soolla straada pehr*
Could you drop me off …?	**Può farmi scendere …?** *pwo faarmee shayndayray*
here	**qui** *kwee*
at the … exit	**all'uscita** *alloosheeta*
in the town center	**in centro** *een chayntro*
Thanks for the lift.	**Grazie per il passaggio.** *gratseeay pehr eel passadjeeo*

TAXI/CAB

All cabs must be metered by law, but it is still wise to ask the fare for longer trips. All rates, including supplements for Sundays, holidays, night trips (11 p.m. – 6 a.m.), airport trips, baggage, are indicated on an official chart, which should be posted inside the taxi. When arriving at or from an airport, remember there is a return trip surcharge to be added to what you read on the meter.

Beware of unlicensed cabs ("**abusivi**") touting for business at airports and stations – they charge greatly over the normal tariffs.

Tipping suggestions: 10-15% for the taxi driver.

Where can I get a taxi?	**Dove si trovano i tassi?** *dovay see trovano ee tassee*
Do you have the number for a taxi?	**Ha il numero dei tassi?** *ah eel noomayro dayee tassee*
I'd like a taxi …	**Vorrei un tassì …** *vorrehee oon tassee*
now/in an hour	**subito/fra un'ora** *soobeeto/ fra oonora*
for tomorrow at 9:00 am	**per domani alle nove** *pehr domaanee allay novay*
The address is …	**L'indirizzo è …** *leendeereetzo eh …*
Please take me …	**Per favore, mi porti …** *pehr favoray mee portee*
to the airport	**all'aeroporto** *allaayroporto*
to the train station	**alla stazione ferroviaria** *alla statseeonay fayrrooveeagreea*
this address	**a questo indirizzo** *ah kwaysto eendeereetso*
How much will it cost?	**Quanto costerà?** *kwanto kostayra*
On the meter it's …	**Il tassemetro segna …** *eel tasseemaytroa saynya*

> ### AT A TAXI STAND
> **Per favore, mi porti all'aeroporto.** *pehr favoray mee portee allaayroporto* (*Please, take me to the airport*)
> **Certo.** *cherto* (*Certainly.*)

CAR/AUTOMOBILE

While driving, the following documents must be carried at all times: valid full driver's license, vehicle registration document and insurance documen-

84

tation. If you don 't hold an EC format license, a translation of the license is also required. Visitors must carry their vehicle registration book/logbook and, if it is not their car, written consent from the owner.

Insurance for minimum Third Party risks is compulsory in Europe. It is recommended that you take out International motor insurance (or a "*Green Card*") through your insurer.

The most common crime against tourists in Italy is theft from rental cars. Always look for secure parking areas overnight and never leave valuables in your car at any time.

Essential equipment: warning triangle, nationality plate. Wearing seat-belts is compulsory. Children under 13 must travel in seats with special restraints.

Traffic on main roads has priority; where 2 roads of equal importance merge, traffic from the right has priority. On 3-lane roads, the central lane is for passing.

Minimum driving age: 18.

Tolls (**il pedaggio**) are payable on expressways (**autostrada**).

Traffic police can give on-the-spot fines (ask for a receipt). The use of horns is prohibited in built-up areas except for emergencies. Alcohol limit in blood: max. 80mg/100ml..

Conversion Chart

km	1	10	20	30	40	50	60	70	80	90	100	110	120	130
miles	0.62	6	12	19	25	31	37	44	50	56	62	68	74	81

Road network

Italy	**autostrada** – toll expressway [motorway]; **superstrada** – non-toll expressway [motorway]; **strata statale** – main road; **strada provinciale** – secondary road; **stada comunale** – local road
Switzerland	**A** – expressway [motorway] toll free; **N** – main road; **E** – secondary road

Speed limits *mph (kmph)*	Built-up area	Outside built-up area	(Toll) expressway/ highway [motorway]
Italy	31 (50)	69 (110) main roads 55 (90) sec. roads	81 (130)
car with trailer/ caravan	31 (50)	44 (70)	50 (80)
Switzerland	31 (50)	50 (80)	62–74 (100–120)

Car rental

Third-party insurance (**R.C.A.**) is included in the basic rental charge, usually with a Collision Damage Waiver.

If you are traveling by air or train, you may want to take advantage of special inclusive arrangements for car rental. Small local firms are generally cheaper than international or major Italian rental companies, but cars can only be booked locally. Some firms require a minimum age of 21; a valid license held for at least one year is a standard requirement.

Where can I rent a car?	**Dove si noleggia un'auto(mobile)?** *dovay see nolaydjaa oonowto (oonowtomobeelay)*
I'd like to rent ...	**Vorrei noleggiare ...** *vorrehee nolaydjaaray*
a 2-/4-door car	**un'auto a due/a quattro porte** *oonowto ah doo-ay/ah kwattro portay*
an automatic car	**un'auto con il cambio automatico** *oonowto kon eel kambeeo owtomaateeko*
with air conditioning	**con aria condizionata** *kon areea kondeetseeonaata*
I'd like it for a day/a week	**Vorrei noleggiarla per un giorno/una settimana.** *vorrehee nolaydjaaray pehr oon jorno/oona saytteemaana*
How much does it cost per day/week?	**Quanto costa al giorno/alla settimana?** *kwanto kosta al jorno/ alla saytteemaana*
Are mileage and insurance included?	**Il chilometraggio e l'assicurazione sono inclusi?** *eel keelomaytradjo ay lasseekooratseeonay sono eengkloosee*
Can I leave the car at ...?	**Posso lasciare la macchina a ...?** *posso lashaaray la makkeena ah*
What kind of fuel does it take?	**Che tipo di benzina prende?** *kay teepo dee bayndzeena praynday*
Where is the high/ low beam?	**Dove sono gli abbaglianti/anabbaglianti?** *dovay sono lyee abbalyeeantee/ anabbalyeeantee*
Could I have full insurance, please?	**Vorrei una polizza di assicurazione completa.** *vorrehee oona poleetsa dee asseekooratseeonay komplayta*

Gas station

Where's the next gas [petrol] station?	**Dov'è la prossima stazione di servizio?** *doveh la prosseema statseeonay dee sayrveetseeo*
Is it self-service?	**È un distributore automatico?** *eh oon deestreebootoray owtomateeko*
Fill it up, please.	**Il pieno, per favore.** *eel peeayno pehr favoray*
… liters of … , please.	**… litri di benzina …, per favore.** *leetree dee bayndzeena … pehr favoray*
super/regular	**super/normale** *super/normaalay*
lead-free/diesel	**verde/il diesel** *vayrday/eel diesel*
Where is the air pump/ water?	**Dov'è la pompa per l'aria/l'acqua?** *doveh la pompa pehr lareea/lakwa*

Parking

Most street parking is limited in town centers. Tokens (**dischi orari**) for parking (up to 1 hour) in blue zones are obtained from tourist organizations, automobile clubs and service stations. Set the disc to show when you arrived and when you must leave.

In Rome, central parking (in the **zona tutelata**) on weekdays is prohibited; punishable by a fine and prison sentence.

Is there a parking lot [car park] nearby?	**C'è un parcheggio qui vicino?** *cheh oon parkaydjo kwee veecheeno*
What's the charge per hour/per day?	**Quanto costa all'ora/al giorno?** *kwanto kosta allora/ al jorno*
Do you have some change for the parking meter?	**Ha qualche moneta per il parchimetro?** *ah kwalkay monayta pehr eel parkeemaytro*
My car has been booted [clamped]. Who do I call?	**La mia auto è stata bloccata con il bloccaruote. A chi devo rivolgermi?** *la meea owto ay staata blokkaata kon eel blokkaroo-otay. a kee dayvo reevoljayrmee*

1 tail lights [back lights]
   i fanali posteriori
2 brakelights **le luci dei freni**
3 trunk [boot] **il portabagagli**
4 gas cap **il tappo del serbatoio**
5 window **il lunotto**
6 seat belt **la cintura di sicurezza**
7 sunroof **il tetto apribile**
8 steering wheel **il volante**
9 ignition/starter **l'accensione**
10 ignition key **la chiave
   dell'accensione**
11 windshield **il parabrezza**
12 windshield [windscreen] wipers
   il tergicristallo
13 windshield [windscreen]
   washers **i lavacristalli**
14 hood **il cofano**
15 headlights **i fari/gli abbaglianti**

16 license plate **la targa**
17 fog lamp **il fanale antinebbia**
18 turn signals [indicators]
   gli indicatori di posizione
19 bumper **il paraurti**
20 tires **i pneumatici**
21 hubcap **la coppa**
22 valve **la valvola**
23 wheels **le ruote**
24 outside mirror **lo specchietto
   retrovisore esterno**
25 automatic locks **la chiusura
   centralizzata**
26 lock **la chiusura**
27 wheel rim **il cerchione**
28 exhaust pipe **il tubo di
   scappamento**
29 odometer **il contachilometri**
30 warning light **le luci
   d'emergenza**
31 fuel gauge **l'indicatore della
   benzina**

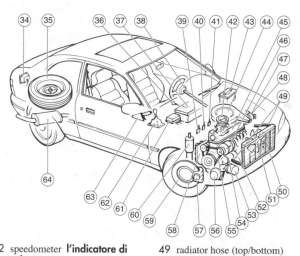

32 speedometer **l'indicatore di velocità**

33 oil gauge **l'indicatore del livello dell'olio**

34 backup lights **le luci di retromarcia**

35 spare tire [wheel] **il pneumatico/ la gomma di ricambio**

36 choke **la valvola d'aria**

37 heater **l'impianto di riscaldamento**

38 steering column il **piantone**

39 accelerator **l'acceleratore**

40 pedal **il pedale**

41 clutch **la frizione**

42 carburetor **il carburatore**

43 battery **la batteria**

44 alternator **l'alternatore**

45 camshaft **l'albero a camme**

46 air filter **il filtro dell'aria**

47 distributor **il distributore**

48 points **le candele**

49 radiator hose (top/bottom) **il tubo del radiatore**

50 radiator **il radiatore**

51 fan **il ventilatore**

52 engine **il motore**

53 oil filter **il filtro dell'olio**

54 starter motor **il motorino d'avviamento**

55 fan belt **la cinghia del ventilatore**

56 horn **il claxon**

57 brake pads **la ganascia dei freni**

58 transmission/gearbox **il cambio di velocità**

59 brakes **i freni**

60 shock absorbers **gli ammortizzatori**

61 fuses **i fusibili**

62 gear shift **la leva del cambio**

63 handbrake **il freno a mano**

64 muffler **la marmitta**

Breakdown

For help in the event of a breakdown refer to your breakdown assistance documents; or contact the **ACI** (**Automobile Club d'Italia**) breakdown service; Italy: ☎ 116.

Where is the nearest garage?	**Dov'è l'autorimessa più vicina?** *doveh lowtoreemayssa peeoo veecheena*
I've had a breakdown.	**Ho un guasto all'automobile.** *o oon goosto allowtomobeelay*
Can you send a mechanic/ tow [breakdown] truck?	**Può mandare un meccanico/un carro attrezzi?** *pwo mandaaray oon maykkaneeko/ oon karro attraytzee*
I belong to ... rescue service.	**Sono socio del servizio soccorso stradale ...** *sono socho dayl sayrveetseeo sokkorso stradaalay*
license plate number	**La targa ...** *la targa*
The car is ...	**L'auto è ...** *lowto eh*
on the highway [motorway]	**sull'autostrada** *soollowtostraada*
2 km from ...	**a due chilometri da ...** *ah doo-ay keelomaytree da*
How long will you be?	**Fra quanto tempo arriva?** *fra kwanto taympo arreeva*

What's wrong?

My car won't start.	**L'auto non parte.** *lowto non partay*
The battery is dead.	**La batteria è scarica.** *la battayreea eh skareeka*
I've run out of gas [petrol].	**Ho finito la benzina.** *oh feeneeto la bayndzeena*
I have a flat [pucture].	**Ho forato.** *oh foraato*
There is something wrong with ...	**C'è qualcosa che non funziona nel ...** *cheh kwalkosa kay non foontseeona nell*
I've locked the keys in the car.	**Ho lasciato le chiavi in macchina.** *o lashyatoh lay keeaavee in makkeena*

Repairs

Do you do repairs?	**Fa riparazioni?** *fa reeparatseeonee*
Can you repair it (temporarily)?	**Può fare una riparazione (provvisoria)?** *pwo faaray oona reeparatseeonay (provveezoreea)*
Please make only essential repairs.	**Faccia solo le riparazioni essenziali, per favore.** *fatcha solo lay reeparatseeonay ayssayntseeaalee pehr favoray*
Can I wait for it?	**Posso aspettare?** *posso aspayttaaray*
Can you repair it today?	**Può ripararla oggi?** *pwo reeparaarla odjee*
When will it be ready?	**Quando sarà pronta?** *kwando sara pronta*
How much will it cost?	**Quanto costerà?** *kwanto kostayra*
That's outrageous!	**Non esageriamo!** *non aysajayreeaamo*
Can I have a receipt for the insurance?	**Mi dia una ricevuta per l'assicurazione, per favore.** *mee deea oona reechayvoota pehr lasseekooratseeonay pehr favoray*

YOU MAY HEAR

... non funziona.	The ... isn't working.
Non ho i pezzi di ricambio necessari.	I don't have the necessary parts.
Devo ordinare i pezzi di ricambio.	I will have to order the parts.
Posso solo fare una riparazione provvisoria.	I can only repair it temporarily.
La sua macchina è inservibile.	Your car is totaled/a write-off.
Non si può riparare.	It can't be repaired.
Sarà pronta ...	It will be ready ...
oggi più tardi	later today
domani	tomorrow
fra ... giorni	in ... days

Accidents

In the event of an accident:
1. put your red warning triangle about 100 meters [metres] behind your car;
2. report the accident to the police (compulsory if there is personal injury); don't leave before they arrive;
3. show your driver's license and green card;
4. give your name, address, insurance company to the other party;
5. report to the appropriate insurance bureaus of the third party and your own company;
6. don't make any written statement without advice of a lawyer or automobile club official;
7. note all relevant details of the other party, any independent witnesses of the accident.

There has been an accident.	**C'è stato un incidente.** *cheh staato oon eencheedayntay*
It's …	**È …** *eh*
on the highway [motorway]	**sull'autostrada** *soollowtostraada*
near …	**vicino a …** *veecheeno ah*
Where's the nearest telephone?	**Dov'è il telefono più vicino?** *doveh eel taylayfono peeoo veecheeno*
Call …	**Chiami …** *keeaamee*
the police	**la polizia/i carabinieri** *la poleetseea/ee karabeenyehree*
an ambulance	**un'ambulanza** *oon amboolantsa*
a doctor	**un medico** *oon maydeeko*
the fire department [brigade]	**i pompieri** *ee pompeeehree*
Help me, please!	**Mi aiuti, per favore!** *mee aeeootee pehr favoray*

Injuries

There are people injured.	**Ci sono dei feriti.** *chee sono day fayreetee*
No one is hurt.	**Non ci sono feriti.** *non chee sono fayreetee*
He is seriously injured.	**È gravemente ferito.** *eh gravaymayntay fayreeto*
She's unconscious.	**Ha perso conoscenza.** *ah payrso konoshayntsa*

Legal matters

What's your insurance company?	**Qual è la sua compagnia d'assicurazione?** *kwaleh la sooa kompanyeea dasseekooratseeonay*
What's your name and address?	**Qual è il suo nome e il suo indirizzo?** *kwaleh eel soo-o nomay ay eel soo-o eendeereetso*
He ran into me.	**Mi ha investito.** *mee ah eenvaysteeto*
She was driving too fast/ too close.	**Andava troppo veloce/era vicino.** *andaava troppo vaylochay/ era veecheeno*
I had the right of way.	**Avevo la precedenza.** *avayvo la praychaydayntsa*
I was only driving ... km/h.	**Andavo solo a ... chilometri all'ora.** *andaavo solo ah ... keelomaytree allora*
I'd like an interpreter.	**Vorrei un interprete.** *vorrehee oon eentayrpraytay*
I didn't see the sign.	**Non ho visto il segnale.** *non oh veesto eel saynyaalay*
The license plate [registration] number was ...	**Il numero di targa era ...** *eel noomayro dee targa ayra*

YOU MAY HEAR

Mi faccia vedere ..., per favore.	Can I see your ..., please?
la patente di guida	driver's license/licence
la polizza d'assicurazione	insurance certificate
i documenti del veicolo.	vehicle registration
A che ora è successo?	What time did it happen?
Dove è successo?	Where did it happen?
C'erano altre persone coinvolte?	Was anyone else involved?
Ci sono testimoni?	Are there any witnesses?
Deve pagare un'ammenda/ una multa subito.	You'll have to pay a fine (on the spot).
Deve fare una dichiarazione in Commissariato.	You have to make a statement at the station.

ASKING DIRECTIONS

Excuse me, please.	**Scusi, per favore.** _skoozee pehr favoray_
How do I get to …?	**Come si arriva a …?** _komay see arreeva ah_
Where is …?	**Dov'è … ?** _doveh_
Can you show me on the map where I am?	**Può indicarmi dove sono sulla cartina?** _pwo eendeekaarmee dovay sono soolla karteena_
I've lost my way.	**Mi sono perso/smarrito.** _mee sono payrso/ smarreeto_
Can you repeat that, please?	**Può ripetere, per favore?** _pwo reepaytayray pehr favoray_
Thanks for your help.	**Grazie (per il Suo aiuto).** _graatseeay (pehr eel soo-o aeeooto)_

Traveling by car

Is this the right road for …?	**È questa la strada per …?** _eh kwaysta la straada pehr_
How far is it to … from here?	**Quant'è lontano/a … da qui?** _kwanteh lontaano/a … da kwee_
Where does this road lead?	**Dove porta questa strada?** _dovay porta kwaysta straada_
How do I get onto the highway [motorway]?	**Come si entra in autostrada?** _komay see ayntra een owtostraada_
What's the next town called?	**Come si chiama la prossima città?** _komay see keeaama la prosseema cheetta_
How long does it take by car?	**Quanto tempo ci vuole in macchina?** _kwanto taympo chee vwolay een makkeena_

ON THE STREET

Scusi, la stazione è lontana da qui? _skoozee la statseeonay eh lontaana da kwee (Excuse me, is the train station far from here?)_

No. È a dieci minuti a piedi. _no eh a deeehchee ah peeaydee (No. It's 10 minutes on foot.)_

Mille grazie. _meelay graatseeay (Thank you very much.)_

Prego. _praygo (You're welcome.)_

94

Town plans

YOU MAY SEE

aeroporto (m)	airport
passaggio (m) pedonale	pedestrian crossing
chiesa (f)	church
cinema (m)	movie theater [cinema]
città (f) storica	old town
commissariato (m)	police station
edifici (mpl) pubblici	public building
fermata (f) d'autobus	bus stop
gabinetti (mpl)	restrooms [toilets]
lei è qui	you are here
parcheggio (m)	parking lot [car park]
parco (m)	park
percorso (m) d'autobus	bus route
posteggio (m) dei tassì	taxi stand [rank]
sottopassaggio (m)	underpass
stadio (m)	stadium
stazione (f) (metropolitana)	subway [metro] station
ufficio (m) postale	post office
via (f) principale	main [high] street
zona (f) pedonale	pedestrian zone

YOU MAY HEAR

È ... da qui	It's ... of here.
al nord/al sud	north/south
all'est/all'ovest	east/west
Prenda la strada per ...	Take the road for ...
È sulla strada sbagliata.	You're on the wrong road.
Deve ritornare a ...	You'll have to go back to ...
Segua le indicazioni per ...	Follow the signs for ...

Road signs

SOLO ACCESSO	access only
PERCORSO ALTERNATIVO	alternative route
DEVIAZIONE	detour [diversion]
METTERSI IN CORSIA	get in lane
DARE LA PRECEDENZA	yield [give way]
PONTE BASSO	low bridge
SENSO UNICO	one-way street
STRADA CHIUSA	road closed
SCUOLA	school
ACCENDERE I FARI	use headlights

YOU MAY HEAR

È ...	It's ...
vicino/lontano	close/a long way
a cinque minuti a piedi	5 minutes on foot
a dieci minuti in auto	10 minutes by car
a circa dieci chilometri	about 10 km away
È ...	It's ...
(sempre) diritto	straight ahead
a sinistra/a destra	on the left/on the right
dall'altro lato della strada	on the other side of the street
all'angolo	on the corner
dietro l'angolo	around the corner
in direzione di ...	in the direction of ...
di fronte .../dietro...	opposite .../behind ...
vicino a .../dopo ...	next to .../after ...
Scenda ...	Go down the ...
la strada (laterale/principale)	street (side/main)
Attraversi ...	Cross the ...
la piazza/il ponte	square/bridge
Prenda la terza svolta a destra.	Take the third turn to the right.
Giri a sinistra ...	Turn left ...
dopo il primo semaforo	after the first traffic light
al secondo incrocio	at the second intersection [crossroad]

SIGHTSEEING

TOURIST INFORMATION OFFICE

Tourist information offices are often situated in the town center; look for **Ufficio turistico**.

Where's the tourist office?	**Dov'è l'Ufficio turistico?** *doveh looffeecho tooreesteeko*
booking office	**l'ufficio prenotazioni** *lufeechio prenotatseeoni*
inquiry	**la richiesta d'informazioni** *la rikyesta deenformatseeoni*
What are the main points of interest?	**Quali sono i principali punti d'interesse?** *kwalay sono ee preencheepaalay poontee deentayrayssay*
We're here for …	**Siamo qui per …** *seeaamo kwee pehr*
only a few hours	**solo poche ore** *solo pochay oray*
a day	**un giorno** *oon jorno*
a week	**una settimana** *oona saytteemaana*
Can you recommend …?	**Può consigliare …?** *pwo konseelyaaray*
a sightseeing tour	**un giro turistico** *oon jeero tooreesteeko*
an excursion	**un'escursione** *oon ayskoorseeonay*
a boat trip	**una gita in barca** *oona jeeta een baarka*
Do you have any information on …?	**Avete informazioni su …?** *avaytay eenformatseeonay soo*
Are there any trips to …?	**Ci sono gite per …?** *chee sono jeetay pehr*

Excursions

How much does the tour cost?	**Quanto costa il giro?** *kwanto kosta*
Is lunch included?	**Il pranzo è compreso?** *eel prandzo eh komprayzo*
Where do we leave from?	**Da dove si parte?** *da dovay partay*
What time does the tour start?	**A che ora comincia la gita?** *ah kay ora komeencha la jeeta*
What time do we get back?	**A che ora si ritorna?** *ah kay ora see reetorna*
Do we have free time in …?	**C'è del tempo libero a …?** *cheh dayl taympo leebayro ah*
Is there an English-speaking guide?	**C'è una guida di lingua inglese?** *cheh oona gooeeda dee eengglayzay*

On tour

Are we going to see …?	**Andiamo a vedere …?** *andeeaamo ah vaydayray*
We'd like to have a look at the …	**Vorremmo dare un'occhiata a …** *vorrehmmo daaray oonokeeaata ah*
Can we stop here …?	**Possiamo fermarci qui …?** *posseeaamo fayrmaarchee kwee*
to take photographs	**per fare fotografie** *pehr faaray fotografeea*
to buy souvenirs	**per comprare dei souvenirs** *pehr kohmpraaray dayee souvenirs*
to go to the restroom	**per andare alla toilette** *pehr andahray allah toaylaytte*
Would you take a photo of us, please?	**Le dispiace farci una fotografia?** *lay deespeeachay farzee oona fotografeea*
How long do we have here/in …?	**Quanto tempo abbiamo qui/a …?** *kwanto taympo abbeeaamo kwee/ah*
Wait! … isn't back yet.	**Aspetti! … non è ancora ritornato(-a).** *aspayttee non eh ankora reetornaato(-a)*

98

RIST GLOSSARY

aforte f etching
arello m watercolor
sco m fresco
wing of building
e m altarpiece
ilievo m high relief
hità fpl antiquities
rtamenti mpl **reali** apartments
zi mpl tapestry
m . arch
m **rampante** buttress
m **trionfale** triumphal arch
nteria f silverware
nto silver
a f weapon
eria f armory
ianato m **d'arte** crafts
m atrium
ga f charioteer
a f abbey
o m **rilievo** bas-relief
oteca f library
f chariot
panile m bell tower
posanto m churchyard
ello m gate
lavoro m masterpiece
ima Cena The Last Supper
mica f ceramic
miche fpl pottery
sa f church
zione f collection
pletato nel ... completed in
erenza f lecture
rafforte f buttress
icione m eaves
m choirstall

corona f crown
cortile m courtyard
costruito(-a) built in
cupola f dome
d'oro golden
da by person
dagherrotipo m daguerreotype
decorato(-a) da decorated by
decorazione f decoration
dettaglio m detail
dipinto m picture
dipinto(-a) da painted by
disegnato(-a) da designed by
disegno m design, drawing
distrutto(-a) da destroyed by
donato(-a) da donated by
dorato(-a) gilded
duomo m dome
edificio m building
eretto(-a) nel/in erected in
facciata facade
fibula f brooch
finestra f **con vetro colorato** stained-glass window
fondato(-a) nel founded in
fonte f font
foro m forum
fossato m moat
fregio m frieze
frontone m pediment
garguglia f gargoyle
giardino f **formale** formal garden
gioielli mpl jewelry
guglia f spire
imperatore m emperor
imperatrice f empress
in prestito a on loan to
incisione f carving, engraving
ingresso m foyer

SIGHTS

Town maps are on display in city centers, train, tram and many bus stations, and at tourist information offices.

Where is/are the ...?	**Dov'è ...?** *doveh*
abbey	**l'abbazia** *labbatseea*
art gallery	**la galleria d'arte** *la gallayreea dartay*
battleground	**i luoghi della battaglia** *ee looogee daylla battalya*
botanical garden	**il giardino botanico** *eel jardeeno botaneeko*
castle	**il castello** *eel kastayllo*
cathedral	**la cattedrale** *la kattaydraalay*
cemetery	**il cimitero** *eel cheemeetayro*
church	**la chiesa** *la keeayza*
downtown area	**il centro** *eel chayntro*
fountain	**la fontana** *la fontaana*
market	**il mercato** *eel mayrkaato*
monastery	**il monastero** *eel monastayro*
museum	**il museo** *eel moozayo*
old town	**la città vecchia** *la cheetta vaykeea*
opera house	**il teatro dell'opera** *eel teeatro dayllopayra*
palace	**il palazzo** *eel palaatso*
park	**il parco/il giardino** *eel parko/eel jordeeno*
parliament building	**il palazzo del Parlamento** *eel palaatso dayl parlamaynto*
ruins	**le rovine** *lay roveenay*
shopping area	**la zona dei negozi** *la dzona dayee naygotsee*
viewpoint	**il punto(m) panoramico** *eel poonto panoraameeko*
Can you show me on the map?	**Può indicarmi sulla cartina?** *pwo eendeekahrmee soollah kahrteenah*

ADMISSION

Check opening times to avoid disappointment: some museums close at 2 p.m. Churches usually close between midday and 4 p.m.

Is the ... open to the public?	**... è aperto(-a) al pubblico?** eh apayrto(-a) al poobleeko
What are the hours?	**Qual è l'orario di apertura?** kwaleh loraareeo dee apayrtoora
When does it close?	**A che ora chiude?** ah kay ora keeooday
Is ... open on Sundays?	**... è aperto(-a) la domenica?** eh apayrto(-a) la domayneeka
When's the next guided tour?	**Quando c'è la prossima visita guidata?** kwando cheh la prosseema veezeeta gooeedaata
Do you have a guide book (in English)?	**C'è una guida (in inglese)?** cheh oona gooeeda (een eengglayzay)
Can I take photos?	**Posso fare fotografie?** posso faaray fotograafeeay
Is there access for the handicapped?	**C'è accesso per disabili?** cheh achaysso pehr deesaabeelee
Is there an audio guide in English?	**C'è una guida registrata in inglese?** cheh oona gooeeda rayjeestraata een eengglaysay

Paying/Tickets

How much is the entrance/entry fee?	**Quant'è il biglietto d'ingresso?** kwanteh eel beelyaytto deenggraysso
Are there any discounts for ...?	**Ci sono riduzioni/tariffe speciali per ...?** chee sono reedootseeonee/tareeffay spaychaalee pehr
children	**bambini** bambeenee
groups	**gruppi** grooppee
the handicapped	**disabili** deesaabeelee
senior citizens	**anziani** antseeaanee
1 adult and 2 children, please.	**Un adulto e due bambini, per piacere.** oon adoolto ay doo-ay bambeenee pehr peeachayray

AT THE TICKET COUNT

Due adulti, per piacere. dooay adoolte peeachayray (Two adults, please.)
Fa trentacinque euro. faa traynta chee (That's 35 euros.)
Ecco a Lei. ekko a lay (Here you are.)

YOU MAY SEE

INGRESSO GRATUITO	free entry
CHIUSO	closed
APERTO	open
ARTICOLI DA REGALO/SOUVENIR	gift shop
L'ULTIMO INGRESSO È ALLE ORE DICIASSETTE.	last entry
LA PROSSIMA VISITA ALLE ...	next tour
INGRESSO VIETATO	no entry
VIETATO USARE IL FLASH.	no flash

IMPRESSIONS

It's ...	È ... eh
amazing	**meraviglioso(-a)** mayra
beautiful	**bello(-a)** bayllo(-a)
boring	**noioso(-a)** noeeozo(-a)
breathtaking	**sensazionale** saynsatse
brilliant	**splendido(-a)** splayndee
great fun	**molto divertente** molto de
interesting	**interessante** eentayrayss
magnificent	**magnifico** manyeefeeko
romantic	**romantico(-a)** romanteel
strange	**strano(-a)** straano(-a)
superb	**stupendo(-a)** stoopaynd
terrible	**terribile** tayrreebeelay
ugly	**brutto(-a)** brootto(-a)
It's a good value.	**Ne vale la spesa.** nay val
It's a rip-off.	**È una bidonata.** eh oona
I like it.	**Mi piace.** mee peeachay

TOU

acqu
acqu
affre
ala
altar
altor
antic
app
roya
araz
arco
arco
arco
arge
arge
arme
arme
artig
atria
auric
badi
bass
bibl
big
cam
cam
canc
cap
L'Ul
cera
cera
chie
colle
com
conf
cont
corr
cor

iniziò nel started in
liberto m freedman
Maestà Madonna and Child in majesty
marmo m marble
mattone m brick
mobilia f/**mobili** mpl furniture
moneta f coin
morto(-a) nel died in
mostra f display, exhibition
muro m wall
nato(-a) nel ... a ... born in ... (year) in ... (town)
navata f nave
oggetto m **esposto/in mostra** exhibit
orecchini mpl earrings
orologio m clock
padiglione m pavilion
paesaggio m landscape (painting)
palcoscenico m stage
paliotto m altar frontal
Papato m Papacy
pastello m pastel
piano m plan
Pietà f Virgin with crucified Christ
pietra f stone
pietra f **angolare** cornerstone
pietra f **preziosa** gemstone
pietra f **tombale** headstone
pilastro m pillar
pittore m, **pittrice** f painter
pittura f **murale** mural
pitture fpl **a olio** oils
placca f plaque
ponte m bridge
porta f **d'ingresso** doorway
ponte m **levatoio** drawbridge
primo livello m level 1
quadro m painting

rappresenta represents
re m king
regina f queen
regno m reign
restaurato nel restored in
ricostruito nel rebuilt in
ritratto m portrait
rocca m fortress/stronghold
rosone m rose window
rovine f ruins
ruderi fpl ruins
sagrestia sacristy
salone m **per cerimonie** stateroom
scala uno:cento scale 1:100
scala f staircase
scavi mpl excavations
schiavo m slave
schizzo m sketch
scoperto(-a) nel discovered in
scultore m, **scultrice** f sculptor
scuola f **di** school of
secolo m century
sette colli fpl Seven Hills
spalti mpl battlement
a spina f **de pesce** herringbone
sporgente overhanging
statua f **di cera** waxwork
tableau f tableau
tapezzerie fpl tapestry
tela f canvas
terme fpl baths
tetto m roof
tomba f grave, tomb
torre f tower
trittico m triptych
vetro m glass
visse lived
volta f vault
zoccolo m molding

103

WHO/WHAT?

What's that building?	**Cos'è quell'edificio?**
	koseh kwayllaydeefeecho
Who was the …?	**Chi era …?** *kee ayra*
architect	**l'architetto** *larkeetaytto*
artist	**l'artista** *larteesta*
What style is that?	**Che stile è?** *kay steelay eh*

Roma repubblicana 753–27 b.c.

After periods of Etruscan (**etrusco**) and Greek (**ellenistico**) influence in Italy, Rome was founded in 753 b.c. The Republic was declared in 509 b.c.; the city expanded its empire across the known world (esp. in Punic Wars against the Carthaginians, ca. 2nd b.c.; and the military successes of Julius Caesar). Caesar's assassination (44 b.c.) brought civil war.

Roma imperiale 27 b.c.–467 a.d.

Caesar's adopted son, Octavius (Augustus), became the first emperor. His descendants (Tiberius, Caligula, Claudius, Nero) were followed by the Flavian, Antonine and Severus dynasties. This period of expansion saw great artistic and architectural achievements. In 382 a.d. Christianity was recognized as the state religion. However, decline set in, the Empire split into two and power was moved to Constantinople. Goths and Vandals plundered Rome, which fell to the Ostrogoths.

Medioevo 467–1300

Italy remained fractured, featuring powerful families such as the Medicis, independent city states like Venice, and increasing Papal power (with Rome as the capital of Western Christianity) through the Holy Roman Empire (**Sacro Romano**). Foreign involvement (Norman, German, French, Spanish and Austrian) continued in Italy beyond the Middle Ages into the nineteenth century.

Impero Risorgimento 1815–1870

The reunification of Italy as one kingdom was achieved by Victor Emmanuel II of Piedmont in 1861, with assistance from his minister Cavour and the exploits of Garibaldi. The final piece came when Rome was captured (1870).

Novecento 20th century

Italy fought with the Allies in World War I, but Benito Mussolini allied with Hitler in World War II with devastating consequences. The Democratic Republic was established in 1946, with numerous fragile governments following. Italy was one of the founding members of the European Economic Community in 1957.

Rulers

What period is that? **Che periodo è …?** _kay payreeodo eh_

Romano(-a) 500 b.c.–467 a.d.

Ruins remain throughout Italy and Western Europe of their forums, basilicas, arenas, theaters, amphitheaters, markets, circuses, libraries, triumphal arches, catacombs, baths, temples, aqueducts, bridges, city walls and mausoleums.

Bizantino 400–1100

Byzantine influence from the Eastern Christian Empire emphasized grandeur and mystery with splendid mosaic-decorated interiors (esp. Ravenna; also later influence in St Mark's in Venice, Sicily and Rome).

Gotico 1300–1400

Gothic style used complex architectural forms, using pointed arches and rib vaults (esp. cathedrals in Genoa and Siena, ornate window openings of Venetian houses, artistic work of Giotto in Padua, Assisi and Florence).

Rinascimento 1400–1650

The Renaissance was a hugely significant cultural and artistic movement, with a fascination with antiquity and admiration of beauty, colors, light, stability and poise. It saw stunning artistic creativity in the Quattrocento (ca. 15th cent.) esp. statues of Donatello, paintings of Botticelli; and Cinquecento (ca. 16th cent.) esp. Michelangelo (statues of David and Moses; Sistine Chapel ceiling), Leonardo da Vinci, Raphael, and the Venetian School (Titian, Tintoretto and El Greco).

Manierismo 1550–1650

Mannerism enjoyed frivolities and exaggerated use of Renaissance features (esp. Tivoli and Bomarzo; artists Caravaggio and Palladio).

Barocco e Rococò 1640–1789

Baroque emphasized movement, using scrolls and ornate embellishments (e.g. Bernini's facade of St Peter's in Rome; artists Canaletto and Bellotto).

CHURCHES

Predominantly Roman Catholic, Italy is rich in cathedrals and churches. Ask permission before taking photographs; cover bare shoulders before entering.

Catholic/Protestant church	**la chiesa cattolica/protestante** _la kee-ehza katoleeka/protaystantay_	
mosque	**la moschea** _la moskeeah_	
synagogue	**la sinagoga** _la seenagoga_	
What time is …?	**A che ora è ….?** _ah kay oara eh_	

IN THE COUNTRY

I'd like a map of …	**Vorrei una cartina di …** *vorrehee oona karteena dee*
this region	**questa regione** *kwaysta rayjonay*
walking routes	**percorsi a piedi** *pehrkorsee ah pee-ehdee*
cycle routes	**percorsi per ciclisti** *pehrkorsee pehr cheekleestee*
How far is it to …?	**Quanto dista …?** *kwanto deesta*
Is there a trail/scenic route to …?	**C'è un sentiero/una strada panoramica per …?** *cheh oon saynteeehro/oona straada panorameeka pehr*
Can you show me on the map?	**Puo indicarmi sulla cartina?** *pwo eendeekaarmee soolla karteena*
I'm lost.	**Mi sono smarrito(-a).** *mee sono smareeto(-a)*

Organized walks

When does the guided walk start?	**A che ora comincia la passeggiata/ l'escursione?** *ah kay ora komeencha la passaydjaata/layskoorseeonay*
When will we return?	**Quando ritorneremo?** *kwando reetornayrehmo*
What is the walk like?	**Com'è la passeggiata?** *komeh la passaydjaata*
gentle/medium/tough	**facile/di media difficoltà/difficile** *facheelay/dee maydeea deeffeekolta/deeffeecheelay*
I'm exhausted.	**Sono esausto(-a).** *sono aysaoosto(-a)*
What kind of … is that?	**Che tipo di … è quello?** *kay teepo dee … eh kwayllo*
animal/bird	**animale/uccello** *aneemaalay/oochayllo*
flower/plant/tree	**fiore/pianta/albero** *feeoray/peeanta/albayro*

106

Geographic features

bridge	**il ponte**	*eel pontay*
cave	**la caverna/la grotta**	*la kavayrna/la grotta*
cliff	**la scogliera/la rupe**	*la sholee-ehra/ la roopay*
field	**il campo**	*eel kampo*
foot path	**il sentiero**	*eel sayntee-ehro*
forest	**la foresta**	*la foraysta*
hill	**la collina**	*la kolleena*
lake	**il lago**	*eel lago*
mountain	**la montagna**	*la montaanya*
mountain pass	**il passo di montagna**	*eel passo dee montaanya*
mountain range	**la catena di montagne**	*la katayna dee montaanyay*
nature reserve	**l'oasi naturale**	*loazee natooraale*
panorama	**il panorama/la vista**	*eel panoraama/ la veesta*
park	**il parco**	*eel parko*
peak	**il picco/la cima**	*eel peeko/la cheema*
picnic area	**l'area da pic nic**	*laraya da peekneek*
pond	**lo stagno**	*lo staanyo*
rapids	**le rapide**	*lay rapeeday*
river	**il fiume**	*eel feeoomay*
sea	**il mare**	*eel maaray*
stream	**il ruscello/il torrente**	*eel rooshayllo/ eel torrayntay*
valley	**la valle**	*la vallay*
viewpoint	**il punto panoramico**	*eel poonto panorameeko*
village	**il paese**	*eel pa-ehsay*
winery [vineyard]	**le vigne**	*lay veenyay*

LEISURE

EVENTS

Local papers and, in large cities, weekly entertainment guides will tell you what's on.

Do you have a program of events?	**Ha un programma delle manifestazioni?** *ah oon programa dayllay maneefaystatseeonee*
Can you recommend ? a good ...	**Può consigliare un(a) buon(a) ...?** *pwo konseelyaaray oon(a) bwon(a)*
Is there a ... somewhere?	**C'è ...?** *cheh*
ballet/concert	**un balletto/un concerto** *oon ballaytto/oon konchayrto*
movie [film]	**un film** *oon film*
opera	**un'opera** *oonopayra*

Tickets for concerts, theater, and other cultural events are on sale at special ticket agencies (e.g. Anteprima, Prenoticket, Prontobiglietto) or major music stores (e.g. Messaggerie Musicali, Ricordi).

Availability

When does it start?	**A che ora comincia?** *ah kay ora komeencha*
When does it end?	**A che ora finisce?** *ah kay ora feeneeshay*
Are there any seats for tonight?	**Ci sono posti per questa sera?** *chee sono postee pehr kwaysta sayra*
Where can I get tickets?	**Dove si comprano i biglietti?** *dovay see kompraano ee beelyayttee*
There are ... of us.	**Siamo in ...** *see-aamo een*

Tickets

How much are the seats?	**Quanto costano i posti?**	
	kwanto kostano ee postee	
Do you have anything cheaper?	**Ha qualcosa di meno caro?**	
	ah kwalkosa dee mayno karo	
I'd like to reserve …	**Vorrei prenotare …**	
	vorrehee praynotaaray	
3 for Sunday evening	**tre posti per domenica sera**	
	tray postee pehr domayneeka sayra	
May I have a program, please?	**Ha un programma, per piacere?**	
	ah oon programma pehr peeachayray	
Where's the coat room?	**Dov'è il guardaroba?** _doveh eel_	
	goo-ardaroba	

YOU MAY HEAR

… della sua carta di credito?	What's your credit card …?
il numero	number
il tipo	type
la data di scadenza	expiration date
Ritiri i biglietti … per favore.	Please pick up the tickets …
alle … di sera	by … p.m.
al banco prenotazioni	at the reservation desk

YOU MAY SEE

PRENOTAZIONI	Bookings
TUTTO ESAURITO	Sold out
BIGLIETTI PER LO SPETTACOLO DI OGGI	Tickets for today's show

AT THE BOX OFFICE

Avete un programma delle manifestazioni?
avaytay oon programa dayllay maneefaystatseeonee
(_Do you have a program of events?_)
Certo. Ecco a Lei. _cherto ekko a lay_
(_Of course. Here you are._)
Grazie. _graatseeay_ (_Thank you._)

Movies

Foreign films are always dubbed into Italian, but a few movie houses show films in the original version. Italy has a film industry of its own, with famous directors such as Fellini, Antonioni and Visconti, Bertolucci, the Taviani Brothers, Roberto Benigni, Salvatores and Nanni Moretti. For a view of Italian humor, try a film by Carlo Verdone.

Is there a movie theater [cinema] near here?	**C'è un cinema qui vicino?** *cheh oon cheenayma kwee veecheeno*
What's playing at the movies tonight?	**Cosa danno al cinema questa sera?** *kosa danno al cheenayma*
Is the film dubbed/subtitled?	**Il film è doppiato/ha i sottotitoli?** *eel film eh doppeeaato/af ee sottoteetolee*
Is the film in the original English?	**Il film è in lingua originale (inglese)?** *eel film eh een leengwa oreejeenaalay eengglayzay*
A …, please.	**…, per favore.** *pehr favoray*
box of popcorn	**un pacchetto di popcorn** *oon pachetto dee popcorn*
chocolate ice cream	**un cremino** *oon kremeeno*
hot dog	**un hot dog** *oon hot dog*
soft drink/soda	**una bibita** *oona beebeeta*
small/regular/large	**piccolo(-a)/medio(-a)/grande** *peekolo(a)/maydeeo(-a)/graanday*

Theater

What's playing at the … Theater?	**Cosa danno al teatro …?** *…kosa danno al teeatro*
Who's the playwright?	**Di chi è?** *dee kee eh*
Do you think I'd enjoy it?	**Pensa che mi piacerà?** *paynsa kay mee peeachayra*
I don't know much Italian.	**Non so bene l'italiano.** *non so baynay eetaleeaano*

Opera/Ballet/Dance

In addition to the La Scala in Milan, excellent productions are found at the opera houses in Bologna, Florence, Naples, Parma, Rome and Turin. Also look for open-air productions in the summer, often held in Greek and Roman ruins.

Where's the opera house?	**Dov'è il teatro dell'Opera?** *doveh eel teeatro dayllopayra*
Is formal dress required?	**È necessario l'abito da sera?** *eh naychayssaareeo labeeto da sayra*
Who's dancing?	**Chi sono i ballerini?** *kee sono ee ballayreenee*
I'm interested in contemporary dance.	**Mi interessa la danza contemporanea.** *mee eentayraysa la dantsa kontaymporaaneha*

Music/Concerts

Where's the concert hall?	**Dov'è la sala concerti?** *doveh la sala konchayrtee*
Which orchestra/ band is playing?	**Che orchestra/gruppo sta suonando?** *kay orkaystra/groopo sta soo-onando*
What are they playing?	**Cosa stanno suonando?** *kosa stanno soo-onando*
Who is the conductor/soloist?	**Chi è il direttore d'orchestra/il (la) solista?** *kee eh eel deerayttoray dorkaystra/eel (la) soleesta*
Who is the support band?	**Chi è il gruppo di supporto?** *kee eh eel grooppo dee soopporto*
I really like …	**Mi piace molto…** *mee peeachay molto*
country music	**la musica country** *la moozeeka country*
folk music	**la musica folk** *la moozeeka folk*
jazz	**il jazz** *eel djaz*
pop	**la musica pop** *la moozeeka pop*
rock music	**il rock** *eel rock*
soul music	**il soul** *il soul*

NIGHTLIFE

What is there to do in the evenings?	**Cosa si può fare la sera?** _kosa see pwo faaray la sayra_
Can you recommend a …?	**Può consigliare …?** _pwo konseelyaaray_
Is there a … in town?	**C'è … in città?** _cheh een cheetta_
bar	**un bar** _oon bar_
casino	**un casinò** _oon kazeeno_
discotheque	**una discoteca** _oona deeskotayka_
gay club	**un locale gay** _oon lokaalay gay_
nightclub	**un nightclub** _oon nightclub_
restaurant	**un ristorante** _oon reestorantay_
What type of music do they play?	**Che tipo di musica suonano?** _kay teepo dee moozeeka soo-onano_
How do I get there?	**Come ci si arriva?** _komay chee see arreeva_

Admission

What time does the show start?	**A che ora comincia lo spettacolo?** _ah kay ora komeencha lo spayttakolo_
Is evening dress required?	**È necessario l'abito da sera?** _eh naychayssareeo labeeto da sayra_
Is there a cover charge?	**Si paga il coperto?** _see paga eel kopayrto_
Is a reservation necessary?	**Si deve prenotare?** _see dayvay praynotaaray_
Do we need to be members?	**Bisogna essere soci?** _eh beesonya ayssayray sochee_
How long will we have to stand in line [queue]?	**Quanto tempo si deve aspettare/ fare la coda?** _kwanto taympo see dayvay aspayttaaray/faaray la koda_
I'd like a good table.	**Vorrei un buon tavolo.** _vorrehee oon bwon tavolo_

YOU MAY SEE

È COMPRESA UNA BIBITA	includes 1 complimentary drink

CHILDREN

Can you recommend something for the children? **Può consigliare qualcosa per i bambini?** *pwo konseelyaaray kwalkosa pehr ee bambeenee*

Are there changing facilities here for infants? **Dove si possono cambiare i pannolini?** *dovay see possono kambeeaaray ee pannoleenee*

Where are the restrooms [toilets]? **Dove sono le toilette/i bagni?** *dovay sono lay toaylayttay/ ee bannee*

amusement arcade **la sala da giochi** *la sala dah jokee*

fairground **la fiera** *la fee-ehra*

kiddie [paddling] pool **la piscina per bambini** *la peesheena pehr bambeenee*

playground **il parco giochi** *eel parko jokee*

zoo **lo zoo** *lo dzoh*

Baby-sitting

Can you recommend a reliable baby-sitter? **Può consigliare una buona babysitter?** *pwo konseelyaaray oona bwona babysitter*

Is there constant supervision? **La sorveglianza è continua?** *la sorvaylyaantsa eh konteenoo-a*

Are the helpers properly trained? **Gli assistenti sono professionisti?** *lyee asseestayntee sono professioneestee*

When can I drop them off? **Quando posso lasciarli(-le)?** *kwando posso lashaarlee(-lay)*

I'll pick them up at … **Li (Le) passo a prendere alle …** *lee (lay) passo ah prayndayray allay*

We'll be back by … **Ritorniamo alle …** *reetrneeamo allay*

She's 3 and he's 18 months. **Lei ha tre anni e lui diciotto mesi.** *layee ah tray annee ay looee deechotto mayzee*

SPORTS

Soccer [football], tennis, boxing, wrestling, windsurfing and bicycle, car and horseracing are the most popular sports.

il calcio *eel kalcho*

Soccer is the overriding passion in Italy, which boasts probably the best league in the world (Serie A) with teams of the calibre of Juventus (Turin), Inter, Milan, Roma and Lazio. The intensity with which fans support their team creates a thrilling atmosphere during matches. In addition, the stadiums in Rome (Stadio Olimpico), Milan (Stadio San Siro) and Naples (Stadio San Paolo) are particularly striking.

Spectator Sports

Is there a soccer game [football match] this Saturday?	**C'è una partita di calcio stasera** *cheh oona parteeta dee kalcho stasayra*
Which teams are playing?	**Che squadre giocano?** *keh skwadray jokano*
Can you get me a ticket?	**Può comprarmi un biglietto?** *pwo kompraaray oon beelyaytto*
What's the admission charge?	**Quanto costa l'entrata?** *kwanto kosta layntraata*
Where's the racetrack [race course]?	**Dov'è l'ippodromo?** *doveh leeppodromo*
Where can I place a bet?	**Dove si scommette?** *dovay see skommayttay*
What are the odds on ...?	**Qual è il pronostico su ....?** *kwaleh eel pronosteeko soo*
athletics	**l'atletica** *l'atlayteeka*
basketball	**la pallacanestro** *la pallakanaystro*
cycling	**il ciclismo** *eel cheekleesmo*
golf	**il golf** *eel golf*
horseracing	**l'ippica** *leepeeka*
soccer [football]	**il calcio** *eel kalcho*
swimming	**il nuoto** *eel noo-oto*
tennis	**il tennis** *eel tennis*
volleyball	**la pallavolo** *la pallavollo*

Playing

Where's the nearest …?	**Dov'è … più vicino(-a)?**
	doveh peeoo veecheeno(-a)
golf course	**il campo da golf** *eel kampo da golf*
sports club	**la palestra**
	la palaystra
Where are the tennis courts?	**Dove sono i campi da tennis?**
	dovay sono ee kampee da tennis
What's the charge per …?	**Quanto costa a/al/all' …?**
	kwanto kosta a/aal/al
day/round/game/hour	**giorno/giro/partita/ora**
	jorno/jeero/parteeta/ora
Where can I rent …?	**Dove posso noleggiare …?**
	dovay posso nolaydjaaray
boots	**gli scarponi** *lyee skaarponee*
clubs	**le mazze** *lay matsay*
equipment	**l'attrezzatura**
	lattraytsatooray
a racket	**la racchetta** *la rakaytta*
I'd like to take lessons.	**Vorrei prendere qualche lezione.**
	vorrehee prayndray kwalkay laytseeonay
Do you have a fitness room?	**C'è una sala attrezzi?**
	cheh oona sala atrayzzee

YOU MAY SEE

SPOGLIATOI	Locker rooms
PESCA VIETATA	No fishing
RISERVATO AI DETENTORI DI LICENZA	Permit holders only

YOU MAY HEAR

Mi dispiace, è tutto prenotato.	I'm sorry, we're booked.
C'è una caparra/un anticipo di …	There is a deposit of …
Che taglia/che misura ha ?	What size are you?
Deve avere una fotografia formato passaporto.	You need a passport-size photo.

At the beach

Italy abounds in beaches and sea resorts, and it is not too difficult to locate near-deserted coves for a quieter time. Nearly all beaches have private bathing establishments where you can rent cabins, deck chairs and sunbeds. Often the beach boys (**bagnini**) are also lifeguards, distinguished by their red shorts and vests.

A red flag signifies rough sea, a white flag denotes calm.

Is the beach …?	**La spiaggia è …?**	*la spee__a__dja eh*
pebbly/sandy	**rocciosa/sabbiosa**	*rockee__o__sa/sabbee__o__sa*
Is there a … here?	**C'è … ?**	*cheh …*
children's pool	**una piscina per bambini** *__oo__na peesh__ee__na pehr bamb__ee__nee*	
swimming pool	**una piscina** *__oo__na peesh__ee__na*	
indoor/outdoor	**invernale/all'aperto** *eenvayrn__aa__lay/allap__ay__rto*	
Is it safe to swim/dive here?	**Si può nuotare/tuffare senza pericolo?** *see pwo noot__aa__ray/too-__fah__-ray __say__ntsa pay__ree__kolo*	
Is it safe for children?	**È sicuro per i bambini?** *eh seek__oo__ro pehr bamb__ee__nee*	
Is there a lifeguard?	**C'è un bagnino?** *cheh oon ban__yee__no*	
I want to rent a/some…	**Vorrei noleggiare …** *vorr__eh__ee nolaydj__aa__ray*	
deck chair	**una sedia a sdraio** *__oo__na s__ay__deea ah sdr__a__eeo*	
jet ski	**una moto acquatica** *__oo__na m__o__to ak__wa__tika*	
motorboat	**una barca a motore** *__oo__na b__a__rka ah mot__o__ray*	
diving equipment	**attrezzature da sub** *attraytsat__oo__ray da soob*	
umbrella [sunshade]	**un ombrellone** *oon ombrayll__o__nay*	
surfboard	**una tavola da surf** *__oo__na t__a__vola da surf*	
waterskis	**degli sci d'acqua** *d__ay__lyee shee d__ak__wa*	
For … hours.	**Per … ore.** *pehr … __o__ray*	

Skiing

There is excellent skiing, in the Dolomites and the Italian Alps (Valle D'Aosta); the Apennines and the slopes of Etna also offer skiing.

What's the snow like?	**Com'è la neve?**	_komeh la nayvay_

heavy/icy	**spessa/ghiacciata**
	spayssa/geeachaata

powdery/wet	**farinosa/bagnata**
	fareenosa/banyaata

I'd like to rent …	**Vorrei noleggiare …**
	vorrehee nolaydjaaray

poles	**le racchette**	_le rachettay_

skates	**i pattini (da ghiaccio)**
	ee patteenee (da geeacho)

ski boots	**gli scarponi (da sci)**
	lyee skarponee (da shee)

skis	**gli sci**	_lyee shee_

These are too …	**Questi(-e) sono troppo …**
	kwaystee(-ay) sono troppo

big/small	**grandi/piccoli(e)**
	graandee/peekolee(-ay)

They're uncomfortable.	**sono scomodi(-e).**	_sono skomodee(-ay)_

A lift pass for a day/ 5 days, please.	**Uno ski pass per un giorno/cinque giorni, per favore.**
	oono ski pass pehr oon jorno/ cheengkway jornee pehr favoray

I'd like to join the ski school.	**Vorrei iscrivermi alla scuola sci.** _vorrehee eeskreevayrmee alla skooola shee._

I'm a beginner.	**Sono un principiante.**
	sono oon preencheepeeantay

I'm experienced.	**Ho esperienza.** _oh ayspayree-ehntsah_

YOU MAY SEE

LA FUNIVIA	cable car/gondola
LA SEGGIOVIA	chair lift
LA SCIOVIA	tow lift

MAKING FRIENDS

INTRODUCTIONS

Greetings vary according to how well you know someone. The following is a guide:

It's polite to shake hands, both when you meet and say good-bye.

Begin any formal conversation, whether with a shop assistant or policeman, with a "**Buongiorno**".

Ciao! is an informal, universal expression, meaning both "hello, hi" and "so long, good-bye."

In Italian, there are two forms for "you" (taking different verb forms):

tu (singular) and **voi** (plural) are used when talking to relatives, close friends and children (and between young people);

Lei (singular) and **Loro** (plural) are used in all other cases (with the 3rd person singular/plural of the verb).

Hello, I don't think we've met.	**Buongiorno, non ci conosciamo.** *bwonjorno non chee konosheeaamo*
My name is …	**Sono …** *sono*
May I introduce …?	**Posso presentarle …?** *posso praysayntaarlay*
Pleased to meet you.	**Piacere/Molto lieto(-a).** *peeachayray/molto leeehto(-a)*
What's your name?	**Come si chiama?** *komay see keeaama*
How are you?	**Come sta?** *komay sta*
Fine, thanks. And you?	**Bene, grazie, e Lei?** *baynay graatseeay ay layee*

AT A RECEPTION

Sono Sheryl. *sono sheryl* (*My name is Sheryl.*)
Piacere. Sono Franco. *peeachayray sono fraanko*
(*Pleased to meet you. My name is Franco.*)
Piacere. *peeachayray* (*Pleased to meet you.*)

Where are you from?

Where do you come from?	**Di dov`è?**	*dee dovay eh*
Where were you born?	**Dove è nato(-a)?**	*dovay eh naato(-a)*
I was born in …	**Sono nato(-a) …**	*sono naato(-a)*
Australia	**in Australia**	*in allowstraaleea*
Britain	**in Gran Bretagna**	*in gran braytanya*
Canada	**in Canada**	*in kanada*
England	**in Inghilterra**	*in eenggeeltayrra*
Ireland	**in Irlanda**	*in eerlanda*
Scotland	**in Scozia**	*in skotseea*
U.S.	**negli Stati Uniti**	*neglee staatee ooneetee*
Wales	**in Galles**	*in gallayss*
Where do you live?	**Dove vive?**	*dovay veevay*
What part of … are you from?	**Da quale parte … viene?**	*da kwalay partay … vee-ehnay*
Italy	**dell'Italia**	*daylleetaaleea*
Sicily	**della Sicilia**	*daylla seecheeleea*
Switzerland	**della Svizzera**	*daylla sveetsayra*
We come here every year.	**Veniamo ogni anno.**	*vayneeaamo onyee anno*
It's my/our first visit.	**È la mia/nostra prima visita.**	*eh la meea/nostra preema veezeeta*
Have you ever been to …?	**È già stato in …?**	*eh ja staato een*
Do you like it here?	**Le piace questo posto?**	*lay peeachay kwaysto posto*
What do you think?	**Cosa pensa?**	*kosa paynsa*
I love the … here.	**Mi piace molto …**	*mee peeachay molto*
I don't really like the … here.	**Non mi piace molto …**	*non mee peeachay molto*
food/people	**la cucina/la gente**	*la koocheena/la jayntay*

What weather!

What a lovely day!	**Che bella giornata!**	_kay baylla jornaata_
What awful weather!	**Che tempo orribile!**	
	kay taympo orreebeelay	
Isn't it cold/hot today!	**Che caldo/freddo oggi!**	
	kay kaldo/frayddo odjee	
Is it usually as warm as this?	**Di solito fa così caldo?**	_dee soleeto faa kosee kaldo_
Do you think it's going to … tomorrow?	**Pensa che domani …?**	
	paynsa kay domaanee	
be a nice day	**sarà una bella giornata**	
	sara oona baylla jornaata	
rain	**pioverà** _peeovayra_	
snow	**nevicherà** _nayveekayra_	
What is the weather forecast?	**Che previsioni ci sono?**	
	kay prayveeseeonay chee sono	
It's …	**È …** _eh_	
cloudy	**nuvoloso** _noovoloso_	
foggy	**nebbioso** _naybbeeoso_	
frosty	**gelato** _jaylaato_	
icy	**ghiacciato** _geeachaato_	
thundering	**temporalesco** _taymporalaysko_	
windy	**ventoso** _vayntoso_	
It's raining.	**Piove.** _peeovay_	
It's snowing.	**Nevica.** _nayveeka_	
It's sunny.	**C'è il sole.** _chay eel solay_	
Has the weather been like this for long?	**Il tempo è così da molto tempo?**	_eel taympo eh kosee da molto taympo_
What's the pollen count?	**Com'è il conteggio del polline?**	
	komeh eel kontaydjo dayl polleenay	
high/medium/low	**alto/medio/basso** _alto/maydeeo/basso_	
What's the forecast for skiing?	**Che previsioni ci sono per sciare?**	_kay prayveeseeonee chee sono pehr sheeaaray_

Enjoying your trip?

I'm here on …	**Sono qui …** _sono kwee_
a business trip	**per affari** _pehr affaaree_
vacation [holiday]	**in vacanza** _een vakantsa_
We came by …	**Siamo venuti(-e) in …** _seeaamo vaynootee(-ay) een_
train/bus/plane	**treno/pullman/aereo** _trayno/pullman/aayreeo_
car/ferry	**auto/traghetto** _owto/tragaytto_
I have a rental car.	**Ho noleggiato una macchina** _o nolaydjaato oona makeena_
We're staying at …	**Alloggiamo …** _allodjaamo_
an apartment	**in un appartamento** _een oon appartamaynto_
a hotel/campsite	**in un albergo/un campeggio** _een oon albayrgo/oon kampaydjo_
with friends	**con amici** _kon ameechee_
Can you suggest …?	**Può consigliare …?** _pwo konseelyaaray_
things to do	**cose da fare** _kosay da faaray_
places to eat	**posti per mangiare** _postee pehr manjaaray_
places to visit	**posti da visitare** _postee da visitaaray_
We're having a great/ an awful time.	**Ci stiamo divertendo/annoiando.** _chee steeaamo deevayrtayndo/ annoeeando_

YOU MAY HEAR

È in vacanza?	Are you on vacation?
Come è arrivato?	How did you travel here?
Dove alloggia?	Where are you staying?
Da quanto tempo è qui?	How long have you been here?
Quanto tempo si trattiene?	How long are you staying?
Dove andrà dopo?	Where are you going next?
Si sta divertendo?	Are you enjoying your vacation?

INVITATIONS

Would you like to have dinner with us on …?	**Vuole venire a cena da noi …?** _vwolay vayneeray a chayna da noee_
May I invite you to lunch?	**Posso invitarla a pranzo?** _posso eenveetaarla ah prandzo_
Can you come for coffee this evening?	**Vuole venire a prendere il caffè da noi questa sera?** _vwolay vayneeray ah prayndayray eel kaffeh da noee kwaysta sayra_
We're having a party. Can you come?	**Facciamo una festa. Vuole venire?** _fachaamo oona faysta. vwolay vayneeray_
May we join you?	**Possiamo venire anche noi?** _passeeaamo vayneeray ankay noee_
Would you like to join us?	**Vuole venire anche Lei?** _vwolay vayneeray ankay layee_

Going out

What are your plans for …?	**Cosa fa …?** _kosa fa_
today/tonight	**oggi/stasera** _odjee/stasayra_
tomorrow	**domani** _domaanee_
Are you free this evening?	**È libero(-a) stasera?** _eh leebayro(-a) stasayra_
Would you like to …?	**Le piacerebbe …?** _lay pee-achayraybbay_
go dancing	**andare a ballare** _andaaray ah ballaaray_
go for a drink/meal	**andare al bar/al ristorante** _andaaray al bar/al reestorantay_
go for a walk	**fare una passeggiata** _faaray oona passaydjaata_
go shopping	**fare acquisti** _faaray akweestee_
I'd like to go to …	**Mi piacerebbe andare …** _mee pee-achayraybbay andaaray_

I'd like to see …	**Mi piacerebbe vedere …**
	mee pee-achayraybbay vaydayray
Do you enjoy …?	**Le piace …?** *lay pee-achay*

Accepting or declining

Great. I'd love to.	**Sarebbe magnifico.**
	saraybbay manyeefeeko
Thank you, but I'm busy.	**Grazie, ma ho un altro impegno.**
	graatseeay ma ho oon altro eempaynyo
May I bring a friend? (male/female)	**Posso portare un amico/un'amica?**
	posso portaaray oon ameeko(-a)
Where shall we meet?	**Dove ci incontriamo?**
	dovay chee eenkontreeaamo
I'll meet you …	**Ci vediamo …** *chee vaydeeaamo*
in front of your hotel	**di fronte al suo albergo**
	dee frontay al soo-o albayrgo
I'll pick you up at 8 p.m.	**La chiamo alle otto.**
	la keeaamo allay otto
Could we make it a bit later/earlier?	**Facciamo un po' più tardi/prima?**
	fachaamo oon po peeoo tardee/preema
How about another day?	**Facciamo un altro giorno?**
	fachaamo oonaltro jorno
That will be fine.	**Va bene.** *va baynay*

Dining out/in

Punctuality varies from region to region in Italy. 15 minutes late may be acceptable in the south, but even 5 minutes would be frowned upon in the north.

Let me buy you a drink.	**Mi permetta di offrirle una bibita.**
	mee payrmeeta dee offreerlay oona beebeeta
Do you like …?	**Le piace …?** *lay peeachay*
What are you having?	**Cosa prende?** *kosa praynday*
That was a lovely meal.	**E'stato squisito!**
	ehstato skweezeeto

ENCOUNTERS

Do you mind if I ...?	**Le dispiace se ...?** *lay deespee<u>a</u>chay say*
sit here	**mi siedo qui** *mee see-<u>e</u>hdo kw<u>ee</u>*
smoke	**fumo** *f<u>oo</u>mo*
Can I get you a drink?	**Posso offrirle qualcosa da bere?** *p<u>o</u>sso off<u>ree</u>rlay kwalk<u>o</u>sa da b<u>ay</u>ray*
I'd love to have some company.	**Mi piacerebbe avere un po' di compagnia.** *me pee-achayr<u>ay</u>bbay av<u>ay</u>ray oon po dee kompany<u>ee</u>a*
Why are you laughing?	**Perché ride?** *payrkeh r<u>ee</u>day*
Is my Italian that bad?	**Parlo così male l'italiano?** *p<u>a</u>rlo kos<u>ee</u> m<u>aa</u>le leetalee<u>aa</u>no*
Shall we go somewhere quieter?	**Andiamo in un posto più tranquillo?** *andee<u>aa</u>mo een oon p<u>o</u>sto pee<u>oo</u> trankw<u>ee</u>llo*
Leave me alone, please!	**Mi lasci in pace!** *mee l<u>a</u>shee een p<u>a</u>chay*
You look great!	**Sei stupendo(-a)!** *s<u>a</u>yee stoop<u>ay</u>ndo(-a)*
Thanks for the evening.	**Grazie per la serata.** *gr<u>a</u>atseeay pehr la sayr<u>aa</u>ta*
I'm afraid we've got to leave now.	**Penso che sia ora di andare.** *p<u>e</u>nso che s<u>ee</u>-a <u>o</u>ra dee and<u>a</u>ray*
Can I see you again tomorrow?	**Posso rivederla domani?** *p<u>o</u>sso reevayd<u>ay</u>rla dom<u>aa</u>nee*
See you soon.	**A presto.** *ah pr<u>ay</u>sto*
Can I have your address?	**Posso avere il suo indirizzo?** *p<u>o</u>sso av<u>ay</u>ray eel s<u>oo</u>-o eendeer<u>ee</u>tso*

TELEPHONING

Most payphones take phonecards, available in units of €1, €2.5, €5 and €8 from newsstands or tobacco shops. You need to snap off the corner of the card for it to work. You can also often use your credit card for calling home.

To phone home from Italy, dial 00 followed by:

Australia 61	Canada 1	Ireland 353
New Zealand 64	South Africa 27	UK 44 US 1

Note that you will usually have to omit the initial 0 of the area code.

Can I have your telephone number?	**Mi dà il suo numero di telefono?** *mee da eel soo-o noomayro dee taylayfono*
Here's my number.	**Ecco il mio numero.** *ehko eel meeo noomayro*
Please call me.	**Mi chiami, La prego.** *mee keeaamee la praygo*
I'll give you a call.	**La chiamerò.** *la keeamayro*
Where's the nearest telephone booth?	**Dov'è il telefono pubblico più vicino?** *doveh eel taylayfono poobbleeko peeoo veecheeno*
May I use your phone?	**Posso usare il suo telefono?** *posso oozaaray eel soo-o taylayfono*
It's an emergency.	**È un'emergenza.** *eh oon aymayrjayntsa*
I'd like to call someone in England.	**Vorrei fare una chiamata in Inghilterra.** *vorrehee faaray oona keeamaata een eenggeeltayrra*
What's the area [dialling] code for …?	**Qual è il prefisso per …?** *kwaleh eel prayfeesso pehr*
What's the number for Information?	**Qual è il numero del Servizio Informazioni?** *kwaleh eel noomayro del serveezeeoh eenformatseeony*
I'd like the number for …	**Vorrei il numero per …** *vorrehee eel noomayro pehr*
I'd like to call collect [reverse the charges].	**Vorrei telefonare a carico del destinatario.** *vorrehee taylayfonaaray ah kareeko dayl daysteenatareeo*

On the phone

Hello. This is …	**Pronto. Sono …** _pronto. sono_
I'd like to speak to …	**vorrei parlare con …** _vorrehee parlaaray kon_
Extension …	**Interno …** _eentayrno_
Speak louder/ more slowly, please.	**Parli più forte/più lentamente, per piacere.** _parlee peeoo fortay/peeoo layntamayntay pehr peeachayray_
Could you repeat that, please?	**Può ripetere, per piacere?** _pwo reepaytayray pehr peeachayray_
I'm afraid he/she's not in.	**Mi dispiace, non c'è.** _mee deespeeaachay non che_
You have the wrong number.	**Ha sbagliato numero.** _ah zbalyaato noomayro_
Just a moment.	**Un momento.** _oon momaynto_
Hold on, please.	**Resti in linea, per piacere.** _een leeneea pehr peeachayray_
When will he/she be back?	**Quando rientra?** _kwando reeayntra_
Will you tell him/her that I called?	**Per favore, gli/le dica che ho chiamato.** _pehr favoray lyee/lay deeka kay o keeamaato_
My name is …	**Mi chiaimo …** _mee keeamo_
Would you ask him/her to phone me?	**Può dirgli/dirle di richiamarmi?** _pwo deerlyee/deerlay dee reekeeamaarmee_
I must go now.	**Ora devo andare.** _ora dayvo andaaray_
Nice to speak to you.	**È stato un piacere parlare con Lei.** _eh staato oon peeachayray parlaaray kon layee_
I'll be in touch.	**La contatterò.** _la kontattayro_
Bye.	**Arrivederci.** _arreevaydayrchee_

Stores & Services

For a view of what Italians are buying, take a look in the big chain stores **La Rinascente**, **Upim** and **Oviesse**, which have branches in most towns.

Check locally for the location and times of open-air markets, generally held at least once a week in most tourist resorts.

I'd like …	**Vorrei …** *vorrehee*
Do you have …?	**Ha …?** *ah*
How much is that?	**Quanto costa?** *kwanto kosta*
Thank you.	**Grazie.** *graatseeay*

STORES AND SERVICES
Where is …?

Where's the nearest …?	**Dov'è … più vicino(-a)?** *doveh … peeoo veecheeno*
Where's there a good …?	**Dove'è un(a) buon(a) …?** *doveh oon (a) bwon(a)*
Where's the main shopping mall [centre]?	**Dov'è la zona dei negozi?** *doveh la dzona dayee naygotsee*
Is it far from here?	**È lontano da qui?** *eh lontaano da kwee*
How do I get there?	**Come ci arrivo?** *komay chee arreevo*

Stores

antiques shop	**il negozio di antiquariato** *eel naygotseeo dee anteekwareeaato*
bakery	**la panetteria** *la panayttayreea*
bank	**la banca** *la banka*
bookstore	**la libreria** *la leebrayreea*
butcher shop	**la macelleria** *la machayllayreea*
camera shop	**il negozio di ottica/foto** *eel naygotseeo dee otteeka/foto*
pharmacy	**la farmacia** *la farmacheea*
clothing store [clothes shop]	**il negozio di abbigliamento** *eel naygotseeo dee abbeelyamaynto*
delicatessen	**la salumeria** *la saloomayreea*

129

department store	**il grande magazzino** *eel granday magatseeno*
drugstore [chemist]	**la farmacia** *la farmacheea*
fish store [fish monger]	**la pescheria** *la payskayreea*
florist	**il fioraio** *eel feeoraeeo*
gift shop	**il negozio di articoli da regalo** *eel naygotseeo de arteekolee da raygalo*
produce store [greengrocer]	**il fruttivendolo** *eel frooteevayndolo*
grocery store	**la drogheria** *la drogayreea*
health food store [shop]	**il negozio di dietetica** *eel naygotseeo dee deeaytayteeka*
jewelry store	**la gioielleria** *la joeeayllayreea*
liquor store [off licence]	**l'enoteca** *lenotekah*
market	**il mercato** *eel mayrkaato*
newsstand	**l'edicola** *laydeekola*
pastry shop	**la pasticceria** *la pasteetchayreea*
record [music] shop	**il negozio di musica** *eel naygotseeo dee moozeeka*
shoe store	**il negozio di scarpe** *eel naygotseeo dee skarpay*
shopping mall [centre]	**il centro commerciale** *eel chayntro kommayrchaalay*
souvenir store	**il negozio di souvenir** *eel naygotseeo dee souvenir*
sporting goods store	**il negozio di articoli sportivi** *eel naygotseeo dee arteekolee sporteevee*
supermarket	**il supermercato** *eel soopayrmayrkaato*
cigarette stand	**la tabaccheria** *la tabakkayreea*
toy store	**il negozio di giocattoli** *eel naygotseeo dee jokattolee*

Services

dentist	**il/la dentista** *eel/la daynteesta*
doctor	**il medico/il dottore(-ressa)** *eel maydeeko/eel dottoray(-rayssa)*
dry cleaner	**la tintoria/la lavanderia** *la teentoreea/la lavandayreea*
hairdresser (ladies/men)	**il parrucchiere/la parrucchiera** *eel parrookkeeayray/parrookkeeayra*
hospital	**l'ospedale** *lospaydaalay*
launderette	**la lavanderia a gettone** *la lavandayreea ah jaytonay*
library	**la biblioteca** *la beebleeoatayka*
optician	**l'ottico/il negozio di ottica** *lotteeko/eel naygotseeo dee otteeka*
police station	**il commissariato/la questura** *eel kommeessareeato/la kwaystoora*

Opening hours

In major cities like Rome, Milan, Bologna and Florence, during the August holidays (**Ferragosto**) you may find very few stores open as most locals have fled to the sea or mountains to escape the humidity.

When does the … open/close?	**Quando apre/chiude …?** *kwando apray/keeooday*
Are you open in the evening?	**È aperto la sera?** *eh apayrto la sayra*
Do you close for lunch?	**Chiude per pranzo?** *keeooday pehr prandzo*
Where is the …?	**Dov'è …?** *doveh*
cashier/cash desk	**la cassa** *la kassa*
store directory [guide]	**la guida al magazzino** *la gooeeda al magatseeno*
first floor [ground floor]	**pianterreno** *peeano tayrra*
second floor [first floor]	**primo piano** *preemo peeano*

	Opening	Closing	Lunch break	Closed
stores (winter)	9.30	8	1–3/4	Sun, one half day
(summer)	9.30	8	1–4/5	during the week
some shopping areas	10	7	none	Sun, Mon a.m
post office	8.30	6	none	Sat p.m., Sun
banks (main offices)	8.30	4	1.30–3	weekend

Service

Can you help me?	**Può aiutarmi?**	pwo aeeootaarmee
I'm looking for …	**Cerco …**	chayrko
I'm just browsing.	**Sto solo dando un'occhiata.** sto solo dando oonokkeeaata	
Do you have any …?	**Avete …?**	avaytay
I'd like to buy …	**Vorrei comprare …**	vorrehee kompraaray
Could you show me …?	**Può farmi vedere …?** pwo faarmee vaydayray	
How much is this/that?	**Quant'è questo/quello?**	kwanteh kwaysto/kwayllo
That's all, thanks.	**È tutto, grazie.** eh tootto graatseeay	

YOU MAY SEE

ORARIO DI APERTURA	business hours
CHIUSO PER LA PAUSA DI MEZZOGIORNO	closed for lunch
ORARIO CONTINUATO	open all day
L'USCITA	exit
L'INGRESSO	entrance
LA SCALA MOBILE	escalator
L'USCITA D'EMERGENZA	emergency/fire exit
L'ASCENSORE	elevator

IN A STORE

Desidera qualcosa? deseederah kwalkosa (Can I help you?)
No grazie. Sto solo dando un'occhiata. no graatseeay sto solo dando oonokeeaata (No, thanks. I'm just browsing.)

Preference

I want something …	**Voglio qualcosa di …**	_volyo kwalkosa dee_
It must be …	**Deve essere …**	_dayvay ayssayray_
big/small	**grande/piccolo(-a)**	_granday/peekkolo(-a)_
cheap/expensive	**economico(-a)/caro(-a)**	_aykonomeeko(-a)/kaaro(-a)_
dark/light	**scuro(-a)/chiaro(-a)**	_skooro(-a)/ keearo(-a)_
light/heavy	**leggero(-a)/pesante**	_laydjayro(-a) payzantay_
oval/round/square	**ovale/rotondo(-a)/quadrato(-a)**	_ovaalay/rotondo(-a)/kwadraato(-a)_
genuine/imitation	**autentico(-a)/imitazione**	_autenteeko(-a)/eemeetatseeonay_
I don't want anything too expensive.	**Non voglio niente di troppo caro.**	_non volyo neeayntay dee troppo kaarao_
Around … euros.	**Sulle … euro.**	_soollay … ayooro_
Do you have anything …?	**Ha qualcosa di …?**	_ah kwalkosa dee_
larger	**più largo**	_peeoo largo_
better quality	**di qualità migliore**	_dee kwaleeta meelyoray_
smaller	**più piccolo**	_peeoo peekkolo_

ESSENTIAL

Che cosa … desidera?	What … would you like?
colore/forma	color/shape
qualità/quantità	quality/quantity
Che tipo preferisce?	What kind would you like?
Su che prezzo vuole rimanere?	What price range are you thinking of?

YOU MAY HEAR

Buongiorno/buonasera, signora/signore.	Good morning/afternoon, madam/sir.
Desidera qualcosa?	Can I help you?
Che cosa desidera?	What would you like?
Glielo(-a) controllo subito.	I'll just check that for you.
È tutto?	Is that everything?
Nient'altro?	Anything else?

cheaper	**più economico/meno caro**
	pee<u>oo</u> aykon<u>o</u>meeko/<u>may</u>no <u>ka</u>ro
Can you show me …?	**Può mostrarmi …?** *pwo mostr<u>aar</u>mee*
that/this one	**quello/questo** *kw<u>ay</u>llo/kw<u>ay</u>sto*
these/those	**questi/quelli** *kw<u>ay</u>stee/kw<u>ay</u>llee*

Conditions of purchase

Is there a guarantee?	**C'è la garanzia?** *cheh <u>la</u> garant<u>see</u>a*
Are there any instructions with it?	**Ci sono anche le istruzioni?** *chee <u>so</u>no <u>an</u>kay leh eestrootsee<u>o</u>nee*

Out of stock

Can you order it for me?	**Può ordinarmelo(-a)?** *pwo ordee<u>naar</u>maylo(-la)*
How long will it take?	**Quanto tempo ci vuole?** *kwanto <u>taym</u>po chee vol<u>ay</u>*

Decision

That's not quite what I want.	**Non è esattamente quello che voglio.** *non eh ayssatta<u>mayn</u>tay kw<u>ay</u>llo kay <u>vo</u>lyo*
No, I don't like it.	**No, non mi piace.** *no non mee pee<u>a</u>chay*
That's too expensive.	**È troppo caro.** *eh <u>tro</u>ppo <u>ka</u>ro*
I'll take it.	**Lo (La) prendo.** *lo (la) <u>prayn</u>do*

YOU MAY HEAR

Mi dispiace, non ne abbiamo.	I'm sorry, we don't have any.
È esaurito(-a).	We're out of stock.
Posso mostrarle qualcos'altro/ un tipo diverso?	Can I show you something else/ a different kind?
Glielo(-a) ordino?	Shall we order it for you?

IN A STORE

Accetta traveller's cheques? *at<u>chay</u>tta traveller's checks (Do you accept traveler's ckecks?)*

No, mi dispiace. Ma accettiamo carte di credito. *no mee deespee<u>a</u>chay maa atchaytt<u>ia</u>mo <u>kar</u>teh dee <u>kray</u>deeto (No, I'm sorry. But we accept credit cards.)*

Paying

Most stores, restaurants and hotels, and some highway service stations accept major credit cards, traveler's checks and Eurocheques–look for the signs on the door.

Tax can be reclaimed on larger purchases when returning home (outside the EU).

Where do I pay?	**Dove si paga?** _dovay see paga_
How much is that?	**Quant'è/Quanto costa?** _kwanteh/kwanto kosta_
Could you write it down, please?	**Può scrivermelo, per favore?** _pwo skreevayrmaylo pehr favoray_
Do you accept traveler's checks?	**Accetta traveller's cheques?** _atchaytta traveller's checks_
I'll pay …	**Pago …** _pago_
by cash	**in contanti** _een kontantee_
by credit card	**con carta di credito** _kon karta dee kraydeeto_
I don't have any small change.	**Non ho spiccioli.** _non o speecholee_
Sorry, I don't have enough money.	**Mi dispiace, non ho abbastanza soldi.** _mee deespeeachay non o abbastantsa soldee_
Could I have a receipt, please?	**Mi dà la ricevuta, per favore?** _mee da la reechayvoota pehr favoray_
I think you've given me the wrong change.	**Credo che si sia sbagliato(-a) nel darmi il resto.** _kraydo kay see see-a zbalyeeaato(-a) nayl daarmee eel raysto_

YOU MAY SEE	
CASSA	cashier
I TACCHEGGIATORI SARANNO	shoplifters will
PUNITI A NORMA DI LEGGE	be prosecuted

Complaints

This doesn't work.	**E' difettoso(-a).** *eh deefayttoso(-a)*
Can you exchange this, please?	**Può cambiarlo, per favore?** *pwo kambeeaarlo pehr favoray*
I'd like a refund.	**Vorrei un rimborso.** *vorrehee oon reemborso*
Here's the receipt.	**Ecco la ricevuta.** *eko la reechayvoota*
I don't have the receipt.	**Non ho la ricevuta.** *non o la reechayvoota*
I'd like to see the manager.	**Vorrei parlare con il direttore.** *vorrehee parlaaray kon eel deerettoray*

Repairs/Cleaning

This is broken. Can you repair it?	**E' rotto(-a). Può ripararlo(-a)?** *eh rotto(-a) pwo reeparaarlo(-la)*
Do you have … for this?	**Ha … per questo?** *ah … pehr kwaysto*
a battery	**una pila** *oona peela*
replacement parts	**dei pezzi di ricambio** *dayee paytsee dee reekambeeo*
There's something wrong with …	**C'è qualcosa che non va …** *cheh kwalkosa kay non va*
Can you … this …?	**Può … questo(-a) …?** *pwo … kwaysto(-a)*
clean	**pulire** *pooleeray*
press	**stirare** *steeraaray*
mend	**riparare** *reeparaaray*
Can you alter this?	**Può aggiustarlo(-a)?** *pwo ajeeoostaarlo(-a)*
When will it be ready?	**Quando sarà pronto(-a)?** *kwando sara pronto(-a)*
This isn't mine.	**Questo non è mio.** *kwaysto non eh meeo*
… is missing.	**Manca …** *manka*

BANK/CURRENCY EXCHANGE OFFICE

At some banks, cash can be obtained from ATMs [cash machines] with Visa, Eurocard, American Express and many other international cards. Instructions are often given in English. You can also change money at most hotels, but the rate will not be as good. Main railway stations and airports also have currency exchange offices. Remember your passport when you want to change money.

In 2002 the currency in most EU countries, including Italy, changed to the euro (€), divided into 100 cents (**centesimi**). Switzerland is not in the EU and the currency is the Swiss franc (**franco**), divided into 100 **centesimi**.

Italy	*Coins:* 1, 2, 5, 10, 20, 50 ct.; €1, 2
	Notes: €5, 10, 20, 50, 100, 200, 500
Switzerland	*Coins:* 5, 10, 20, 50 ct.; 1, 2, 5 SF.
	Notes: 10, 20, 50, 100, 500, 1000 SF.

Where's the nearest …?	**Dov'è … più vicino/a?** _dovay_ peeoo vee_chee_no/aa
bank	**la banca** la _ban_kaa
currency exchange	**l'ufficio di cambio** loof_ee_zeeo dee _kam_beeo

Changing money

Can I exchange foreign currency here?	**Si può cambiare valuta straniera ?** see pwo kambee_aa_ray va_loo_ta stranyeh_ray
I'd like to change some dollars/pounds into euros.	**Vorrei cambiare alcuni dollari/sterline in euro.** vor_reh_ee kambee_aa_ray al_koo_nee dol_laree/stayr_lee_nay een _ayoo_ro
I want to cash some traveler's checks [cheques].	**Voglio incassare dei traveller's cheques/degli Eurocheques.** _vol_yo eenkas_saa_ray travellers cheques/deli eurocheques
What's the exchange rate?	**Quant'è il cambio?** kwan_teh_ eel _kam_beeo
How much commission do you charge?	**Quanto prendete di commissione?** _kwan_to _prayn_dayte de kommeessee_o_nay
Could I have some small change, please?	**Posso avere delle banconote di taglio più piccolo?** _posso a_vay_ray _dayl_lay banko_no_tay dee _tal_yo peeoo _peek_kolo
I've lost my traveler's checks.These are the numbers.	**Ho perso i miei traveller's cheques. Ecco i numeri.** oa _payr_so ee mee_ayee_ travellers cheques. _eko_ ee _noo_mayree

Security

Posso vedere …?	Could I see …?
il suo passaporto	your passport
un documento d'identità	some identification
la sua carta bancaria	your bank card
Qual' è il suo indirizzo?	What's your address?
Dove alloggia?	Where are you staying?
Compili/riempia questo modulo, per favore.	Fill out this form, please.
Per favore firmi qui.	Please sign here.

ATMs [Cash machines]

Can I withdraw money on my credit card here?	**Posso fare un prelievo con la mia carta di credito?** _posso faaray oon prayleeayvo kon la meea karta dee kraydeeto_
Where are the ATMs [cash machines]?	**Dove' è il Bancomat/la cassa automatica?** _doveh il bankomat/ lay kassa owtomateeka_
Can I use my … card in the ATM [cash machine]?	**Posso usare la mia carta … nel Bancomat?** _posso oozaaray la meea karta … nayl bankomat_
The ATM [cash machine] has eaten my card.	**Il Bancomat si è mangiato la mia carta.** _eel bankomat see eh manjaato la meea karta_

BANCOMAT/CASSA AUTOMATICA	automated teller [cash machine]
TUTTE LE OPERAZIONI	all transactions
SPINGERE/TIRARE/PREMERE	push/pull/press
APERTO/CHIUSO	open/closed
CASSA	cashiers

PHARMACY

Pharmacies are easily recognized by their sign: a green cross, usually lit up. If you are looking for a pharmacy at night, on Sundays or holidays, you'll find the address of emergency pharmacies (**farmacia di turno**) listed in the newspaper or displayed in all pharmacy windows.

Where's the nearest (all-night) pharmacy?	**Dov'è la farmacia (notturna) più vicina?** *doveh la farmacheea (nottoorna) peeoo veecheena*
What time does the pharmacy open/close?	**A che ora apre/chiude la farmacia?** *ah kay ora apray/keeooday la farmacheea*
Can you make up this prescription for me?	**Può farmi questa ricetta?** *pwo faarmee kwaysta reechaytta*
Shall I wait?	**Devo aspettare?** *dayvo aspayttaaray*
I'll come back for it.	**Passerò a ritirarla.** *passayro ah reeteeraarla*

Dosage instructions

How much should I take?	**Quanto devo prenderne?** *kwanto dayvo prayndayrnay*
How often should I take it?	**Con quale frequenza devo prenderlo(-la)?** *kon kwalay fraykwehntsa dayvo prayndayrlo(-la)*
Is it suitable for children?	**È adatto ai bambini?** *eh adatto ay bambeenee*

YOU MAY SEE

SOLO PER USO ESTERNO	for external use only
NON PER USO INTERNO	not to be taken internally

YOU MAY HEAR

Prenda ... pastiglie/cucchiaini ...	Take ... tablets/teaspoons ...
prima/dopo i pasti	before/after meals
con acqua	with water
intero(-a)	whole
la mattina/la sera	in the morning/at night
per ... giorni	for ... days

Asking advice

What would you recommend for …?	**Che cosa mi consiglia per …?** _kay kosa mee konseelya pehr_
a cold	**un raffreddore** _oon raffraydoray_
a cough	**la tosse** _la tossay_
diarrhea	**la diarrea** _la deearraya_
a hangover	**i postumi di una sbornia** _ee postoomee dee oona zborneea_
hayfever	**la febbre da fieno** _la faybbray da fee-ayno_
insect bites	**le punture d'insetto** _lay poontooray deensaytto_
a sore throat	**il mal di gola** _eel mal dee gola_
sunburn	**una bruciatura di sole** _oona broochatoorah dee soleh_
motion [travel] sickness	**la cinetosi** _la cheenaytozee_
an upset stomach	**mal di stomaco** _mal dee stomako_

Over-the-counter treatment

Can I have …?	**Ha …?** _ah_
an antiseptic cream	**una pomata antisettica** _oona pomaata anteesaytteeka_
(soluble) aspirin	**dell'aspirina (solubile)** _dayllaspeereena (soloobeelay)_
bandage	**delle bende** _dayllay baynday_
condoms	**dei profilattici** _dayee profeelatteechee_
cotton	**del cotone idrofilo** _dayl kotonay eedrofeelo_
an insect repellent/spray	**una pomata contro gli insetti/dello spray insetticida** _oona pomaata kontro lyee eensayttee/dayllo spray eensaytteecheeda_
pain killer	**dell'antinevralgico** _dayllanteenayvraljeeko_
vitamin pills	**delle vitamine** _dayllay veetameenay_

140

Toiletries

I'd like …	**Vorrei …** *vorrehee*
aftershave	**un dopobarba** *oon dopobarba*
deodorant	**un deodorante** *oon deeodorantay*
moisturizing cream	**una crema idratante** *oona krayma eedratantay*
razor blades	**delle lamette da barba** *dayllay lamayttay da barba*
sanitary napkins [towels]	**degli assorbenti** *daylyee assorbayntee*
soap	**del sapone** *dayl saponay*
sun block	**un blocco antisolare** *oon block anteesolaaray*
suntan lotion	**una crema/una lozione abbronzante** *oona krayma/oona lotseeonay abbrondzantay*
factor …	**fattore …** *fattoray*
tampons	**dei tamponi** *dayee tamponee*
tissues	**dei fazzoletti di carta** *dayee fatsolayttee dee karta*
toilet paper	**della carta igienica** *daylla karta eejayneeka*
toothpaste	**un dentifricio** *oon daynteefreecho*

For the baby

baby food	**degli alimenti per neonati** *daylyee aleemayntee pehr neonaatee*
baby wipes	**dei fazzolettini/delle salviette per neonati** *dayee fatzolaytteenee/dayllee salveeayttee pehr neeonaatee*
diapers [nappies]	**dei pannolini** *dayee pannoleenee*

Haircare

comb	**un pettine** *oon paytteenay*
conditioner	**del balsamo** *dayl balsamo*
hair mousse	**della schiuma per capelli** *daylla skeeooma per kapellee*
hair spray	**della lacca per capelli** *daylla lakka pehr kapayllee*
shampoo	**dello shampoo** *dayllo shampoo*

CLOTHING

The fashion capital of Italy is Milan, where many of the great designers, such as **Armani**, **Versace**, **Trussardi**, **Ferré**, **Moschino** and **Krizia** have salons.

You'll find that airport boutiques offering tax-free shopping may have cheaper prices but less selection.

General

I'd like …	**Vorrei …** vor<u>re</u>hee
Do you have any …?	**Avete ….?** a<u>vay</u>tay

YOU MAY SEE

ABBIGLIAMENTO DA DONNA	ladies wear
ABBIGLIAMENTO DA UOMO	menswear
ABBIGLIAMENTO DA BAMBINO	children's wear
SALDI/LIQUIDAZIONI	sale

Color

I'm looking for something in …	**Cerco qualcosa in …** <u>chayr</u>ko kwal<u>ko</u>sa een
beige	**beige** beige
black	**nero** <u>nay</u>ro
blue	**blu** bloo
brown	**marrone** mar<u>ro</u>nay
green	**verde** <u>vayr</u>day
gray	**grigio** <u>gree</u>jo
orange	**arancione** aran<u>cho</u>nay
pink	**rosa** <u>ro</u>sa
purple	**viola** vee<u>o</u>la
red	**rosso** <u>ros</u>so
white	**bianco** bee<u>an</u>ko
yellow	**giallo** <u>jal</u>lo
light …	**chiaro** kee<u>aa</u>ro
dark …	**… scuro** … <u>skoo</u>ro
Do you have the same in …?	**Ce l'ha anche in …?** chay la <u>an</u>kay een

belt	**la cintura**	*la cheentoora*
bikini	**il bikini**	*eel beekeenee*
blouse	**la camicetta**	*la kameechaytta*
bra	**il reggiseno**	*eel raydjeesayno*
briefs	**le mutandine**	*lay mootandeenay*
cap	**il berretto**	*eel bayrraytto*
coat	**il cappotto**	*eel kappotto*
dress	**il vestito**	*eel vaysteeto*
handbag	**la borsetta**	*la borsaytta*
hat	**il cappello**	*eel kapayllo*
jacket	**la giacca**	*la jakka*
jeans	**i jeans**	*ee jeans*
jumper	**la maglia**	*la malya*
leggings	**i fuseaux**	*ee fooso*
pants	**i pantaloni**	*ee pantalonee*
pullover	**il maglione**	*eel malyonay*
raincoat	**l'impermeabile**	*leempayrmeeabeelay*
scarf	**la sciarpa/il foulard**	*la sharpa/eel foolar*
shirt	**la camicia**	*la kameecha*
shorts	**gli shorts**	*lyee shorts*
skirt	**la gonna**	*la gonna*
socks	**i calzini**	*ee kaltseenee*
stocking	**le calze**	*lay kaltsay*
suit	**il completo**	*eel komplayto*
sweatshirt	**la felpa**	*la faylpa*
swimming trunks	**i calzoncini da bagno**	*ee kaltsoncheenee da banyo*
swimsuit	**il costume da bagno**	*eel kostoomay da banyo*
T-shirt	**la T-shirt/la maglietta**	*la tee shirt/la malyaytta*
tie	**la cravatta**	*la kravatta*
tights	**il collant**	*eel kollant*
tracksuit	**la tuta da ginnastica**	*la toota da jeennasteeka*
underpants	**le mutande**	*lay mootanday*

Shoes

A pair of ...	**un paio di** *oon pa-yo dee*
boots	**gli scarponi** *lyee skarponay*
flip-flops	**le ciabatte** *lay cheeabattay*
sandals	**i sandali** *ee sandalee*
shoes	**le scarpe** *lay skarpay*
slippers	**le pantofole** *lay pantofolay*
running shoes [trainers]	**le scarpe da ginnastica**
	lay skarpay da jeennasteeka

Walking/hiking gear

windbreaker	**la giacca a vento** *la jakka ah vaynto*
knapsack	**lo zaino** *lo dza-eeno*
walking boots	**gli scarponi** *lyee skarponee*
waterproof jacket	**la giacca a vento** *la jakka ah vaynto*

Fabric

I want something in ...	**Vorrei qualcosa in ...**
	vorrehee kwalkosa een
cotton	**cotone** *kotonay*
denim	**tela jeans** *tayla "jeans"*
lace/leather	**pizzo/pelle** *peetso/ payllay*
linen	**lino** *leeno*
wool	**lana** *lana*
Is this ...?	**È ...?** *eh*
pure cotton	**in puro cotone** *een pooro kotonay*
synthetic	**in fibra sintetica**
	een feebra seentayteeka
Is it hand washable/ machine washable?	**Si può lavare a mano/in lavatrice?** *see pwo lavaaray ah maano/een lavatreechay*

YOU MAY SEE	
LAVARE A SECCO	dry clean only
NON STIRARE	do not iron
COLORI SOLIDI	colorfast

Does it fit?

Can I try this on?	**Me lo/la posso provare?**
	may lo/la posso provaaray
Where's the fitting room?	**Dov'è la cabina di prova?**
	doveh la kabeena dee prova
It fits well. I'll take it.	**Mi va bene. Lo/La prendo.**
	mee va baynay. lo/la prayndo
It doesn't fit.	**Non mi va bene.** *non mee va baynay*
It's too…	**È troppo …** *eh troppo*
short/long	**corto(-a)/lungo(-a)** *korto(-a)/loonggo(-a)*
tight/loose	**stretto(-a)/largo(-a)** *straytto(-a)/largo(-a)*
Do you have this in size …?	**Ha questo nella taglia/misura …?**
	ah kwaysto naylla talya/meesoora
What size is this?	**Che taglia è?** *kay talya eh*
Could you measure me?	**Può prendermi le misure?**
	pwo prendermee leh meesooreh
What size do you take?	**Cha taglia/misura prende?**
	kay talya/meesoora praynday
I don't know Italian sizes.	**Non conosco le misure italiane.**
	non konosko lay meesooray eetaleeaanay

	Dresses/Suits						Women's shoes			
American	8	10	12	14	16	18	6	7	8	9
British	10	12	14	16	18	20	4½	5½	6½	7½
Continental	38	40	42	44	46	48	37	38	39	40

	Shirts				Men's shoes							
American **British**	15	16	17	18	6	7	8	8½	9	9½	10	11
Continental	38	41	43	45	38	39	41	42	43	43	44	44

YOU MAY SEE

EXTRA GRANDE	extra large (XL)
GRANDE	large (L)
MEDIA	medium (M)
PICCOLA	small (S)

HEALTH AND BEAUTY

I'd like a …	**Vorrei fare…** *vorrehee fare*
facial	**un trattamento per il viso** *oon trattamaynto pehr eel veezo*
manicure	**una manicure** *oona maneekooray*
massage	**un massaggio** *oon massadjo*
waxing	**la ceretta** *la chayraytta*

Hairdresser

Tipping: up to 15% is normal.

I'd like to make an appointment for …	**Vorrei un appuntamento per …** *vorrehee oon appoontamaynto pehr*
Can you make it a bit earlier/later?	**Può un po' prima/più tardi?** *pwo oon po preema/peeoo tardee*
I'd like a …	**Vorrei …** *vorrehee*
cut and blow-dry	**taglio e asciugatura con fon** *talyo ay ashoogatoora kon fon*
shampoo and set	**shampoo e messa in piega** *shampoo ay mayssa een peeayga*
trim	**una spuntatina** *oona spoontateena*
I'd like my hair …	**Vorrei …** *vorrehee*
colored/tinted	**fare il colore** *faaray eel koloray*
permed	**la permanente** *la payrmanayntay*
Don't cut it too short.	**Non li tagli troppo corti.** *non lee talyee troppo kortee*
A little more off the …	**Tagli ancora un po' …** *talyee ankora oon po*
back/front	**dietro/davanti** *deeaytro/davantee*
neck/sides	**sul collo/ai lati** *sool kollo/ay lattee*
top	**sopra** *soprah*
That's fine, thanks.	**Va bene, grazie.** *va baynay graatseeay*

HOUSEHOLD ARTICLES

I'd like a(n)/some …	**Vorrei …** *vorrehee*
adapter	**una presa multipla** *oona praysa moolteepla*
aluminum foil	**della carta stagnola** *daylla karta stanyolay*

bottle opener	**un apribottiglie** *oon apreebotteelyay*
candles	**delle candele** *dayllay kandaylay*
clothespins [pegs]	**delle mollette da bucato** *dayllay mollayttay da bookaato*
plastic wrap [cling film]	**della pellicola** *daylla paylleekola*
corkscrew	**un cavatappi** *oon kavatappee*
lightbulb	**una lampadina** *oona lampadeena*
matches	**dei fiammiferi** *dayee feeammeefayree*
paper napkins	**dei tovaglioli di carta** *dayee tovalyolee dee karta*
plug *(electrical)*	**una spina elettrica** *oona speena aylayttreeka*
scissors	**un paio di forbici** *oon paeeo dee forbeechee*
screwdriver	**un cacciavite** *oon katchaveetay*
can [tin] opener	**un apriscatole** *oon apreeskatolay*

Cleaning products

bleach	**della candeggina** *daylla kandaydjeena*
dish cloth [tea towel]	**uno strofinaccio per i piatti** *oono strofeenatcho pehr ee peeattee*
detergent [washing powder]	**un detersivo per lavatrice** *oon daytayrseevo pehr lavatreechay*
dishwashing [washing-up] detergent	**un detersivo per lavastoviglie** *oon daytayrseevo pehr lavastoveelyay*
dishwashing [washing-up] liquid	**un detersivo per i piatti** *oon daytayrseevo pehr ee peeattee*
garbage [refuse] bags	**dei sacchetti per i rifiuti** *dayee sakkayttee pehr ee reeffeeootee*

China/Cutlery

cups	**delle tazze** *dayllay tatsay*
forks	**delle forchette** *dayllay forkayttay*
glasses	**dei bicchieri** *dayee beekkeeehree*
knives	**dei coltelli** *dayee koltayllee*
mugs	**dei boccali** *dayee bokkaalee*

JEWELER

Even if you can't afford the wares of **Bulgari** and **Buccellati**, Italy's most famous jewelers, you will find the jewelry is generally beautifully crafted and 18-carat gold is a good buy.

Could I see …?	**Vorrei vedere …** *vor<u>reh</u>ee vay<u>day</u>ray*
this/that	**questo/quello** *kwehsto/k<u>weh</u>llo*
It's in the window/ display case.	**È in vetrina.** *eh eenvay<u>tree</u>na*
I'd like a(n)/some …	**Vorrei …** *vor<u>reh</u>ee*
alarm clock	**una sveglia** *<u>oo</u>na <u>zvay</u>lya*
bracelet	**un braccialetto** *oon bratcheea<u>lay</u>tto*
brooch	**una spilla** *<u>oo</u>na <u>spee</u>lla*
chain	**una catenina** *<u>oo</u>na katay<u>nee</u>na*
clock	**un orologio** *oon oro<u>lo</u>jo*
earrings	**degli orecchini** *<u>day</u>lyee oraykk<u>ee</u>nee*
necklace	**una collana** *<u>oo</u>na ko<u>lla</u>na*
ring	**un anello** *oon a<u>nay</u>llo*
watch	**un orologio** *oon oro<u>lo</u>jo*
watch battery	**una pila per orologi** *<u>oo</u>na <u>pee</u>la pehr oro<u>lo</u>jee*

MATERIALS

Is this real silver/gold?	**È argento/oro vero?** *eh ar<u>jay</u>nto/<u>o</u>ro <u>vay</u>ro*
Is there a certificate for it?	**C'è il certificato di garanzia?** *cheh eel chayrteefeek<u>aa</u>to dee garants<u>ee</u>a*
Do you have anything in …?	**Ha qualcosa …?** *ah kwal<u>ko</u>sa*
copper/pewter	**in rame/in peltro** *een <u>ra</u>may/een <u>pay</u>ltro*
crystal (quartz)	**in cristallo** *een krees<u>ta</u>llo*
cut glass	**in vetro tagliato** *een <u>vay</u>tro tal<u>yaa</u>to*
diamond/pearl	**con diamante/con perle** *kon deea<u>man</u>tay/kon <u>payr</u>lay*
enamel	**in smalto** *een <u>smal</u>to*
gold/silver	**in oro/in argento** *een <u>o</u>ro/een ar<u>jay</u>nto*
gold-plated	**placcato d'oro** *plak<u>aa</u>to d<u>o</u>ro*
platinum	**in platino** *een pla<u>tee</u>no*

Foreign newspapers can usually be found at rail stations or airports, or on newsstands in major cities.

Tobacco is a state monopoly in Italy. Licensed tobacconists are marked by a large white "**T**" on a black background. Cigarettes are also sold in some cafés and bars with a tobacco license.

Do you sell English-language books/newspapers?	**Avete libri/giornali inglesi?** *avaytay leebree/jornaalee eengglayzee*
I'd like a(n)/some …	**Vorrei …** *vorraiee*
book	**un libro** *oon leebro*
candy [sweets]	**dei dolci** *dayee dolchee*
chewing gum	**della gomma da masticare** *daylla gomma da masteekaaray*
chocolate bar	**una tavoletta di cioccolata** *oona tavolaytta dee chokkolaata*
pack of cigarettes	**un pacchetto di sigarette** *oon pakkaytto dee seegarayttay*
cigars	**dei sigari** *dayee seegaaray*
dictionary	**un dizionario** *oon deetseeonaareeo*
Italian-English	**Italiano-Inglese** *eetaleeano eengglayzay*
envelopes	**delle buste** *dayllay boostay*
guidebook for …	**una guida di …** *oona gooeeda dee*
lighter	**un accendino** *oon atchayndeeno*
magazine	**una rivista** *oona reeveesta*
road map of …	**una carta stradale di …** *oona karta stradaalay*
matches	**dei fiammiferi** *dayee feeaammeefayree*
newspaper	**un giornale** *oon jornaalay*
American/English	**americano/inglese** *amayreekaano/eengglayzay*
paper	**della carta** *daylla karta*
pen	**una penna** *oona paynna*
pencil	**una matita** *oona mateeta*
postcard	**una cartolina** *oona kartoleena*
stamps	**dei francobolli** *dayee frankobollee*
tobacco	**del tabacco** *dayl tabako*

PHOTOGRAPHY

I'm looking for a(n) ... camera.	**Cerco una macchina fotografica ...** _chayrko oona makkeena fotografeeka_
automatic	**automatica** _owtomateeka_
compact	**compact** _kompakt_
disposable	**usa-e-getta** _ooza ay jaytta_
SLR	**SLR** _ayssay ayllay ayrray_
battery	**la pila** _la peela_
camera case	**la custodia della macchina fotografica** _la koostodeea dela makkeena fotografeeka_
flash	**il flash** _eel flash_
filter	**il filtro** _eel feeltro_
lens	**l'obiettivo** _lobeeaytteevo_
lens cap	**il tappo per l'obiettivo** _eel tappo pehr lobyaytteevo_

Film/Processing

I'd like a ... film for this camera.	**Vorrei una pellicola ... per questa macchina (fotografica).** _vorrehee oona paylleekola... pehr kwaysta makkeena (fotografeeka)_
black and white	**in bianco e nero** _een beeanko ay nayro_
color	**a colori** _ah koloree_
24/36 exposures	**da 24/36 pose** _da vaynteekwatro/trayntasay pozay_
I'd like this film developed, please.	**Vorrei fare sviluppare questo film.** _vorrehee faaray zveeloopaaray kwehsto film_
Would you enlarge this, please?	**Può ingrandire questa, per favore?** _pwo eenggrandeeray kwaysta pehr favoreh_
How much do ... exposures cost?	**Quanto costa lo sviluppo ...?** _kwanto kosta lo zveelooppo_
When will the photos be ready?	**Quando saranno pronte le foto?** _kwando saranno prontay lay foto_
I'd like to pick up my photos. Here's the receipt.	**Vorrei ritirare le mie foto. Ecco la ricevuta.** _vorrehee reeteeraaray lay meeay foto. eko la reechayvoota_

POLICE

In Italy, dial ☎ 113 for all emergency services and ☎ 118 for fire. Dial ☎ 7 for the police in Switzerland.

Beware of pickpockets, particularly in crowded places. Report all thefts to the local police within 24 hours for your own insurance purposes.

Where's the nearest …?	**Dov'è … più vicino(-a)?** _doveh … peeoo veecheeno(-a)_
police station	**il commissariato/la questura** _eel kommeessareeaato/la kwehstoora_
Does anyone here speak English?	**C'è qualcuno che parla inglese?** _cheh kwalkoono kay parla eengglayzay_
I want to report a(n) …	**Voglio denunciare …** _volyo daynoonchaaray_
accident/attack	**un incidente/un'aggressione** _oon eencheedayntay/oonaggraysseeonay_
mugging/rape	**un'aggressione per rapina/uno stupro.** _oonaggraysseeonay pehr rapeena/oono stoopro_
My child is missing.	**Il/La mio(-a) bambino(-a) è scomparso(-a).** _eel/la meeo(-a) bambeeno(-a) eh skompaarso(-a)_
Someone's following me.	**Qualcuno mi sta seguendo.** _kwalkoono mee sta saygoo-ayndo_
I've seen a suspicious package.	**Ho visto un pacco sospetto.** _o veesto oon pakko sospaytto_
I need an English-speaking lawyer.	**Vorrei un avvocato che parli inglese.** _vorrehee oon avokaato kay parlee leengglayzay_
I need to contact the Consulate.	**Devo contattare il consolato.** _dayvo kontataaray eel konsolaato_

YOU MAY HEAR

Lo/la può descrivere?	Can you describe him/her?
uomo/donna	male/female
biondo(-a)/bruno(-a)	blonde/brunette
con i capelli rossi/grigi	red-headed/gray
con i capelli lunghi/corti/stempiato	long/short hair/balding
altezza approssimativa …	approximate height …
di (circa) … anni	aged (approximately) …
indossava …	He/She was wearing …

Lost property/Theft

I want to report a theft/break-in.	**Voglio denunciare un furto/una rapina.** _volyo daynoonchaaray oon foorto/oona rapeena_
I've been mugged/robbed.	**Sono stato aggredito/derubato.** _sono staato aggraydeto/dayroobaato_
I've lost my …	**Ho perso …** _o payrso_
My … has been stolen.	**Mi hanno rubato …** _mee anno roobaato_
bicycle	**la bicicletta** _la beecheeklaytta_
camera	**la macchina fotografica** _la makeena fotografeeka_
(rental) car	**l'auto (noleggiata)** _lowto (nolaydjaata)_
credit cards	**le carte di credito** _lay kartay dee kraydeeto_
handbag	**la borsetta** _la borsaytta_
money	**i soldi** _ee soldee_
passport	**il passaporto** _eel passaporto_
purse	**il portamonete** _eel poartamonaytay_
ticket	**il biglietto** _eel beelyaytto_
wallet	**il portafoglio** _eel portafolyo_
watch	**l'orologio** _lorolojo_
What shall I do?	**Cosa faccio?** _kosa fatcho_
I need a police report for my insurance claim.	**Devo avere una copia della mia denuncia per la mia assicurazione.** _dayvo avayray oona kopeea daylla meea daynooncha pehr la meea asseekooratseeonay_

POST OFFICE

Italian post offices bear the sign PT. Mail boxes are red in Italy, though some post offices have yellow boxes for express mail.

In major towns, the main post offices are normally open from 8.30 a.m. through to 6 p.m., while smaller branches close at 2 p.m. Stamps can be bought from tobacconists **(tabaccaio),** some hotel desks, as well as from the Post Office.

General queries

Where is the main post office?

Dov'è l'ufficio postale centrale? *dovai looffeecho postaalay chentraleh*

What time does the post office open/close?

A che ora apre/chiude l'ufficio postale? *ah kay oray apray/keeooday looffeecho postaalay*

Does it close for lunch?

Chiude per pranzo? *keeooday pehr prandzo*

Where's the mailbox [postbox]?

Dov'è la cassetta delle lettere? *doveh la kassaytta dayllay layttayray*

Where's the general delivery?

Dov'è il Fermo Posta? *doveh eel fayrmo posta*

Buying stamps

A stamp for this postcard, please.

Un francobollo per questa cartolina, per favore. *oon frankobollo pehr kwaysta kartoleena pehr favoray*

A ...-cent stamp, please.

Un francobollo da ... centesimi, per favore. *oon frankobollo da ... chentehseemee pehr favoray*

What's the postage for a letter to ...?

Quanto costa spedire una lettera a ...? *kwanto kosta spaydeeray oona layttayra ah*

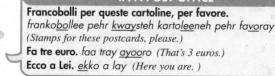

IN A POST OFFICE

Francobolli per queste cartoline, per favore. *frankobollee pehr kwaysteh kartoleeneh pehr favoray* *(Stamps for these postcards, please.)*

Fa tre euro. *faa tray ayooro* *(That's 3 euros.)*

Ecco a Lei. *ekko a lay* *(Here you are.)*

Sending packages

I want to send this package [parcel] by …	**Voglio spedire questo pacco …** *volyo spaydeeray kwaysto pahkko*
airmail	**per via aerea** *pehr veea aayreea*
express/special delivery	**per espresso** *pehr ayspraysso*
It contains …	**Contiene …** *konteeaynay*

Telecommunications

YOU MAY HEAR	
Deve compilare il modulo per la dogana.	Please fill out the customs declaration form.
Che valore ha?	What is the value?
Cosa c'è dentro?/Cosa contiene?	What's inside?

I'd like a phonecard, please.	**Vorrei una carta telefonica, per favore.** *vorraiee oonah kahrtah taylayfoneekah pair fahvoray*
5/8 euros.	**Da cinque/otto euro.** *da cheengkway/otto ayooro*
Do you have a photocopier?	**Avete il servizio fotocopie?** *avaytay eel sayrveetseeo fotokopeeay*
I'd like … copies.	**Vorrei … copie.** *vorrehee … kopee-eh*
I'd like to send a message …	**Vorrei trasmettere un messaggio …** *vorrehee trasmayttayray oon mayssajeeo*
by E-mail/fax	**per posta elettronica/fax.** *pehr posta aylaytroneeka/fax*
What's your E-mail address?	**Qual è il suo indirizzo di e-mail?** *kwalay eel soo-o eendeereetso dee e-mail*
Can I access the Internet here?	**Posso accedere a Internet?** *posso achaydayray a eentaynet*
What are your charges per hour?	**Quanto si paga all'ora?** *kwanto see paaga allora*
How do I log on?	**Come ci si collega?** *komay chee see kollayga*

SOUVENIRS

Italy is a shopping wonderland and you'll find no shortage of souvenirs and gifts to take home.

Italian designer clothes for men, women and children are internationally renowned, as well as shoes, accessories and other leather goods (handbags, beauty cases, luggage). You'll also find knitwear, cloth (silk, linen) and lace; or jewelry, including gold and silverware.

Regional crafts include pottery, ceramics, olivewood, glass and crystal work, straw and raffia goods. If you're still stuck for a souvenir, try a bottle of fine Italian wine, liqueur or aperitif or an art book or reproduction.

antiques	**gli oggetti di antiquariato**
	lyee ojayttee dee anteekwareeaato
ceramics	**la ceramica** la chayraameeka
doll	**la bambola** la bambola
glassware	**gli articoli di vetro**
	lyee arteekolee dee vehtro
jewelry	**i gioielli** ee joeeehllee
knitware	**la maglieria** la malyayreea
needlework	**il ricamo** eel reekaamo
silk	**la seta** la sehta
woodwork	**il lavoro in legno**
	eel lavoro een lehnyo

Gifts

bottle of wine	**una bottiglia di vino**
	oona botteelya dee veeno
box of chocolates	**una scatola di cioccolatini**
	oona skatola dee chokkolaateenee
calendar	**un calendario** oon kalayndaareeo
key ring	**un portachiavi** oon portakeeavee
postcard	**una cartolina** oona kartoleena
souvenir guide	**una guida-ricordo**
	oona gooeeda reekordo
ceramic plate	**un piatto di ceramica**
	oon peeatto dee cerameekaa
T-shirt	**una maglietta** oona malyaytta

Music

I'd like a …	**Vorrei …** *vorrehee*
cassette	**un nastro/una cassetta** *oon nastro/oona kassaytta*
compact disc	**un compact/un CD** *oon compact/oon cheedee*
record	**un disco** *oon deesko*
videocassette	**una videocassetta** *oona veedeeokassaytta*
Who are the popular Italian singers/bands?	**Chi sono i cantanti/gruppi italiani più famosi?** *chee sono ee kantantee/grooppee eetaleeaanee peeoo famozee*

Toys and games

I'd like a toy/game …	**Vorrei un giocattolo/un gioco …** *vorrehee oon jokattolo/oon joko*
for a boy	**per un bambino** *pehr oon bambeena*
for a 5-year-old girl	**per una bambina di cinque anni** *pehr oona bambeena dee cheenkway annee*
pail and shovel [bucket and spade]	**un secchiello e una paletta** *oon saykeeayllo ay oona palaytto*
chess set	**un gioco degli scacchi** *oon joko daylyee skakee*
doll	**una bambola** *oona bambola*
electronic game	**un gioco elettronico** *oon joko aylayttroneeko*
teddy bear	**un orsacchiotto** *oon orsakkeeotto*

Antiques

How old is this?	**Di che anno è?** *dee kay anno ay*
Do you have anything from the … era?	**Ha qualcosa del periodo … ?** *ah kwalkosa dayl payreeodo*
Can you send it to me?	**Può spedirmelo(-la)?** *pwo spaydeermeelo(-la)*

156

Will I have problems with customs?	**Avrò problemi con la dogana?**
	avro proablaymee kon la dogaana
Is there a certificate of authenticity?	**C'è il certificato di autenticità?** _cheh_
	eel chayrteefeekato dee owtaynteecheeta

SUPERMARKET/FOODSTORE

Supermarkets and convenience stores are found in most tourist resorts and all towns; however, Italy is still rich in markets, smaller stores and delicatessens (**salumeria**), where it can be more fun to shop.

At the supermarket

Excuse me. Where can I find …?	**Scusi. Dove posso trovare …?**
	skoozee. dovay posso trovaaray
Do I pay for this here or at the checkout?	**Pago qui o alla cassa?**
	pago kwee o alla kassa
Where are the baskets/ shopping carts [trolleys]?	**Dove sono i cestelli/carrelli?**
	dovay sono ee karrayllee/chestayllee
Is there a … here?	**C'è … ?**
	cheh …
delicatessen	**una salumeria**
	oona saloomayreea
pharmacy	**farmacia** _farmacheea_

YOU MAY SEE	
PANE E DOLCI	bread and cakes
PRODOTTI DI PULIZIA	cleaning products
LATTICINI	dairy products
PESCE FRESCO	fresh fish
CARNI FRESCHE	fresh meat
PRODOTTI FRESCHI	fresh produce
PRODOTTI SURGELATI	frozen foods
ARTICOLI CASALINGHI	household goods
POLLAME	poultry
FRUTTA E VERDURA	fruit and vegetables
VINI E LIQUORI	wines and spirits

Food hygiene

AT THE GROCERY STORE

I'd like some of that/these.	**Vorrei un pò di quello/questo.** *vorrehee oon po dee kwayllo/kwaysto*
this one/those	**questo/quelli** *kwaysto/kwayllee*
to the left/right	**a sinistra/destra** *ah seeneestra/daystra*
over there/Here	**lì/qui** *lee/kwee*
Which one/ones?	**Quale/quali** *kwalay/kwalee*
That's all, thanks.	**È tutto, grazie.** *eh tootto graatseeay*
I'd like a(n) …	**Vorrei …** *vorrehee*
kilo of apples	**un chilo di mele** *oon keelo dee maylay*
half-kilo of tomatoes	**mezzo chilo di pomodori** *maytso keelo dee pomodoree*
100 grams of cheese	**100 grammi di formaggio** *chaynto grammee dee formadjo*
liter of milk	**un litro di latte** *oon leetro dee lattay*
half-dozen eggs	**mezza dozzina di uova** *maytsa dotseena dee ooova*
… slices of ham	**… fette di prosciutto** *… fehttay dee proshootto*
piece of cake	**un pezzo di torta** *oon paytso de torta*
box of chocolates	**una scatola di cioccolatini** *oona skatola dee chokkolateenee*
bottle of wine	**una bottiglia di vino** *oona botteelya dee veeno*
carton of milk	**una confezione di latte** *oona konfeceeoneh dee lattay*
jar of jam	**un vasetto di marmellata** *oon vasaytto dee marmayllaata*

IN A SUPERMARKET

Scusi. Dove posso trovare lo zucchero? _skoozee_ _do_vay _posso_
trovaaray lo tsookkayro (Excuse me, where can I find sugar?)
Lì, a sinistra. _lee ah seeneestra_ (Over there, to the left.)
Grazie. _graatseeay_ (Thanks.)

PROVISIONS/PICNIC

beer	**birra** _beerra_
butter	**burro** _boorro_
cheese	**formaggio** _formadjo_
cookies [biscuits]	**biscotti** _beeskottee_
chips	**patatine** _patateenay_
eggs	**uova** _oo-ova_
grapes	**uva** _oova_
ice cream	**gelato** _jaylaato_
instant coffee	**caffè solubile** _kaffeh soloobeelee_
loaf of bread	**pagnotta di pane** _panyotta dee panay_
milk	**latte** _lattay_
rolls (bread)	**i panini** _ee paneenee_
sausages	**salciccie** _salcheechay_
soft drink/soda	**bibita analcolica** _beebeeta analkoleeka_
tea bags	**bustine di tè** _boosteenay dee teh_
bottle of wine	**bottiglia di vino** _botteelyay dee veeno_

del pane _dayl paanay_

Bread; look for **pane all'olio** (olive oil white bread), **pane al latte** (milk
bread), **panettone** (Christmas bread enriched with butter and candied fruit,
sultanas and raisins), **pandoro** (a large sponge cake topped with powdered
vanilla), **pangiallo** and **panforte** (firm nut and honey cake), **panpepato**
(spicy nut cake) and **veneziana** (sweet holiday bread with whole almonds).

focaccia _fokatcha_

Savory flatbread; which may be flavored ~ **alla salvia** (sage bread), ~ **alla
salsiccia** (sausage bread) or ~ **alle noci** (walnut bread).

CONVERSION CHARTS

The following conversion charts contain the most commonly used measures.

1 grammo (gr)	= 1000 milligrams	= 0.035 oz.
1 etto (hg)	= 100 grams	= .22 lb
1 mezzo chilo	= 500 grams	= 1.1 lb
1 chilo (kg)	= 1000 grams	= 2.2 lb
1 litro (l)	= 1000 milliliters	= 1.06 U.S / 0.88 Brit. quarts
		= 2.11 /1.8 US /Brit. pints
		= 34 /35 US /Brit. fluid oz.
1 centimetro (cm)	= 10 millimeter	= 0.4 inch
1 metro (m)	= 100 centimeters	= 39.37 inches/3.28 ft.
1 chilometro (km)	= 1000 meters	= 0.62 mile
1 metro quadrato (m2)		= 10.8 square feet
1 ettaro (ha)	= 10,000 sq meters	= 2.5 acres
1 chilometro quadrato (km2)		= 247 acres

Not sure whether to put on a bathing suit or a winter coat? Here is a comparison of Fahrenheit and and Celsius/Centigrade degrees.

					Oven Temperatures	
-40°C	–	-40°F	5° C	–	41°F	
-30°C	–	-22°F	10°C	–	50°F	100° C – 212° F
-20°C	–	-4° F	15°C	–	59°F	121° C – 250° F
-10°C	–	14° F	20°C	–	68°F	154° C – 300° F
-5° C	–	23° F	25°C	–	77°F	177° C – 350° F
-1° C	–	30° F	30°C	–	86°F	204° C – 400° F
0° C	–	32° F	35°C	–	95°F	260° C – 500° F

When you know	Multiply by	To find
ounces	28.3	grams
pounds	0.45	kilograms
inches	2.54	centimeters
feet	0.3	meters
miles	1.61	kilometers
square inches	6.45	sq. centimeters
square feet	0.09	sq. meters
square miles	2.59	sq. kilometers
pints (US/Brit)	0.47 / 0.56	liters
gallons (US/Brit)	3.8 / 4.5	liters
Fahrenheit	5/9, after subtracting 32	Centigrade
Centigrade	9/5, then add 32	Fahrenheit

HEALTH

Before you leave, make sure your health insurance policy covers any illness or accident while on vacation [holiday]. If not, ask your insurance representative, automobile association or travel agent for details of special health insurance. In Italy, EU citizens with a Form E111 are eligible for free medical treatment from the Italian national health system.

Hospital emergency departments (**Pronto Soccorso**) will treat all emergencies. However, it you are a non-EU citizen or without an E111 form, you will later have to sign a declaration that either you or your consulate will pay.

DOCTOR (GENERAL)

Where can I find a doctor/dentist?	**Dove posso trovare un medico/ un dentista?** _dovay posso trovaaray oon maydeeko/oon daynteesta_
Where's there a doctor who speaks English?	**C'è un medico che parla inglese?** _cheh oon maydeeko kay paarla eengglayzay_
What are the office hours?	**Quando apre l'ambulatorio?** _kwando apray lamboolatoreeo_
Could the doctor come to see me here?	**Posso avere una visita domiciliare?** _posso avayray oona veeseeta domeecheelyaaray_
Can I make an appointment …?	**Vorrei (fissare) un appuntamento …?** _vorrehee (feessaaray) oon appoontamaynto_
for tomorrow	**per domani** _pehr domaanee_
for as soon as possible	**al più presto** _al peeoo praysto_
It's urgent.	**È urgente.** _eh oorjayntay_
I've got an appointment with Doctor …	**Ho un appuntamento con il dottor/ la dottoressa …** _oh oon appoontamaynto kon eel dottor/la dottorayssa_

161

Accident and injury

My ... is hurt/injured.	**... si è fatto(-a) male/è ferito(-a).**
	see eh fatto(-a) malay/eh fayreeto(-a)
husband/wife	**Mio marito/Mia moglie**
	meeo mareeto/meea molyeeay
son/daughter	**Mio figlio/Mia figlia** *meeo feelyo/meea feelya*
friend	**Il mio amico/La mia amica**
	eel meeo ameeko/la meea ameeka
He/She is unconscious.	**Ha perso conoscenza.** *ah payrso konoshayntsa*
He/She is bleeding . (heavily)	**Perde (molto) sangue.**
	payrday (molto) sanggway
He/She is injured	**È ferito(-a).** *eh fayreeto(-a)*
I've got a/an ...	**Ho ...** *o*
burn	**una scottatura** *oona skottatoora*
cut	**un taglio** *oon talyo*
insect bite	**una puntura d'insetto**
	oona poontoora deensaytto
rash	**un'eruzione sulla pelle** *oonayrootseeonay*
	soollah payllay
swelling	**un gonfiore** *oon gonfeeoray*

Short-term symptoms

I've been feeling sick [ill] for ... days.	**Mi sento male da ... giorni.** *mee saynto*
	malay da ... jornee
I feel faint.	**Mi sento svenire.** *mee saynto svayneeray*
I feel feverish.	**Mi sento la febbre.** *mee saynto la faybbray*
I've been vomiting.	**Ho vomitato.** *o vomeetaatao*
I have diarrhea.	**Ho la diarrea.** *o la deeaarraya*
I have a/an...	**Ho ...** *o*
cold	**il raffreddore** *eel raffrayddoray*
cramps	**i crampi** *ee krampee*
headache	**mal di testa** *mal dee taysta*
sore throat	**mal di gola** *mal dee gola*
stiff neck	**il collo rigido** *eel kollo reejeedo*
stomachache	**mal di stomaco** *mal dee stomako*

Health conditions

I have arthritis.	**Ho l'artrite** o lartreetay
I have asthma.	**Ho l'asma** o lasma
I am …	**Sono …** sono
diabetic	**diabetico(-a)** deeabayteeko(-a)
epileptic	**epilettico(-a)** aypeelaytteeko(-a)
handicapped	**disabile** deesabeelay
(… months) pregnant	**incinta di … mesi** eencheenta dee … maysee
I have a heart condition.	**Ho disturbi cardiaci.** o deestoorbee kardeeachee
I have high blood pressure.	**Ho la pressione alta.** o la praysseeonay alta
I had a heart attack … years ago.	**Ho avuto un infarto … anni fa.** o avooto oon eenfaarto … annee fa

Parts of the body

appendix	**l'appendice** lappayndeechay	kidney	**il rene** eel raynay
arm	**il braccio** eel bratcho	knee	**il ginocchio** eel jeenokkeeo
back	**il dorso/la schiena** eel dorso/la skeeehna	leg	**la gamba** la gamba
bladder	**la vescica** la vaysheeka	lip	**il labbro** eel labbro
bone	**l'osso** losso	liver	**il fegato** eel faygato
breast	**il petto/il seno** eel paytto/eel sayno	mouth	**la bocca** la bokka
chest	**il torace** eel toraachay	muscle	**il muscolo** eel mooskolo
ear	**l'orecchio** loraykkeeo	neck	**il collo** eel kollo
eye	**l'occhio** lokkeeo	nose	**il naso** eel naaso
face	**la faccia/il viso** la fatcha/eel veezo	rib	**la costola** la kostola
finger	**il dito** eel deeto	shoulder	**la spalla** la spalla
foot	**il piede** eel peeehday	skin	**la pelle** la payllay
gland	**la ghiandola** la geeandola	stomach	**lo stomaco** lo stomako
hand	**la mano** la mano	thigh	**la coscia** la kosha
head	**la testa** la taysta	throat	**la gola** la gola
heart	**il cuore** eel koooray	thumb	**il pollice** eel polleechay
jaw	**la mascella** la mashehlla	toe	**il dito del piede** eel deeto dayl peeehday
joint	**l'articolazione** larteekolatseeonay	tongue	**la lingua** la leenggooy
		tonsils	**le tonsille** lay tonseellay
		vein	**la vena** la vayna

Doctor's Inquiries

Da quanto tempo si sente così?	How long have you been feeling like this?
È la prima volta che ha questo disturbo?	Is this the first time you've had this?
Prende altre medicine?	Are you taking any other medicines?
È allergico(-a) a qualcosa?	Are you allergic to anything?
È vaccinato(-a) contro il tetano?	Have you been vaccinated against tetanus?
Ha perso l'appetito?	Have you lost your appetite?

Examination

Le misuro la temperatura/ la pressione del sangue.	I'll take your temperature/ blood pressure.
Arrotoli/tiri sù la manica.	Roll up your sleeve.
Si spogli fino alla vita.	Undress to the waist.
Si sdrai, per favore.	Please lie down.
Apra la bocca.	Open your mouth.
Respiri profondamente.	Breathe deeply.
Tossisca, per favore.	Cough please.
Dove le fa male?	Where does it hurt?
Fa male qui?	Does it hurt here?

Diagnosis

Deve fare una radiografia.	I want you to have an x-ray.
Voglio un campione di sangue/feci/urina.	I want a specimen of your blood/stool/urine.
Deve farsi visitare da uno specialista.	I want you to see a specialist.
Deve andare in ospedale.	I want you to go to the hospital.
È rotto(-a)/slogato(-a).	It's broken/sprained.
È lussato(-a)/strappato(-a).	It's dislocated/torn.
Ha …	You've got (a/an) …
l'appendicite	appendicitis
la cistite	cystitis

la febbre	temperature
l'influenza	flu
un'avvelenamento alimentare	food poisoning
una frattura	fracture
la gastrite	gastritis
l'ernia	hernia
un'infiammazione al/alla ...	inflammation of ...
il morbillo	measles
la polmonite	pneumonia
la sciatica	sciatica
la tonsillite	tonsilitis
un tumore	tumor
una malattia venerea	venereal disease
È infetto(-a).	It's infected.
È contagioso(-a)	It's contagious.

Treatment

Le do ...	I'll give you ...
un antisettico	an antiseptic
un analgesico	a pain killer
Le prescrivo ...	I'm going to prescribe ...
una cura di antibiotici	a course of antibiotics
delle supposte	some suppositories
È allergico(-a) a qualche medicina?	Are you allergic to any medicines?
Prenda una pillola ...	Take one pill ...
ogni ... ore/... volte al giorno	every ... hours/... times a day
prima dei/dopo i pasti	before/after meals
in caso di dolore	if there is any pain
per ... giorni	for ... days
Ritorni fra ... giorni.	I'd like you to come back in ... days.
Consulti un medico quando ritorna a casa.	Consult a doctor when you get home.

DICTIONARY
ENGLISH-ITALIAN

A

a few alcuni(e)
a little un poco
a lot molto(-a)
a.m. di mattina
abbey abbazia f
able, to be potere
about *(approximately)* circa
above *(place)* sopra
abroad all'estero
abscess ascesso
accept, to accettare
access accesso m
accessories accessori mpl
accident incidente; *(road)* incidente stradale m
accidentally accidentalmente
accommodations sistemazione f
accompaniments condimenti mpl, salse f
accompany, to accompagnare
accountant contabile m/f
ace *(cards)* asso m
activities le attività fpl
acne acne f
across attraverso
action film film m d'azione
actor/actress attore m/attrice f
adaptor presa f multipla
address indirizzo m
adhesive bandage bende fpl adesive
adjoining room camera f adiacente
admission charge prezzo m d'entrata
adult adulto m
advance, in in anticipo
aerial *(car/tv)* antenna f
aerobics aerobica f
after *(time)* dopo; *(place)*
aftershave dopobarba m
after-sun lotion lozione f doposole
afternoon, in the nel pomeriggio
age: what age? età: quanti anni?
aged, to be avere … anni

ago fa
agree: I agree sono d'accordo
air conditioning aria f condizionata
air mattress materasso m di gomma
air pump pompa f per l'aria
air-freshener deodorante m per ambienti
airline linea f aerea
airmail via f aerea
airplane aeroplano m
airport aeroporto m
air steward/hostess assistente m/f di volo
aisle seat posto m nel corridoio
alarm clock sveglia f
alcoholic *(drink)* alcolico(-a)
all tutto(-a)
all-night bar bar m aperto tutta la notte
all-night pharmacy farmacia f notturna
allergic, to be essere allergico(-a) a
allergy allergia f
allowed: is it allowed? è permesso?
almost quasi
alone solo(-a)
alphabet alfabeto m
already già
also anche
alter, to ritoccare
aluminum foil carta f stagnola
always sempre
am: I am sono
amazing meraviglioso(-a)
ambassador ambasciatore m
amber ambra f
ambulance ambulanza f
American *(person/adj)* americano(-a) m/f
American football calcio m americano
amethyst ametista f
amount ammontare m, cifra (f)
and e
anesthetic anestetico m
angling pesca f con la lenza
animal animale m
announcement: what was that announcement? cos'era quell'annuncio?
another un altro/un'altra
another time un'altra volta

antacid antiacido m
antibiotics antibiotici mpl
antifreeze antigelo m
antique oggetti mpl di antiquariato
antiques shop negozio m di antiquariato
antiseptic antisettico m; ~ **cream** pomata f antisettica
any qualsiasi
anyone: does anyone speak English? c'è qualcuno che parla inglese?
anyone else altre persone
anything cheaper qualcosa di più economico
anything else? nient'altro?
apartment appartamento m
apologies scuse fpl
apologize: I apologize chiedo scusa
appendicitis appendicite f
apples mele fpl
appointment appuntamento m
approximately circa/approssimativamente
architect architetto m/f
architecture architettura f
area regione f; ~ **code** codice m, prefisso m
arm braccio m
armbands (swimming) bracciali mpl salvagente
around (place) attorno, intorno; (time) circa
arrange: can you arrange it? può organizzarlo(-a)?
arrest, to be under essere in arresto
arrive, to arrivare
art arte f
art gallery galleria d'arte f, pinacoteca f
artery arteria f
arthritic, to be essere artritico(-a)
artificial sweetener dolcificante m
artist artista m/f
ashtray posacenere m
asked for ... ho ordinato ...
asking the way chiedere la strada
asleep, to be essere addormentato(-a)
aspirin aspirina f
asthmatic, to be essere asmatico(-a)

astringent astringente m/f
at (place) a; (time) a/alle
at least almeno, minimo
ATM (cash machine) Bancomat m
attack (crime) aggressione f; (medical) attacco m
attendant guardiano m
attractive attraente m/f
aunt zia f
Australian (n) australiano(-a) m/f
Austrian (person) austriaco(-a) m/f
authentic: is it ? è autentico(-a)?
automatic (car) auto f con cambio automatico
automatic camera macchina f fotografica automatica
autumn autunno m
avalanche valanga f
away via
awful orribile

B

baby bambino m/bambina f; neonato(-a) m/f
baby food alimenti per neonati
baby seat seggiolino m
baby wipes fazzolettini mpl/salviette fpl per neonati
baby's bottle biberon f
babysitter babysitter f
back dorso m, schiena f
backache mal m di schiena
backpack zaino m
backpacking girare il mondo con lo zaino
bad cattivo(-a)
baked al forno
bakery panetteria f
ball palla f
ballet balletto m
ballroom sala f da ballo
bandage bende fpl
bank banca f
bank account conto m bancario
bank card carta bancaria f
bank loan prestito m bancario
bar (hotel) bar m
barber shop barbiere m

barge *(long boat)* lancia f
basic expressions espressioni comuni
basin catino m
basket cestello m
basketball pallacanestro f
bath towel asciugamano m
bath: to take a fare il bagno
bathroom bagno m; sala f da bagno
battery batteria f; pila f
be able, to potere
be, to essere
beach spiaggia f
beard barba f
beautiful bello(-a); stupendo(-a)
because perché
because of a causa di
bed letto m
bed: I'm going to vado a letto
bedding biancheria f da letto
bee ape f
beer birra f
before *(time)* prima di
begin, to *(see also to start)* iniziare
beginner principiante m/f
beginning inizio m
belong: this belongs to me questo è mio
below °C sotto i °C
belt cintura f
beneath sotto
berth cuccetta f
best migliore m/f
better migliore
between fra, tra
bib bavaglino m
bicycle bicicletta f
bicycle parts parti della bicicletta
bicycle rental noleggio *(m bicicletie)*
big grande
bill conto m; **put it on the ~** lo metta sul conto
bin liner sacco m di plastica per bidoni di spazzatura
binoculars binocolo m
bird uccello m
birthday compleanno m
biscuits biscotti m
bite *(insect)* puntura f

bitten: I've been bitten by a dog sono stato morso da un cane
bitter amaro(-a)
bizarre bizzarro(-a)
black nero(-a)
black and white film *(camera)* bianco e nero
black coffee *(weak)* caffè m (lungo)
bladder vescica f
blanket coperta f
bleach candeggina f
bleeding, to be perdere sangue
blind tapparella f
blister vescica f
blocked bloccato(-a); **the drain is ~** le fognature sono bloccate; **the road is ~** la strada è bloccata
blood sangue m
blood group gruppo m sanguigno
blood pressure pressione f (del sangue)
blouse camicetta f
blow-dry asciugatura f a fon
blue blu
blush *(rouge)* fard m
board, on a bordo
boarding pass carta f d'imbarco
body: parts of the body parti fpl del corpo
boiled bollito
bone osso m
book libro m
book of tickets blocchetto m di biglietti
book, to prenotare
booked up, to be essere prenotato(-a)
booking prenotazione f
booking office ufficio m prenotazioni
bookstore libreria f
boots stivali mpl; *(for sport)* scarponi mpl
border *(country)* frontiera f
boring noioso(-a)
born: I was born in sono nato a/nel
borrow: may I borrow your ...? posso prendere in prestito il suo...?
bottle bottiglia f
bottle-opener apribottiglie m
bowel intestino m

box of chocolates scatola f di cioccolatini
box office biglietteria f
boxing pugilato m
boy bambino m; ragazzo m
boyfriend ragazzo m
bra reggiseno m
bracelet braccialetto m
brass ottone m
bread pane m
break, to rompere; ~ **the journey** interrompere il viaggio
break-in rapina f
breakage rottura f
breakdown guasto m
breakfast (prima) colazione f
breast petto m, seno m
breathe, to respirare
breathtaking mozzafiato
bridge ponte m; (cards) bridge m
briefcase valigetta f portadocumenti
briefs mutandine fpl
brilliant splendido(-a)
bring, to portare
Britain Gran Bretagna f
British (person/adj) britannico(-a) m/f
brochure opuscolo m
broken rotto(-a)
bronchitis bronchite f
bronze (adj) bronzeo(-a)
brooch spilla f
broom scopa f
brother fratello m
brown marrone
browse, to dare un'occhiata
bruise contusione f
brush spazzola f
bubble bath schiuma f da bagno
bucket secchio m
buffet car vagone m ristorante
build, to costruire
building edificio m
built costruito(-a)
buoy boa f
burger hamburger m
burger stand chiosco m degli hamburger
burn bruciatura f
burn: it's burned è bruciato(-a)

bus autobus m
bus route percorso m d'autobus
bus station stazione f d'autobus
bus stop fermata f d'autobus
business trip viaggio m d'affari
business, on per lavoro
businessman uomo m d'affari
businesswoman donna f d'affari
busy, to be (occupied) occupato(-a)
but ma
butane gas butano m, gas m
butcher shop macelleria f
butter burro m
button bottone m
buy, to comprare
bye! arrivederci
bypass circonvallazione f / bypass (medicine)

C

cabaret cabaret m
cable car funivia f
café bar m
cake torta f
cake shop pasticceria f
calendar calendario m
call, to chiamare; (phone) telefonare; ~ **call the police!** chiami la polizia!
camcorder videocamera f
camera macchina f fotografica
camera case custodia f per macchina fotografica
camera store [shop] negozio m di ottica/foto
campbed lettino m da campeggio
camping campeggio m
camping equipment attrezzatura f da campeggio
campsite campeggio m
can I posso
can opener apriscatole m
cancel, to annullare
cancer (disease) cancro m
candles candele fpl
candy caramella f
cap berretto m
cap (dental) capsula f corona f
capital city capitale f

car auto(mobile) f, macchina f; **by ~** in auto/macchina
car alarm antifurto m per auto
car rental noleggio auto m, autonoleggio m
car pound deposito auto m
car repairs meccanico m
car wash lavaggio auto m
cardphone telefono m a scheda
cards carte
careful: be careful! faccia attenzione!
carpet *(fitted)* moquette f; *(rug)* tappeto m
carrier bag sacchetto m
carry-cot portabebè m
carton scatola f (di cartone); **~ of milk** confezione f di latte
cartoon cartoni mpl animati
cash contanti mpl, soldi mpl
cash card carta f bancaria
cash desk cassa f
cash machine Bancomat m
cash, to incassare
cassette cassetta f, nastro m
castle castello m
cat gatto m
catch, to *(bus)* prendere (l'autobus)
cathedral cattedrale f
cave caverna m, grotta f
CD compact m, CD m
CD-player lettore m di compact
cent centesimo m
central heating riscaldamento m centralizzato
center of town centro m città
ceramics ceramica f
certificate certificato m
certification certificato m
chain catenina f
chair sedia f
chair-lift seggiovia f
change *(coins)* moneta f; resto m, spiccioli mpl
change lanes, to cambiare corsìa
change, to cambiare
change: keep the change tenga il resto
chapel cappella f
charcoal carbone m
charter flight volo m charter

cheap a buon prezzo, economico
cheaper più economico(-a); meno caro(-a)
check conto m
check in, to registrare
check out, to *(hotel)* saldare il conto
checkbook libretto m degli assegni
checkers *(draughts)* gioco m della dama
checkout cassa f
check guarantee card carta f bancaria
cheek quancia f
cheers! salute!
cheese formaggio m
chemist farmacia f
chess scacchi
chess set gioco m degli scacchi
chest torace m
chewing gum gomma f da masticare
chickenpox varicella f
child bambino m/bambina f; figlio m/figlia f
child seat *(in car)* seggiolino m
children bambini mpl; figli mpl
children's meals piatti mpl per bambini
chin mento m
Chinese *(cuisine)* (cucina) cinese
chips patatine fpl
choc-ice cremino m
chocolate cioccolata f; **box of ~** scatola f di cioccolatini
chocolate bar tavoletta f di cioccolata
chop *(meat)* braciola f
Christian *(adj)* cristiano(-a)
Christmas Natale m
church chiesa f
cigarette machine distributore m automatico di sigarette
cigarettes, pack of pacchetto m di sigarette fpl
clamps *(car)* i ceppi bloccaruote fpl
class: first class prima classe f
clean *(adj)* pulito(-a)
clean, to pulire
cleaning person cameriera f
cliff scogliera f/rupe f
cling film pellicola f trasparente
cloakroom guardaroba m

clock orologio m
close *(near)* vicino(-a)
close, to chiudere
clothes abbigliamento m, vestiti
clothes dryer asciugatore m elettrico
clothes line corda f per il bucato
clothing store *(clothing store)* negozio m di abbigliamento
cloudy, to be essere nuvoloso
clown clown, pagliaccio m
clubs *(golf)* mazze fpl
coach corriera f, pullman m; *(train compartment)* carrozza f
coat cappotto m
code *(area/dialling)* codice m telefonico
coffee caffè m
coin moneta f
cold freddo(-a)
cold *(flu)* raffreddore m
cold meats affettati mpl
collapse: he's collapsed ha avuto un collasso
collect, to ritirare
color colore m; *(film)* a colori
comb pettine m
come back, to *(return)* ritornare; *(for collection)* passare a ritirare
communication difficulties difficoltà di comunicazione
compact camera macchina f compact
company *(business)* azienda f; *(companionship)* compagnia f
compartment *(train)* scompartimento m
complaints reclami mpl; **to make a ~** fare un reclamo
computer computer m, ordinatore m
concert hall sala f concerti
concession tariffa f speciale
concussion, to have a avere la commozione cerebrale
condoms profilattici mpl
conductor direttore m d'orchestra
conference conferenza f
confirm, to *(reservation)* confermare
confirmation conferma f
congratulations! congratulazioni!
connection *(transport)* coincidenza f

conscious, to be *(medical)* riprendere conoscenza
Consulate consolato m
consult, to consultare
consultant *(medical)* specialista m/f
contact lens lenti fpl a contatto
contact, to contattare
contact lens fluid fluido m per lenti a contatto
contagious, to be essere contagioso(-a)
contain, to contenere
contraceptive contraccettivo m
convenience store negozio m di alimentari
convenient conveniente
convertible *(car)* auto f decappottabile
cook cuoco m, cuoca f
cook, to cucinare
cooker cucina f a gas/elettrica
cookies biscotti mpl
cooking *(cuisine)* cucina f
copper rame m
copy copia f
corkscrew cavatappi m
corn pad callifugo m
corner angolo m
correct *(also right)* giusto
cosmetics cosmetici mpl
cottage villa f, cottage m
cotton cotone m
cotton wool *(absorbent cotton)* cotone m idrofilo
cough tosse f
cough syrup sciroppo m per la tosse
cough, to tossire
counter *(shop)* bancone m *(post office, bank)* sportello m
country *(nation)* paese m
countryside campagna f
couple *(pair)* paio m
courier *(guide)* guida m/f, l'accompagnatore m
course *(meal)* portata f
courthouse palazzo m di giustizia
cousin cugino m, cugina f
cover *(lid)* coperchio m
cover charge coperto m
craft shop negozio m di artigianato
cramps crampi mpl

crash: I've had a crash ho avuto un incidente d'auto
creche asilo-nido m
credit card carta f di credito
credit status posizione f finanziaria
credit credito m
crib culla f
crisps chips fpl
crockery stoviglie fpl
cross, to (road) attraversare
cross-country skiing trail pista f per sci di fondo
crossroads incrocio m
crowded affollato(-a)
crown (dental) corona f
cruise crociera f
crutches stampelle f
cup tazza f
cupboard credenza f, l'armadio m
currency valuta f
currency exchange office ufficio m cambio
curtains tende fpl
cushion cuscino m
customs dogana f
customs declaration dichiarazione f doganale
cut taglio m
cut and blow-dry taglio m e asciugatura a fon
cutlery posate fpl
cycle helmet casco m da ciclista
cycle path pista f ciclabile
cycling ciclismo m
cyclist ciclista m/f
cystitis cistite f

daily giornalmente
damaged, to be essere danneggiato(-a)
damp (n) umidità f; (adj) umido(-a)
dance (performance) danza f
dancing, to go andare a ballare
dangerous pericoloso(-a)
dark scuro(-a); buio(-a)
daughter figlia f
daughter-in-law nuora f
day giorno m; (ticket) giornaliero

day trip gita f di un giorno
dead morto(-a); (battery) scarico(-a)
deaf, to be essere sordo(-a)
dear (greeting) caro(-a)
decide: we haven't decided yet non abbiamo ancora deciso
deck (ship) ponte m
deck chair sedia f a sdraio
declare, to dichiarare
deduct, to (money) detrarre
deep profondo(-a)
deep frozen surgelato(-a)
defrost, to scongelare
degrees (temperature) gradi mpl
delay ritardo m
delicatessen salumeria f
delicious (food) squisito(-a); delizioso(-a)
deliver, to consegnare
dental floss filo m interdentale
dentist dentista m/f
dentures dentiera fsing
deodorant deodorante m
depart, to (train, bus) partire
department store grande magazzino m
departure (train) partenza f
departure lounge sala f partenze
depend: it depends on dipende da
deposit caparra f; anticipo m
describe, to descrivere
design (dress) disegno m
designer stilista m/f
desk scrivania f
dessert dolce m
destination destinazione f
details dettagli mpl
detergent detersivo m
develop, to (photos) sviluppare
diabetes diabete m
diabetic diabetico(-a)
dialing (area) code codice m, prefisso m
diamond diamante m; (cards) quadri mpl
diapers pannolini mpl
diarrhea diarrea f; to have ~ avere la diarrea
dice dadi mpl
dictionary dizionario m

diesel diesel m
diet: I'm on a diet sono a dieta
difficult difficile
digital digitale
dine, to mangiare
dining car carrozza ristorante f
dining room sala f da pranzo
dinner jacket smoking m
dinner, to have cenare
direct diretto
direct, to indicare la via
direct-dial telephone telefono m a linea diretta
direction direzione f; **in the ~ of** in direzione
director *(of company)* direttore m; *(film)* regista m/f
directory *(telephone)* elenco m telefonico
Directory Inquiries Informazioni Elenco Abbonati
dirty sporco(-a)
disabled disabili m/fpl
discount sconto m; **can you offer me a ~?** può farmi uno sconto?
disgusting disgustoso(-a)
dish *(meal)* piatto m
dish cloth strofinaccio m per i piatti
dishes posate fpl
dishwashing detergent detersivo m per lavastoviglie
dislocated, to be essere lussato(-a)
display cabinet armadietto m vetrina
display case astuccio m
disposable camera macchina f usa-e-getta
distilled water acqua f distillata
district zona f
disturb: don't non disturbare
dive, to tuffarsi
diversion deviazione f
divorced, to be essere divorziato(-a)
dizzy, to feel avere il capogiro
do: things to do cose fpl da fare
doctor dottore(ssa) m/f, medico m
dog cane m
doll bambola f
door porta f
dosage dose f

double bed letto m matrimoniale
double room camera f doppia
down giù
downstairs al piano inferiore
downtown area centro m
dozen dozzina f
drain fognatura f
draught *(wind)* corrente f d'aria
dress vestito m
drink bibita f
drinking water acqua f potabile
drinks bevande f
drip: the faucet [tap] drips rubinetto perde
drive, to guidare
driver conducente m; *(bus, etc)* autista m/f
driver's [driving] license patente di guida f
drop someone off, to fare scendere
drowning: someone is ~ qualcuno sta annegando
drugstore farmacia f
drunk ubriaco(-a)
dry-clean, to lavare a secco
dry cleaner lavanderia f
dry clothes, to asciugare i vestiti
dubbed, to be essere doppiato
during durante
dusty polveroso(-a)
duty: to pay duty pagare il dazio
duvet piumone m

each: how much each? quant'è ciascuno?
ear orecchio m; **~ache** mal d'orecchio m; **~drops** le gocce fpl per le orecchie; **~rings** orecchini mpl
earlier più presto/prima
early di buon'ora, presto
east est m
Easter Pasqua f
easy facile
eat, to mangiare; **places ~** posti mpl per mangiare
eaten: have you ~? ha già mangiato?; **we've already ~** abbiamo già mangiato

economical economico(-a)
economy class in classe turistica
eggs uova fpl
either ... or ... o ... o ...
elastic *(adj)* elastico(-a)
electric: ~ meter contatore m dell'elettricità; **~ shaver** rasoio m elettrico
electrical items articoli mpl elettrici
electrician elettricista m
electricity elettricità f
electronic: ~ flash flash m elettronico; **~ game** gioco m elettronico
elevator ascensore m
else: something ~ qualcos'altro
embark, to *(boat)* imbarcarsi
embassy ambasciata f
emerald smeraldo m
emergency emergenza f; **it's an ~** è un'emergenza; **~ room** pronto soccorso m
emergency exit uscita f d'emergenza
empty vuoto(-a)
enamel smalto m
end, to finire
end: at the end in fondo
engaged, to be essere fidanzato(-a)
engine motore m
engineer ingegnere m/f
England Inghilterra f
English *(language)* inglese m
enjoy, to piacere
enlarge, to *(photos)* ingrandire
enough abbastanza
entertainment: what ~ is there? che divertimenti/spettacoli ci sono?
entertainment guide guida degli spettacoli
entirely completamente
entrance fee tariffa f d'ingresso
entry visa visto m d'entrata
envelope busta f
epileptic epilettico(-a); **to be ~** essere epilettico(-a)
equally equamente
equipment *(sports)* attrezzatura f
error errore m
escalator scala mobile f
essential essenziale
estate agent agente m/f immobiliare

EU Unione f Europea, UE
euro (€) euro m
evening dress abito m da sera
events manifestazioni fpl
every day ogni giorno
every week ogni settimana
examination *(medical)* visita f medica
example, for per esempio
excellent *(adj)* eccellente
except eccetto
excess baggage eccedenza bagaglio f
exchange rate tasso m di cambio
exchange, to cambiare
excluding meals pasti m esclusi
excursion escursione f, gita f
excuse me *(apology. attention)* scusi
exhausted, to be essere esausto(-a)
exhibition mostra f
exit uscita f; **at the ~** all'uscita
expensive caro(-a)
expiration date data f di scadenza
expire, to: when does it expire? quando scade?
exposure *(photos)* posa f
expressway autostrada f
extension interno
extension cord prolunga f
extra *(additional)* supplementare
extracted, to be *(tooth)* avere un'estrazione
extremely estremamente
eye occhio m

fabric *(material)* stoffa f
face faccia f, viso m
facial trattamento per il viso m
facilities servizi mpl; attrezzature f
factor *(sun protection)* fattore
factory outlet vendita diretta in fabbrica
faint, to feel sentirsi svenire
fall *(season)* autunno m
fall: he's had a fall è caduto
family famiglia f
famous famoso(-a)
fan *(air)* ventaglio m
far lontano(-a); **how ~ is it?** quanto dista?; **is it ~?** è lontano?

farsighted presbite

fare tariffa f

fashionable, to be essere alla moda

fast-food restaurant tavola calda f, self-service m

fast, to be *(clock)* anticipare

fat grasso m

father padre m

fault: it's my/your fault è colpa mia/sua

faulty difettoso(-a)

faulty, to be essere difettoso(-a)

favorite favorito(-a)

fax facilities servizio m fax

fax, to spedire un fax

feeding bottle biberon m

feel ill, to sentirsi male

feel sick, to sentirsi male/vomitare

female donna f; femmina f

festival festival m

fetch help! chiami aiuto!

feverish, to feel sentirsi la febbre

few pochi (e)

fiancé(e) fidanzato(-a) m/f

field campo m

fight *(brawl)* rissa f

fill out, to compilare/riempire

filling *(dental)* otturazione f; *(in sandwich)* ripieno m

filling station stazione f di servizio

film *(camera)* pellicola f; film m

film speed velocità f della pellicola

filter filtro m; **~ paper** *(for coffee)* filtro m del caffè

find out: could you find that out? può informarsi?

fine *(penalty)* multa f; *(well)* bene

finger dito m

fire alarm allarme m antincendio

fire department pompieri (pl)

fire escape uscita f di sicurezza

fire extinguisher estintore m

fire: there's a fire! al fuoco!

fireplace caminetto m

first primo(-a)

first class in prima classe; di prima classe

first course primo (piatto) m

first floor *(UK)* primo piano m

first floor *(US)* pianterreno m

first name nome m

first-aid kit astuccio m di pronto soccorso

fish store pescheria f

fishing rod canna f da pesca

fishing, to go andare a pesca

fit, to *(clothes)* andare bene

fitting room cabina di prova f

fix, to: can you fix it? può ripararlo(-a)?

flag bandiera f

flash *(photography)* flash m elettronico

flashlight *(torch)* pila f

flat *(tire)* pneumatico m scoppiato

flavor: what flavors do you have? che gusti avete?

flea pulce f

flea market mercato m delle pulci

flight volo m; **~ number** numero m del volo; **~ attendant** assistente m/f di volo

flip-flops ciabatte fpl

flood inondazione f

floor *(level)* piano m

floor mop mocho m; Vileda (trademark)

floor show spettacolo m di varietà

florist fiorista f

flour farina f

flower fiore m

flu influenza f

fluent: to speak fluent Italian parlare italiano correntemente

fly *(insect)* mosca f

fly, to volare

foggy, to be essere nebbioso(-a)

folding chair/table sedia/tavola f pieghevole

folk art arte f popolare

folk music musica f folk

follow, to seguire

food poisoning avvelenamento m alimentare

foot piede m

football *(soccer)* calcio m

footpath sentiero m

for a week per una settimana

forecast previsioni fpl

foreign straniero(-a)

foreign currency valuta f straniera

forest foresta f

forget, to dimenticare
fork forchetta f; *(in the road)* incrocio m
form modulo m
formal dress tenuta f da sera
forms moduli mpl
fortunately fortunatamente
forward: please forward my mail per favore faccia proseguire la mia posta
foundation *(make-up)* crema f base
fountain fontana f
four-door car auto f a quattro porte
four-wheel drive auto fuoristrada f
foyer *(hotel/theater)* atrio m
frame *(glasses)* montatura f
France Francia f
free *(available, not busy)* libero(-a); *(of charge)* gratuito(-a)
French *(cuisine)* (cucina) Francese
French *(language)* francese m
frequent: how frequent? con che frequenza?
frequently frequentemente
fresh fresco(-a)
freshly squeezed fruit juice spremuta f di frutta
fridge frigorifero m
fried fritto(-a)
friend amico m/amica f
friendly amichevole, simpatico(-a)
fries patate f fritte
frightened, to be essere spaventato(-a)
fringe frangia f
from da; ~ ... **to** *(time)* da ... a
front door porta f d'ingresso; ~ **key** chiave f della porta d'ingresso
frosty, to be *(weather)* essere gelato(-a)
frozen congelato(-a)
fruit juice succo m di frutta
fuel *(gasoline/petrol)* carburante (benzina) m
full pieno(-a)
full board *(A.P.)* pensione f completa
full insurance polizza f di assicurazione completa
fun, to have divertirsi

funny *(amusing/odd)* buffo/divertente
furniture i mobili mpl
fuse fusibile m
fuse box fusibili mpl
fuse wire filo m a piombo

G

gallon gallone m
gambling giocare d'azzardo
game *(toy)* gioco m
garage garage m, autorimessa f
garden giardino m
gardener giardiniere m
gardening giardinaggio m
gas bottle bombola f del gas
gas: I smell gas! c'è odore di gas!
gasoline benzina f
gastritis gastrite f
gate *(airport)* uscita f
gay club locale m gay
generous: that's very ... è molto generoso
genuine autentico(-a)
get, to *(find)* cercare
get by: may I get by? permesso?
get off, to *(transport)* scendere
get out, to *(of vehicle)* scendere
get to, to arrivare a; **how do I get to ...?** come si arriva a ...?
gift regalo m
gift shop negozio m di articoli da regalo
girl ragazza f; bambina f
girlfriend ragazza f
give way, to *(on the road)* dare la precedenza
give, to dare
glacier ghiacciaio m
gland ghiandola f
glass bicchiere m
glasses *(optical)* occhiali mpl
gliding volare con il deltaplano
gloomy tetro(-a)
glossy finish *(photos)* smaltato(-a)
glove guanto m
go, to andare; **let's go!** andiamo!; **where does this bus go?** dove va questo autobus?
go away! vada via!

go back, to *(turn around)* ritornare
go for a walk, to fare una passeggiata
go out, to *(in evening)* uscire
go shopping, to fare acquisti
goggles occhialini per il nuoto
gold oro m
goldplate placcato d'oro
good buono(-a)
good afternoon buonasera *(from pm)*
good evening buonasera
good morning buongiorno
good night buonanotte
good-bye arrivederci
gorge gola f
got: have you got any ...? avete pl de... ?
grade *(fuel)* grado del carburante m
gram grammo m
grandparents nonni mpl
grapes uva f
grass erba f
gratuity mancia f
gray grigio
graze escoriazione f
greasy *(hair)* grasso(-a)
great fun molto divertente
Greek (cuisine) (cucina) Greca
green verde
greengrocer fruttivendolo m
greetings saluti
greyhound racing corsa f di levrieri
grilled alla griglia
grocer *(grocery)* drogheria f
ground: camping ~ terreno m del campeggio
ground floor pianterreno
groundsheet telo m per il terreno
group gruppo m
guarantee garanzia f
guarantee: is it guaranteed? è garantito(-a)?
guide *(tour)* guida m/f
guidebook guida f/m turistica
guided tour visita f guidata
guitar chitarra f
gum *(mouth)* gengiva f
gynecologist ginecologo m/f

hair capelli mpl
hair brush spazzola f dei capelli
hair dryer asciugacapelli m, fon m
hair gel gel m dei capelli
hair spray lacca f
haircare prodotti per i capelli
haircut taglio di capelli m
hairdresser's parrucchiera f, parrucchiere m
half, a mezzo
half board *(M.A.P.)* mezza pensione f
half fare metà prezzo
half past e mezza/... e trenta
hammer martello m
hand mano f
hand cream crema f per le mani
hand luggage bagaglio a mano m
hand towel asciugamano m
hand washable lavaggio a mano
handbag borsetta f
handicapped, to be essere disabile
handicrafts artigianato m
handkerchief fazzoletto m
handle maniglia f
hang-gliding fare il deltapiano
hanger gruccia f
hangover postumi mpl della sbornia
happen: what happened? che cosa è successo?
happy: I'm not happy with the service non sono soddisfatto(-a) del servizio
harbor porto m
hard shoulder *(road)* corsia f d'emergenza
hardware store negozio m di ferramenta
hat cappello m
hatchback auto f a cinque porte
have, to avere
have to, to *(must)* dovere
hayfever febbre f da fieno
head testa f
head waiter capocameriere m
headache mal di testa m
heading, to be *(in a direction)* andare in direzione di

health food store [shop] negozio *m* di dietetica
health insurance assicurazione *f* medica
hear, to sentire
hearing aid protesi *f* per udito
heart cuore *m*
heart attack infarto *m*
heart condition condizione *f* del cuore
hearts *(cards)* cuori *mpl*
heating riscaldamento *m*
heavy pesante
height altezza *f*
helicopter elicottero *m*
hello buongiorno; salve
help aiuto *m*
help, to aiutare; **help me!** aiuto!
helper assistente *m/f*
hemorrhoids emorroidi *fpl*
her lei; suo(-a)
here qui
hernia ernia *f*
hers suo(-a)
hi! ciao!
high alto(-a)
high/main street via principale *f*
high tide alta marea *f*
hike *(walk)* escursione *f* a piedi
hiking fare escursioni a piedi
hill collina *f*
him lui
hire out, to *(rent out, to)* noleggiare
hire, for libero
hire, to noleggiare
his suo(-a)
history storia *f*
hitchhike, to fare l'autostop
HIV-positive sieropositivo(-a)
hobby *(pastime)* hobby
hockey field campo *m* di hockey
hold, to *(contain)* contenere
hold on, to restare in linea
hole *(in clothes)* buco *m*
holiday resort posto *m* di villeggiatura
holiday, on per/in vacanza
home casa *f*; **to go ~** rientrare
homeopathic remedy rimedio *m* omeopatico

homosexual *(adj)* omosessuale
honeymoon, to be on essere in luna di miele
hopefully speriamo!
horse cavallo *m*
horseracing ippica
horseback trip escursione *f* a cavallo
hospital ospedale *m*, policlinico *m*
hot caldo(-a); *(weather)* caldissimo(-a)
hot chocolate cioccolata *f* calda
hot dog hot dog
hot spring sorgente *f* calda
hot water acqua *f* calda; **~ bottle** bottiglia *f* dell'acqua calda
hotel albergo *m*
hour ora *f*; **in an ~** fra un'ora
hours *(opening)* orario *m* di apertura
house casa *f*
household articles casalinghi *mpl*
housewife casalinga *f*
how? come?
how are you? come sta?
how far? quanto dista?
how long? quanto (tempo)?
how many? quanti?
how much? quanto?; quanto costa?
how often? con che frequenza?; ogni quanto?
how old? quanti anni?
however comunque
hungry, to be avere fame
hurry, to be in a avere fretta
hurt, to be essere ferito(-a); farsi male; **it hurts** fa male
husband marito *m*,

I

I'd like vorrei
I'll have prendo
I've lost ho perso
ice ghiaccio *m*
ice cream gelato *m*
ice cream parlor gelateria *f*
ice dispenser distributore *m* di ghiaccio
ice lolly ghiacciolo *m*
ice pack borsa *f* da ghiaccio
ice rink pista *f* di pattinaggio su ghiaccio, palazzo *m* del ghiaccio
ice-hockey hockey *m* su ghiaccio

icy, to be essere ghiacciato(-a)
identification documento m d'identità
ill, to be stare male
illegal, to be essere illegale
illness malattia f
imitation imitazione f
immediately immediatamente
impressive di grande effetto
in *(place)* in; *(time)* fra
in-law: father/mother-in-law suocero(-a)
included: is it included? è incluso/compreso?
inconvenient scomodo(-a)
Indian (cuisine) (cucina) indiana
indicate, to indicare
indigestion indigestione f
indoor al coperto
indoor pool piscina f invernale
inexpensive economico(-a)
infection infezione f
inflammation infiammazione f
informal *(dress)* abbigliamento m casual
information informazione f
information desk banco m informazioni
information office ufficio m informazioni
injection iniezione f
injured, to be essere ferito(-a)
innocent innocente
inquiry desk banco m informazioni
insect insetto m
insect bite puntura f d'insetto
insect repellent [spray] pomata f contro gli insetti/ dello spray insetticida
inside dentro
inside lane corsia f interna
insist: I insist insisto
insomnia insonnia f
instant coffee caffè m solubile
instead of invece di
instructions istruzioni fpl
instructor istruttore m
insulin insulina f
insurance assicurazione f
insurance certificate polizza f d'assicurazione

insurance claim richiesta f di rimborso assicurazione
insurance company compagnia f d'assicurazione
interest *(hobby)* gli interessi
interest rate tasso m d'interesse
interesting interessante
international internazionale
International Student Card Carta f Internazionale dello studente
interpreter interprete m/f
intersection intersezione f
interval intervallo m
into dentro, in
introduce oneself, to presentarsi
introductions presentazioni
invitation invito m
invite, to invitare
involved, to be essere coinvolto(-a)
iodine iodio m
Ireland Irlanda f
Irish *(n)* irlandese m/f
iron *(for clothing)* ferro m da stiro
iron, to stirare
is there ...? c'è...?
island isola f
it is è
Italian *(language)* italiano m; *(person)* italiano(-a) m/f
itch: it itches prude
itemized bill conto m dettagliato

jack *(cards)* fante m
jacket giacca f
jam marmellata f/conserva f di frutta
jammed: it's jammed è bloccato(-a)
jar vasetto m
jaw mascella f
jellyfish medusa f
jet lag: I have soffro il cambiamento di fuso orario
jewelry store/jeweler's gioielleria f
Jewish *(adj)* ebreo(-a)
job: what's your job? che lavoro fa?
join: may we join you possiamo venire anche noi?
joint *(body)* articolazione f; *(meat)* pezzo m (di carne)

joke scherzo m barzelletta f
joker *(cards)* jolly m
journalist giornalista m/f
journey viaggio m
jug *(of water)* brocca f
jumper maglia f
junction *(exit)* uscita f autostrada; *(intersection)* intersezione f autostrada

K

kerosene cherosene m
ketchup ketchup m
kettle bollitore m
key chiave f
key ring portachiavi m
kidney rene m
kilo(gram) chilo(grammo) m
kilometer chilometro m
kind *(pleasant)* gentile
kind: what kind of …? che tipo di …?
king *(cards, chess)* re m
kiosk chiosco m
kiss, to baciare
kitchen paper carta f da cucina
kitchenette zona cottura f
knee ginocchio m
knife coltello m
knight *(chess)* cavallo m
knocked down, to be essere buttato a terra
know: I don't know non lo so
kosher puro(-a)

L

label etichetta f
lace pizzo m
ladder scala f
ladies room *(toilet)* toilette f signore
lake lago m
lamp lampada f
land, to atterrare
landing *(house)* pianerottolo m
landlord/landlady padrone m, padrona f di casa
lane corsìa f
language course corso m di lingua
large grande

last ultimo(-a)
last, to *(time)* durare
late *(delayed)* in ritardo; tardi
later più tardi
laugh, to ridere
launderette lavanderia f a gettone
lavatory bagno m
lawn prato m coltivato
lawyer avvocato m
laxative lassativo m
lead, to *(road)* portare
lead-free *(gas/petrol)* benzina verde f
leader *(of group)* capogruppo m/f
leaflet opuscolo m
leak, to *(roof/pipe)* perdere; *(car)*
learn, to *(language/sport)* imparare
learner studente m, studentessa f
least expensive meno caro m, meno cara f
leather pelle f
leave, to *(exit)* partire; *(abandon)* lasciare; **leave me alone!** mi lasci in pace!
lecturer docente, insegnante m/f
left-hand side dal lato sinistro
left, on the a sinistra
left-handed mancino(-a)
left-luggage office *(baggage check)* deposito m bagagli
leg gamba f
legal matters *(car accident)* questioni legali
legal, to be essere legale
lemon limone m
lemonade limonata f
lend: could you lend me …? può prestarmi …?
length lunghezza f
lens obiettivo m; lenti fpl
lens cap tappo m per obiettivo
lesbian club club m per lesbiche
less *(di)* meno
lesson lezione f
letter lettera f; **by ~** per lettera
letterbox cassetta f per lettere
level *(ground)* livellato, piano
library biblioteca f
license plate number numero di targa m

lie down, to sdraiarsi
lifebelt cintura f di salvataggio
lifeboat scialuppa f di salvataggio
lifeguard bagnino m
lifejacket giubba f di salvataggio
lift pass ski pass f
light *(color)* chiaro(-a); *(weight)* leggero(-a)
light bulb lampadina f
lighter accendino m
lighthouse faro m
lightning fulmine m
like, to piacere; **I'd like ...** vorrei ...;
I don't like it non mi piace
like this *(similar)* come questo(-a)
limousine berlina f
line *(subway [metro])* linea f; *(profession)* professione f, lavoro m
line: an outside line, please una linea esterna, per favore
linen lino m
lip(s) labbro m, labbra fpl
lipsalve balsamo m per le labbra
lipstick rossetto m
liqueur liquore m
liter/litre litro m
little piccolo(-a)
live, to vivere; **~ together** abitare insieme
liver fegato m
loaf of bread pagnotta f di pane
lobby *(theater/hotel)* atrio m
local regionale, locale
local anesthetic anestesia f locale
local road strada f comunale
lock *(key)* serratura f; *(canal)* chiusa f
lock oneself out, to chiudersi fuori
locked, to be essere chiuso(-a); **it's locked** è chiuso a chiave
locker armadietto m
locker rooms spogliatoi mpl
lollipop leccalecca m
long *(clothing)* lungo(-a)
long *(time)* molto; **how long?** quanto tempo?; **how much longer?** per quanto tempo?
long-distance call telefonata f interurbana

look: I'm just looking sto solo guardando
look for, to cercare
loose *(clothing)* largo(-a)
lose, to perdere; **I've lost ...** ho smarrito ...; ho perso
lost, to be essere smarrito
lost-and-found/lost property office ufficio m oggetti smarriti
lotion lozione f
lots molti (e)
loud, it's too è troppo rumoroso(-a)
louder più forte
love: I love Italian food amo la cucina italiana;
I love you ti amo
low-fat magro(-a)
lower berth cuccetta f in basso
lubricant lubrificante m
luck: good luck buona fortuna
luggage *(baggage)* bagaglio m
luggage allowance peso m consentito
luggage locker deposito m bagagli automatico
luggage tag etichetta f per bagaglio
luggage ticket biglietto m per i bagagli
luggage carts *(trolleys)* carrelli mpl
lumpy *(mattress)* pieno di protuberanze
lunch pranzo m
lung polmone m

M

machine washable lavabile in lavatrice
madam signora
made: what is it made of? di che cosa è fatto(-a)?
magazine rivista f
magician mago m
magnetic north nord m magnetico
magnificent magnifico
maid cameriera f
maiden name nome m da nubile
mail, to imbucare
mail *(post)* posta f
mailbox cassetta f postale
main principale

main course secondo (piatto) m
main train station stazione f
ferroviaria principale
main street via f principale
mains conduttura f principale
make (brand) marca f
makeup cosmetici mpl trucco m
male uomo, maschio m
mallet maglio m
man uomo m
manager direttore m, direttrice f;
gestore m/f
manicure manicure f
manual (car) manuale m
many molti (e)
map carta f, cartina
margarine margarina f
market mercato m; **~ day** giorno m
di mercato
married, to be essere sposato(-a)
mascara mascara f
mask (diving) maschera f subacquea
mass messa f
massage massaggio m
match (game) partita f
matches fiammiferi mpl
material (fabric) stoffa f
matinée spettacolo m del
pomeriggio
matter: what's the matter? cosa
succede?; **it doesn't matter** non
importa
mattress materasso m
may I ...? posso ... ?
maybe forse
me me
meal pasto m;
mean, to significare
measles morbillo m
measure, to misurare
measurement le misure fpl
meat carne f
medical certificate certificato m
medico
medicine medicina f
medium (regular) medio(-a); (steak)
cottura media
meet, to incontrare; **pleased to meet
you** piacere/molto lieto(-a)

meeting place luogo m d'incontro
member (of club) socio m
memorial monumento m
commemorativo
men (toilets) bagno m, signori mpl
mend, to riparare
mention: don't mention it prego
menu menu m
message messaggio m
metal metallo m
meter (taxi) tassametro m
methylated spirits alcol denaturato
microwave (oven) forno m a
microonde
midday mezzogiorno
midnight mezzanotte
migraine emicrania f
mileage chilometraggio m
milk latte m; **with ~** con latte
milk of magnesia latte m di magnesia
million un milione
mince carne f tritata
mine mio(-a)
mineral water acqua f minerale
minibar minibar m
minibus minibus m
minimum (n) minimo m
minister ministro m
minor road strada f secondaria
minute minuto m
mirror specchio m
miss, to passare, mancare; **have I
missed the bus to ...?** ho perso
l'autobus per ...?
missing, to be mancare; scomparire
mistake errore m
misunderstanding: there's been a ~
c'è stato un malinteso
mittens guantoni mpl
mobile home camper m
modern art arte f moderna
moisturizing cream crema f idratante
monastery monastero m
money soldi mpl
money order vaglia m postale
money-belt cintura f portasoldi
month mese m
monthly (ticket) mensile
monument monumento m

moped motorino m
more (di) più; **I'd like some more ...**
vorrei ancora un po' di ...
morning, in the al mattino; di mattina
moslem (adj) mussulmano(-a)
mosquito zanzara f
mosquito bite puntura f di zanzara
mother madre f
motorbike motocicletta f
motorboat barca f a motore
motorcycle motocicletta f
motorcycle parts
motorway autostrada f
mountain montagna f
mountain pass passo m di montagna
mountaineering alpinismo m
mousetrap trappola f per topi
moustache baffi mpl
mouth bocca f
move, to cambiare; (car) spostare la
macchina; (house) traslocare; **don't**
move him! non lo muova!
Mr. signor m
Mrs. signora f
much molto
mugged, to be essere aggredito(-a)
mugging aggressione per rapina f
mugs boccali mpl
multiple trip (ticket) biglietto m
multiplo
mumps gli orecchioni mpl
muscle muscolo m
museum museo m
music musica f
music box carillon m
musician musicista m/f
must: I must devo
mustard senape f
my mio
myself: I'll do it myself lo faccio io

N

nail polish lo smalto m per unghie
nail scissors le forbicine f da unghie
name cognome m
name (first name) nome m; **what's**
your name? come si chiama?
napkin tovagliolo m
narrow stretto(-a)

national health servizio m sanitario
nationality nazionalità f
natural history storia f naturale
nature reserve riserva f naturale
nature trail percorso m naturalistico
nausea nausea f
navy blue blu m marino
near vicino
nearsighted miope
nearest più vicino(-a)
neck collo m; (clothes)
necklace collana f
need: I need to ... ho bisogno di ...
needle ago m
negative (photo) negativo m
neighbor vicino(-a) m/f
nephew nipote m
nerve nervo m
nervous system sistema m nervoso
never mai
never mind non importa
new nuovo(-a)
New Year Anno m Nuovo
New Zealand Nuova Zelanda f
newsagent giornalaio m
newsdealer giornalaio m
newspaper giornale m
newsstand edicola f
next prossimo(-a); **next stop!**
prossima fermata!
next to accanto(-a) a; vicino(-a) a
niece nipote f
night, at di notte; **per night** per notte
night porter portiere m di notte
nightdress camicia f da notte
nobody else nessun altro
noisy rumoroso(-a)
non-alcoholic analcolico(-a)
non-smoking area zona non fumatori f
none nessuno(-a)
noon mezzogiorno
no one nessuno(-a)
normal normale
north nord m
Northern Ireland Irlanda f del nord
nose naso m
nosebleed emoraggia nasale f
not yet non ancora
note banconota f

notebook taccuino m
nothing else nient'altro
nothing to declare niente da dichiarare
notice board bacheca f
notify, to informare
now subito; ora, adesso
nudist beach spiaggia f nudista
number numero m; *(telephone)* numero (di telefono) m
number plate *(registration plate)* numero di targa m
nurse infermiere(-a) m/f
nut *(for bolt)* dado m per bullone
nylon nylon m

<hr>

O

o'clock, it's ... è .../sono le ...
observatory osservatorio m
occasionally occasionalmente
occupations occupazioni mpl
occupied occupato(-a)
of di, da
of course naturalmente, certamente
off-peak bassa stagione f
office ufficio m
often sovente/spesso
oil olio m
oil lamp lampada f a olio
oily *(hair)* grasso(-a)
okay d'accordo./va bene
old vecchio(-a)
old town città f vecchia; città f storica
old-fashioned antiquato(-a)
olive oil olio m d'oliva
omelet frittata f
on *(day, date)* il
on *(place)* in
on the left a sinistra
on the other side all'altro lato
on the right a destra
on/off switch interruttore m
once una volta; ~ **a week** una volta alla settimana
open aperto(-a); ~ **to the public** aperto(-a) al pubblico ~ **to traffic** aperto(-a) al traffico
open, to aprire
opening hours orario m d'apertura
opera house teatro m dell'opera

operation operazione f
operator operatore m
opposite di fronte
optician ottico m; negozio m di ottica
or o/oppure
orange arancione
oranges arance fpl
orchestra orchestra f
order, to ordinare; *(taxi)* chiamare
our nostro
out: he's out è fuori/non c'è
outdoor all'esterno; ~ **pool** piscina f all'aperto
outside fuori
outside lane corsia f di sorpasso
oval ovale
oven forno m
over sopra
over there laggiù
overcharged: I've been prezzo è eccesivo
overdone *(adj)* troppo cotto(-a)
overdraft scoperto m
overdrawn, to be avere uno scoperto bancario
overheat, to surriscaldare
overnight una notte f
overnight service servizio m ventiquattro ore
owe: how much do I owe you? quanto le devo?
own: on my own da solo(-a)
owner proprietario

<hr>

P

pacifier tettarella f
pack, to fare i bagagli
pack of cards mazzo m di carte
pack of cigarettes pacchetto m di sigarette
package pacco m
packed lunch pranzo m al sacco
pack [packet] pacco m, pacchetto m
padlock lucchetto m
pail secchiello m
pain, to be in stare male
painkillers antinevralgico m; analgesico m, antidolorifico m
paint, to dipingere

painted dipinto(-a)
painter pittore m, pittrice f
painting quadro m
pair of, a un paio di
pajamas pigiama m
palace palazzo m
palpitations palpitazioni fpl
panorama panorama m/vista f
pantomime pantomima f
pants pantaloni mpl
pantyhose collant m
paper carta f
paper napkins tovaglioli mpl di carta
paraffin paraffina f
paralysis paralisi f
parcel *(package)* pacco m
pardon? prego?
parents genitori mpl
park parco m, giardini mpl
park ranger guardia f forestale
park, to parcheggiare
parking parcheggio m
parking disk disco m orario
parking lot parcheggio m
parking meter parchimetro m
parliament building palazzo m del
Parlamento
partner *(boyfriend/girlfriend)*
compagno m, compagna f
parts *(components)* pezzi mpl di
ricambio
party *(social)* festa f
pass passo m
pass, to passare
passenger passeggero m, passeggera f
passport passaporto m
passport control controllo m passaporti
pastry shop pasticceria f
patch, to rattoppare
path sentiero m
patient paziente m/f
pavement, on the sul marciapiede m
pay, to pagare; ~ **a fine** pagare
un'ammenda/una multa; ~ **by credit
card** pagare con carta di credito
pay phone telefono m a scheda
payment pagamento m
peak picco m/cima f
pebbly *(beach)* pietroso(-a)

pedalo pedalò m
pedestrian crossing attraversamento
m pedonale
pedestrian zone/precinct isola
f/zona f pedonale
pedicure pedicure f
pen penna f
pencil matita f
penicillin penicillina f
penknife coltellino m
penpal il, corrispondente m/f
people gente f
people carrier *(minivan)* furgoncino m
pepper *(condiment)* pepe m; *(vegetable)*
peperone m
per day al giorno; per giorno
per hour all'ora; per ora
per night per notte
per week alla settimana
performance spettacolo m
perhaps forse
period periodo m; *(menstrual)*
mestruazioni fpl
period pains dolori mpl mestruali
perm *(hair)* permanente f
perm, to fare la permanente
permit permesso m, licenza f
personal stereo stereo m personale
pet *(animal)* animale m domestico
pharmacy farmacia f
phone telefono m
phone call telefonata f
phonecard carta f telefonica
photo, to take a fare una fotografia
photo: passport-size photo
fotografia f formato passaporto
photocopy fotocopia f
photographer fotografo m/negozio m
di ottica
photography fotografia f
phrase frase f
phrase book frasario m
piano pianoforte m
pick up, to passare a prendere; *(ticket)*
ritirare
pick-up truck autocarro m
picnic picnic m, scampagnata f; ~
area area f per pic nic

piece articolo di bagaglio m; pezzo m; a ~ of … un pezzo di …
Pill *(contraceptive)*, **to take the** prendere la pillola (contraccettiva)
pillow cuscino m
pillowcase federa f
pilot light luce f-spia
pink rosa
pint pinta f
pipe *(smoking)* pipa f
pipe cleaners puliscipipa m
pipe tobacco tabacco m da pipa
piste map carta f delle piste
pitch *(for camping)* posto m tenda
pity: it's a pity è un peccato
place *(space)* posto m
place a bet, to scommettere
plain pianura f; *(not patterned)* in tinta unita
plane volo m
plans, to have fare dei progetti
plant pianta f
plastic bags sacchetti mpl di plastica
plate piatto m
platform binario m
platinum platino m
play, to *(drama)* rappresentare *(music)* suonare
playground parco m giochi
playgroup club m per bambini
playing cards carte fpl da gioco
playing field campo m da gioco
pleasant gradevole
please per piacere./per favore
pliers le pinze fpl
plug *(bath)* presa f; *(electric)* spina f elettrica
plumber idraulico m
p.m. di pomeriggio, di sera
pneumonia polmonite f
point of interest luoghi mpl d'interesse
point to, to indicare
poison veleno m
poisonous velenoso(-a)
police polizia f, carabinieri (pl)
police report denuncia f
police station commissariato m, questura f
pollen count conteggio m del polline

polyclinic policlinico m
pond stagno m
pony ride passeggiata f in pony
pop music musica f pop
popcorn popcorn m
port *(harbor)* porto m
porter portiere m; facchino m
portion porzione f
possible: as soon as possible appena possibile
possibly possibilmente
post, to *(mail, to)* imbucare
post *(mail)* posta f
post office ufficio m postale
postbox *(mailbox)* cassetta f delle lettere
postcard cartolina f
poster manifesto m
postman postino m
potato patata f
pottery ceramica f
pound *(sterling)* lira f sterlina
power failure interruzione f della corrente
power point presa f di corrente
practice: to practice speaking Italian praticare l'italiano parlato
pregnant, to be esser incinta
prescribe, to prescrivere
prescription ricetta f
present *(gift)* regalo m
press, to stirare
pretty carino(-a)
priest prete m
primus stove fornello m da campeggio
prison carcere m
private bathroom bagno f privato
probably probabilmente
program programma m; ~ of events programma m delle manifestazioni
prohibited: is it prohibited? è proibito?
promenade deck ponte m di coperta
pronounce, to pronunciare
properly correttamente
Protestant protestante
pub osteria f
public building edifici pubblici mpl
public holidays giorni mpl festivi

pullover maglione m
pump *(gas/petrol)* pompa f
puncture *(flat)* foratura f
pure *(material)* puro(-a)
purple viola
purpose motivo m scopo m
purse portamonete m
push-chair passeggino m
put: where can I put ...? dove posso mettere ..?
put aside, to *(in shop)* mettere da parte
put up: can you put me up for the night? può ospitarmi per una notte?
putting course terreno m da golf

Q

quality qualità f
quantity quantità f
quarantine quarantina f
quarter, a un quarto
quarter past *(after)* e un quarto
quarter to *(before)* meno un quarto
quay molo m
queen *(cards, chess)* regina f
question domanda f
quick veloce
quickest: what's the quickest way to ... qual è la via più breve per ...?
quickly presto!
quiet silenzioso(-a)
quieter più tranquillo(-a)

R

rabbi rabbino m
race *(cars)* gara f automobilistica; *(horses)* corsa f di cavalli
racetrack ippodromo m
racing bike bicicletta f da corsa
racket *(tennis, squash)* racchetta f
rail station stazione f ferroviaria
railroad ferrovia f
rain, to piovere
raincoat impermeabile m
rape stupro m
rapids rapide fpl
rare *(unusual)* raro(-a); *(steak)* poco cotta

rarely raramente
rash eruzione f della pelle
rather piuttosto; ~ **noisy** piuttosto rumoroso(-a);
ravine burrone m
razor rasoio m
razor blades lamette fpl da barba
re-enter, to rientrare
reading *(interest)* lettura f
reading glasses gli occhiali mpl da lettura
ready, to be essere pronto(-a); **are you ready?** è pronto(-a)?
real *(genuine)* vero/autentico
real estate agent agente m/f immobiliare
receipt ricevuta f
reception *(desk)* ricezione f
receptionist ricezionista m/f
reclaim tag talloncino m
reclaim, to ottenere il rimborso m
recommend, to consigliare; raccomandare; **can you recommend?** può consigliare?
record *(lp)* *(disco)* LP m
red rosso(-a)
red wine vino m rosso
reduction sconto m, riduzione f
refreshments rinfreschi (pl)
refrigerator frigorifero m
refund rimborso m
regards to ... saluti a ...
region regione f
register receipt ricevuta f di cassa
registered mail posta f raccomandata
registration form modulo m di registrazione
registration number numero di targa m
regular *(gas/petrol)* normale; *(size of drink)* medio(-a)
regulations: I didn't know the regulations non conoscevo il regolamento
religion religione f
remember: I don't remember non ricordo
removed, to be essere rimossa
rent, to noleggiare
rent: for rent affittasi

rental car auto f noleggiata
repair, to riparare
repairs riparazioni fpl
repeat, to ripetere; **please repeat that** per piacere può ripetere
replacement *(n)* sostituzione f
replacement part pezzo di ricambio m
report, to denunciare
representative rappresentante m/f
required necessario(-a)
reservation prenotazione f
reservation desk botteghino m
reserve, to prenotare
rest, to riposare
retired, to be essere in pensione
return ticket biglietto di andata e ritorno m; biglietto circolare m
return, to *(travel)* ritornare; *(surrender)* restituire
reverse the charges, to *(call collect, to)* telefonare a carico del destinatario
revolting disgustoso(-a)
rheumatism reumatismo m
rib costola f
right *(correct)* giusto(-a)
right, on the a destra
right of way diritto m di passaggio; precedenza f
right-handed che usa la mano destra
ring anello m
rip-off bidonata f
river fiume m
road strada f
road accident incidente m stradale
road assistance soccorso m stradale
road map carta f stradale
road signs segnaletica f, lindicazioni fpl stradali
roasted arrosto(-a)
robbed, to be essere derubato(-a)
robbery rapina f
rock climbing alpinismo m di roccia
rock concert concerto m rock
rocks rocce fpl
roller blades roller blades mpl
rolls panini mpl
romance *(film/play)* romanzo m
romantic romantico(-a)

roof *(house/car)* tetto m
roof-rack portabagagli m esterno
rook *(chess)* torre f
room camera f
room service servizio m in camera
rope corda f
round *(shape)* rotondo(-a); *(of golf)* giro m; **it's my ~** è il mio turno
roundabout rotatoria f
roundtrip ticket biglietto di andata e ritorno m; biglietto circolare m
route strada f, percorso m
row, to remare
rowboat barca f a remi
rude, to be essere maleducato(-a)
rugby rugby m
ruins rovine fpl
run into, to *(crash)* venire addosso
run out, to *(fuel)* finire
run over, to *(people)* investire
rush hour ora f di punta

safe *(lock-up)* cassaforte f
safe *(not dangerous)* sicuro(-a); **to feel ~** sentirsi sicuro(-a)
safety sicurezza f
safety pins spille fpl di sicurezza
sailboat barca f a vela
salad insalata f
sales rep agente m/f di vendita
salt sale m
same day lo stesso giorno
same: the same again please lo stesso, per favore
sand sabbia f
sandals sandali mpl
sandwich panino m
sandwich bar paninoteca f
sandy sabbioso(-a)
sanitary napkins assorbenti mpl
satellite TV televisione f satellitare
satisfied: I'm not satisfied with this non sono soddisfatto(-a) di
sauce salsa f
saucepan pentola f
sausages salcicce fpl
saw *(tool)* sega f

say: how do you say …? come si dice ..?; **what did he say?** cosa ha detto?
scarf sciarpa f
scenic route strada f panoramica
scheduled flight volo m di linea
school scuola f
sciatica sciatica f
scientist scienziato m, scienziata f
scissors un paio di forbici fpl
scooter motoretta f
Scotland Scozia f
Scottish (person/adj.) scozzese m/f
screw vite f
screwdriver cacciavite m
scrub brush spazzola f dura
sculptor scultore m, scultrice f
sea mare m
seafront lungomare m
seasick, I feel ho il mal di mare
season ticket tessera f
seasoning condimenti mpl
seat posto m
second secondo(-a)
second class di seconda classe
second floor (US) primo piano m
secondhand di seconda mano
secretary segretaria f
security guard guardia f di sicurezza
sedative sedativo m
see, to (inspect, witness) vedere; **~ someone again** rivedere
self-catering in affitto
sell, to vendere
send, to mandare; spedire
senior citizens anziani (pl)
separated, to be essere separato(-a)
separately (adv) separatamente
septic tank fognatura f
serious serio
served, to be (meal) essere servito; servire
service servizio m; **~ charge** servizio m; **is service included?** è compreso il servizio?
service station stazione f di servizio
serviette tovagliolo m
set menu menù m fisso
sex (act) sesso m

shade sfumatura f
shady ombreggiato
shallow basso(-a)
shampoo shampoo m
shampoo and set shampoo e messa in piega
shampoo for dry/oily hair shampoo m per capelli secchi/grassi
shape forma f
sharp tagliente
shatter, to (glass) rompere
shaver rasoio m elettrico
shaver socket presa f per rasoio
shaving brush pennello m da barba
shaving cream crema f da barba
she lei
sheet (bedding) le lenzuola fpl
shelf scaffale m
ship nave f
shirt camicia f
shiver, to sentirsi i brividi
shock (electric) scossa f elettrica
shoelaces lacci mpl delle scarpe
shoepolish lucido m da scarpe
shoe repair riparatura f delle scarpe
shoe-cleaning service servizio m pulizia scarpe
shoemaker calzolaio m
shoes scarpe fpl
shop (store) grande magazzino m
shop assistant commesso(-a) m/f
shop/storekeeper negoziante m/f
shopping area zona f dei negozi
shopping basket (bag) cesto f della spesa; cestello m
shopping mall [centre] centro m commerciale
shopping list lista f della spesa
shopping cart [trolley] carrello m
shopping, to go (food) andare a fare la spesa; (other items) andare a fare acquisti
shore (sea/lake) riva f del mare/lago
short corto(-a)
shorts shorts mpl
shoulder spalla f
show spettacolo m
show, to indicare, mostrare; **can you show me?** può indicarmi?

shower gel gel m per doccia
shower room sala f docce (pl)
showers docce f
shutter persiana f
shy timido(-a)
sick, to feel sentirsi male; **I'm going to be ~** mi viene da vomitare
side *(of road)* lato m
side order contorno m
side street strada f laterale
sidewalk marciapiede m
sights luoghi mpl d'interesse
sightseeing tour giro m turistico
sightseeing, to go visitare luoghi d'interesse
sign *(road)* segnali (pl), indicazioni stradali fpl
signpost indicatore m stradale
silk seta f
silver argento m
silverplate placcato d'argento
similar, to be essere simile a
since *(time)* da
singer cantante m/f
single, to be essere single
single *(one-way)* **ticket** biglietto di andata m; biglietto di corsa semplice m
single room camera f singola
sink lavandino m
sister sorella f
sit, to sedersi; sedere
sit down, please si accomodi, prego
six-pack of beer confezione f di sei lattine di birra
size misura f, taglia f
skates pattini mpl da ghiaccio
skating rink palazzo m del ghiaccio
ski bindings gli attacchi mpl per sci
ski boots scarponi mpl da sci
ski instructor istruttore m di sci
ski lift sciovia f ski lift m
ski pants pantaloni mpl da sci
ski poles racchette fpl da sci
ski school scuola f di sci
ski suit tuta f da sci
ski wax cera f per sci
skid: we skidded abbiamo slittato
skiing sci m
skin pelle f, epidermide f

skin-diving equipment attrezzatura f per l'immersione subacquea
skirt gonna f
skis sci mpl
sledge slitta f
sledge run pista f per slitte
sleep, to dormire
sleeping bag sacco m a pelo
sleeping car vagone m letto
sleeping pill sonnifero m
sleeve manica f
slice fetta f
slide film le diapositive fpl
slip *(undergarment)* sottoveste f
slippers pantofole fpl
slope *(ski)* discesa f
slow lento(-a)
slow down! rallenti!
slow, to be *(clock)* ritardare
slowly lentamente
small piccolo(-a); basso(-a)
small change moneta f; spiccioli mpl
small spoon cucchiaino m
smell: there's a bad smell c'è cattivo odore
smoke, to fumare
smoke: I don't smoke non fumo
smoking area zona fumatori f
snacks spuntini mpl
sneakers scarpe fpl da tennis
snorkel maschera f da subacqueo
snow neve f
snow, to nevicare
snowed in, to be essere bloccato dalla neve
snowplow spazzaneve m
soaking solution *(contact lenses)* soluzione f per lenti a contatto
soap sapone m
soap powder detersivo m in polvere
socket presa f
socks calzini mpl
sofa divano m
sofa-bed divano-letto m
soft drink *(soda)* bibita f frizzante; bibita f analcolica
sold out tutto esaurito(-a)
sole *(shoes)* suola f
soluble aspirin aspirina f solubile

some alcuni, del/dei/dell'/della/delle
someone qualcuno
sometimes qualche volta
son figlio m
soon presto; **as ~ as possible** al più presto
sore throat mal m di gola
sore: it's sore fa male
sorry! sono spiacente
sort tipo m
sound-and-light show spettacolo m di suoni e luci
sour acido(-a), aspro(-a)
south sud m
souvenir ricordo m, souvenir m; **~ guide** guida f ricordo
spa stazione f termale
space spazio m
spade *(shovel)* paletta f *(cards)* carta f di picche
speak, to parlare; **~ to someone** parlare con qualcuno; **do you speak English?** parla inglese?
special rate condizioni fpl speciali; tariffa speciale f
special requirements richieste f particolari
specialist specialista m/f
specimen campione m
spectacles occhiali mpl
speed limit limite di velocità m
spell, to sillabare
spend, to spendere
spicy speziato(-a)
spin-dryer asciugatore m elettrico
spine spina f dorsale
sponge spugna f
spoon cucchiaio m
sports club palestra f/associazione f sportiva
sports ground campo m sportivo
sprained, to be essere slogato(-a)
sprained muscle strappo m muscolare
spring *(season)* primavera f; *(water)* fonte f
square *(shape)* quadrato(-a); *(street)* piazza f
stain macchia f
stainless steel acciaio m inossidabile

stairs scale fpl
stale non fresco(-a)
stall: the engine stalls motore s'inceppa
stalls *(orchestra)* platea f
stamp francobollo m; **~ machine** distributore m automatico di francobolli
stand in line, to aspettare, fare la coda
standby ticket biglietto m non prenotato
start inizio m
start, to cominciare **starter** antipasto m
statement *(legal)* dichiarazione f, denuncia f
station stazione f
stay, to fermarsi, rimanere
sterilizing solution soluzione f sterilizzante
stiff neck torcicollo m
still: I'm still waiting sto ancora aspettando
sting puntura f
stocking calze fpl
stolen, to be essere rubato(-a)
stomach stomaco m; **~ ache** dolore m allo stomaco; **~ cramps** crampi mpl allo stomaco
stool *(feces)* feci fpl
stop *(bus, tram, metro)* fermata f
stop, to femarsi; **please stop here** si fermi qui, per favore
stopover sosta f
store detective personale m di sicurezza
store guide guida f al magazzino
stove stufa f
straight ahead (sempre) dritto
strange strano(-a)
straw *(drinking)* cannuccia f
strawberry *(flavor)* fragola f
stream ruscello m, torrente m
string cordino m
stroller passeggino m
strong *(potent)* forte
stuck: the key's stuck la chiave è bloccata

students studenti pl
study, to studiare
stunning magnifico(-a)
stupid: how stupid! che stupidaggine!
style stile m
styling mousse schiuma f per capelli
subtitled, to be avere i sottotitoli
subway metropolitana
subway station stazione f (della) metropolitana
suede pelle f scamosciata
sugar zucchero m
suggest, to suggerire
suit completo m
suitable for adatto(-a) per la
summer estate f
sun block blocco m antisolare
sun lounger sedia f a sdraio
sunbathe, to prendere il sole
sunburn scottatura f solare
suncare prodotti solari
Sunday domenica
sundeck (ship) ponte m superiore
sunglasses occhiali mpl da sole
sunshade (umbrella) ombrellone m
suntan lotion crema f/lozione f abbronzante
sunstroke colpo di sole m
super (gas/petrol) super
superb stupendo(-a)
supermarket supermercato m
supervision sorveglianza f
supplement supplemento m
suppositories supposte fpl
sure: are you sure? è sicuro(-a)?
surfboard tavola f da surf
surname cognome m
suspicious sospettoso(-a)
swallow, to inghiottire
sweatshirt felpa f
sweet (taste) dolce
sweets (dessert) dolci mpl; (candy) caramelle f
swelling gonfiore m
swim, to nuotare
swimming (activity) nuoto m
swimming pool piscina f
swimming trunks calzoncini mpl da bagno

swimsuit costume m da bagno
Swiss (person) svizzero(-a) m/f
switch interruttore m
switch on/off, to accendere/spegnere
Switzerland Svizzera f
swollen, to be essere gonfio(-a)
symptoms sintomi
synagogue sinagoga f
synthetic in fibra sintetica

T-shirt maglietta f
table tavolo m
tablecloth tovaglia f
table tennis tennis m da tavolo
tablet pastiglia f
take away, to da asporto
take photographs/pictures, to fare fotografie
take someone home, to riaccompagnare
take, to (room, bus, medicine) prendere (carry) portare;
taken (occupied) occupato(-a)
talcum powder borotalco m
talk, to parlare
tall alto(-a)
tampons tamponi mpl
tan abbronzatura f
tap (faucet) rubinetto m
tape measure metro m a nastro
tarpaulin telo m per il terreno
taste gusto m
taxi tassì m
taxi driver autista m/f di tassì
taxi stand posteggio m di tassì
tea tè m
tea bags bustine fpl di tè
teacher insegnante m/f
team squadra f
teaspoon cucchiaino m
teat (for baby) tettarella f
teddy bear orsacchiotto m
teenager adolescente m/f
telephone telefono m
telephone bill (in hotel) conto m del telefono
telephone booth cabina f telefonica, telefono m pubblico

telephone directory elenco m telefonico
telephone kiosk cabina f telefonica
telephone number numero m di telefono
telephone token gettone m telefonico
telephone, to telefonare
television televisione f
telex telex m
tell, to dire; **tell me** dimmi
temperature temperatura f
temporary provvisorio(-a)
tendon tendine m
tennis ball palla f da tennis
tennis court campo m da tennis
tent tenda f
tent pegs picchetti mpl
tent pole palo m della tenda
terrible terribile
tetanus tetano m
thank you grazie
that quello(-a)
that one quello(-a)
that's all è tutto
thawing snow neve f fondente
theater [theatre] teatro m
theft furto m
their loro
theirs loro m/f
them loro
theme park parco m a tema
then *(time)* poi
there là
there is ... c'è
thermometer termometro m
thermos bottle [flask] termos m
these questi
they loro
thick spesso(-a)
thief ladro m
thigh coscia f
thin sottile
think, to credere; **I think** penso
think about it, to pensarci
third terzo(-a); **a ~** un terzo
thirsty assetato(-a)
this one questo(-a)
those quelli
thread filo m

throat gola f
throat lozenges pastiglie fpl per la gola
thrombosis trombosi f
through per, attraverso
thumb pollice m
ticket biglietto m
ticket agency/office biglietteria f
tie cravatta f
tie pin spilla f da cravatta
tight *(clothing)* stretto(-a)
tights collant m
till receipt scontrino m di cassa
time *(of day)* ora f; **on ~** in orario; **free ~** tempo m libero; **at what ~?** a che ora?
timetable orario m
tin (can) lattina f; **~ opener** apriscatole m
tin foil carta f stagnola
tint, to fare il colore
tinted *(glass/lens)* colorati (e)
tip mancia f
tipping dare la mancia
tire pneumatico m
tired, to be essere stanco(-a)
tissues fazzoletti mpl di carta
to *(place)* a
toaster tostapane m
tobogganing andare in toboga
today oggi
toe dito m del piede
toilet toilette f
toilet paper carta f igienica
toilets toilettes fpl/bagni mpl
tomorrow domani
tongue lingua f
tonic water acqua f tonica
tonight stasera; **for ~** per questa sera
tonsillitis tonsillite f
tonsils tonsille fpl
too *(also)* anche; *(extreme)* troppo
too much troppo
tooth dente m
toothache mal m di denti
toothbrush spazzolino m da denti
toothpaste dentifricio m
top cima f
top floor ultimo piano m
torch torcia f

totally totalmente
tough *(food)* duro(-a)
tour giro m, gita f
tour guide guida m/f turistica
tour operator agente m di viaggio
tour representative rappresentante m/f dell'agenzia di viaggi
tourist turista m/f
tourist office Ufficio del Turismo m/ Ente del Turismo m
tow, to trainare
tow rope fune f da traino
towards verso
towel asciugamano m
towelling tela f per asciugamani
tower torre f
town città f
town hall Municipio m
town plans cartine f
toy giocattolo m
track sentiero m
tracksuit tuta f da ginnastica
traditional tradizionale
traffic traffico m
traffic jam ingorgo stradale m
traffic light semaforo m
traffic offense/violation infrazione f stradale
tragedy tragedia f
trail sentiero m
trailer roulotte f
trailer park parco m roulotte
train treno m
train times orario m ferroviario
training shoes scarpe fpl da ginnastica
tram tram m
transfer *(transport)* trasferta f
transfer, to trasferire
transit, in durante il viaggio
translate, to tradurre
translation traduzione f
translator traduttore m, traduttrice f
trash rifiuti mpl
trash bags sacchetti mpl per i rifiuti
trash cans bidoni mpl per i rifiuti
travel agency agenzia f di viaggio
travel sickness *(car/air/sea)* mal d'auto/d'aria/di mare
travel, to viaggiare, partire

traveler's checks traveller's cheques mpl
tray vassoio m
tree albero m
tremendous straordinario(-a)
trim *(hair)* spuntatina f
trip gita f
trolley carrello m
trouble: I'm having trouble with ... ho difficoltà con ...
trouser press stirapantaloni m
trousers pantaloni mpl
truck camion m
true: that's not true non è vero
try on, to provare
tube tubo m
tumor tumore m
tunnel tunnel m
turn, to girare
turn down (volume, heat), to abbassare (volume, riscaldamento)
turn off, to spegnere
turn on, to accendere
turn up, to *(volume, heat)* alzare
turn(ing) svolta f
TV room sala f televisione
tweezers le pinzette fpl
twice due volte
twin bed due letti mpl
two-door car auto a due porte f
type: what type? che tipo?
typical tipico(-a)
tyre pneumatico m

ugly brutto(-a)
UK Regno m Unito
ulcer ulcera f
umbrella ombrello m
uncle zio m
unconscious, to be perdere conoscenza
under *(place)* sotto
underdone *(adj)* non abbastanza cotto(-a)
underpants mutande fpl
underpass sottopassaggio m
understand, to capire; **do you understand?** capisce?; **I don't understand** non capisco

undress, to spogliarsi
uneven *(ground)* in dislivello
unfortunately sfortunatamente
uniform uniforme m/f
United States gli Stati Uniti mpl
university università f
unleaded gasoline benzina f senza piombo
unlimited mileage chilometraggio m illimitato
unlock, to aprire a chiave, sbloccare
unpleasant sgradevole
unscrew, to svitare
until fino a
up to fino a
upmarket elegante m/f
upper berth cuccetta superiore f
upset stomach mal m di stomaco
upstairs al piano superiore
urgent urgente
us: for/with ~ per/con noi
U.S. Stati fpl Uniti, USA
use, to usare
use: for my personal use per mio uso personale
useful utile m/f
utensils stoviglie fpl

V

vacancy camere libere
vacant libero(-a)
vacate, to lasciare lbero(-a)
vacation vacanza f
vaccinated against, to be essere vaccinato(-a) contro
vaccination vaccinazione f
vaginal infection infezione f vaginale
valet service servizio m di pulizia
valid valido
validate, to *(ticket)* convalidare
valley valle *f*
valuable prezioso(-a)
value valore m
vanilla *(flavor)* vaniglia f
VAT *(sales tax)* I.V.A. (Imposta Valore Aggiunto) f
VAT receipt Ricevuta f Fiscale
vegan, to be seguire una dieta macrobiotica

vegan: suitable for vegans adatto(-a) per chi non consuma prodotti derivati da animali
vegetables le verdure fpl
vegetarian vegetariano(-a)
vehicle veicolo m
vehicle registration (document) documenti del veicolo
vein vena f
velvet velluto m
vending machine distributore m automatico
venereal disease malattia f venerea
ventilator ventilatore m
very molto
vet veterinario m
video arcade sala f giochi
video game videogioco m
video recorder videoregistratore m
view: with a view of the sea con vista sul mare
viewing point punto m panoramico
village paese m
vineyard vigne fpl
visa visto m
visit visita f
visit, to visitare
visiting hours ore fpl di visita
vitamin pills vitamine fpl
voice voce f
volleyball pallavolo
voltage voltaggio m
vomit, to vomitare

W

wading pool piscina per bambini
waist vita f **~ pouch** borsello m da cintura
wait attesa f
wait for, to aspettare; **wait!** aspetti!
waiter/waitress cameriere(-a) m/f
waiting room sala f d'aspetto
wake, to *(self)* svegliarsi
wake someone, to svegliare qualcuno
wake-up call sveglia f telefonica
Wales Galles m
walk: to go for a walk andare a fare una passeggiata
walk home, to rientrare a piedi

walking passeggiare, camminare
walking boots scarponi mpl
walking distance, within raggiungibile a piedi
walking route percorso m a piedi
walking gear abbigliamento m escursionismo
wall muro m
wallet portafoglio m
want, to volere
ward (*hospital*) reparto m, corsia f
warm (*weather*) caldo(-a)
warm, to riscaldare
warmer più caldo(-a)
wash basin lavello (*kitchen*) m, lavandino (*bathroom*) m
wash, to lavare
washing, to do fare il bucato
washing instructions istruzioni di lavaggio
wasp vespa f
watch orologio m
watch band cinturino m dell'orologio
watch battery pila f per orologi
watch maker orologeria f
watch TV, to guardare la televisione
water acqua f
water carrier bidone m dell'acqua
water heater boiler m
waterfall cascata f
waterproof impermeabile m/f
waterskiing sci m d'acqua
waterskis sci mpl d'acqua
wave onda f
way (*direction*) strada f; **I've lost my ~** mi sono smarrito; **it's in the ~** blocca il passaggio; **on the ~ to** sulla strada di
we noi
weak coffee caffè m lungo
weak: I feel weak mi sento debole
wear, to indossare
weather tempo m
weather forecast previsioni fpl del tempo
wedding matrimonio m
wedding ring fede f nuziale
week settimana f

weekend fine f settimana; **on [at] the ~** al fine settimana
weekend rate tariffa f per fine settimana
weekly (*ticket*) settimanale
weight: my weight is ... peso ...
welcome to ... benvenuto(-a) a
well-done (*steak*) ben cotta
Welsh (*person/adj*) gallese m/f
west ovest m
wetsuit tuta f per immersione
what? cosa?
what kind of ...? che tipo di ... ?
what time ...? a che ora ...?
what's the time? che ora è?
wheelchair carrozzella f
when? quando?
where? dove?; **~ is ...?** dov'è ...?
where are you from? da dove viene?/di dov'è?
where else? dove?
which? quale?; **~ stop?** quale fermata?
while mentre
whist (*cards*) gioco m del whist
white bianco
who? chi?
whole: the whole day tutto il giorno
whose di chi
why? perchè?
wide largo(-a)
wife moglie f
wildlife fauna f
windbreaker giace f a vento
window finestra f; finestrino m; (*shop*) vetrina f
window seat posto m accanto al finestrino
windshield [windscreen] parabrezza m
windy, to be essere ventoso(-a)
wine vino m; **~ bottle** bottiglia f di vino
winery vigne fpl
wine list lista f dei vini
winter inverno m
wishes: best wishes to ... tanti auguri mpl a ...
with con
withdraw, to fare un prelievo
without senza

witness testimone m/f
wood *(forest)* bosco m; *(material)* legno m
wool lana f
work, to lavorare; *(operate)* funzionare; **it doesn't work** non funziona
worry: I'm worried sono preoccupato(-a)
worse peggiore; **it's gotten [got] ~** è peggiorato(-a)
worst *(adv./adj.)* peggio, peggiore m/f
worth: is it worth seeing? vale la pena vederlo?
wound ferita f
wrap up, to impacchettare
write-off *(car)* inservibile
write: write soon! scriva presto!
writing pad carta f da lettere
wrong sbagliato(-a); *(not right)* non funziona; **~ number** numero m sbagliato; **there's something ~ with …** c'è qualcosa che non va con …; **what's ~?** che guasto ha?

XYZ

x-ray radiografia f
yacht yacht m
year anno m
yellow giallo
yes sì
yesterday ieri
yield *(give way)* dare la precedenza
yogurt yogurt m
you *(sing/plur/formal)* tu/voi/Lei
young giovane
your(s) *(formal)* Suo(-a), *(familiar)* tuo(-a)
youth hostel ostello m della gioventù
zero zero
zip(per) cerniera f
zone zona f
zoo zoo m
zoology zoologia f

DICTIONARY
ITALIAN-ENGLISH

This Italian-English Dictionary covers all the areas where you may need to decode written Italian: hotels, public buildings, restaurants, shops, ticket offices and transportation. It will also help with understanding forms, maps, product labels, road signs and operating instuctions (for telephones, parking meters etc.). If you can't locate the exact sign, you may find key words or terms listed separately.

A

a passo d'uomo dead slow
a proprio rischio at the owner's risk
a scelta at your choice …
a stomaco vuoto on an empty stomach
abbazia abbey
abbigliamento da bambino children's wear
abbigliamento da donna ladies wear
abbigliamento da uomo menswear
abbigliamento sportivo sportswear
abiti per uomo menswear
accendere i fari/luci switch on headlights
accettazione admissions
acciaio steel
accostarsi a sinistra/destra keep to the left/right
aceto vinegar
acqua non potabile do not drink water
acqua potabile drinking water
aereo plane
affitasi camere rooms to rent
affitasi appartamento apartment to let
agenzia di assicurazioni insurance agency
agenzia di viaggi travel agency

agenzia immobiliare real estate agency
aggiornato updated
agitare prima dell'uso shake well before use
ai binari to the platforms
al coperto indoor
albergo hotel
alianti gliding
alimentari grocer's
alimenti surgelati frozen foods
aliscafo hydrofoil
all'aperto outdoor/open-air
allacciare le cinture fasten your seatbelt
alle cabine cabin decks
alotto lounge
alpinismo mountaineering, abseiling
alpinismo da roccia rock climbing
alt stop
alta tensione high voltage
altezza height
altezza massima … metri headroom
altitudine altitude
alzare il ricevitore lift receiver
ambasciata embassy
ambulatorio oculistico eye infirmary
ancora meglio improved
andata one-way/single
andata e ritorno round trip
andata semplice one-way
anti-urto shock-proof
antiquario antiques store/shop
aperto open
aperto tutti i giorni anche la domenica open every day including Sundays
aprire qui open here
area di ristoro rest area
area di servizio service area
argenteria silver shop
argento silver
aria condizionata air conditioning
aromi (naturali) (natural) flavoring
arredi per arredamento furnishings
arrivi arrivals

articoli di bellezza e profumeria
makeup and perfume
articoli per cucina kitchen equipment
articoli per il bagno bathroom
accessories
articoli per la camera di letto
bedroom accessories
ascensore elevator
aspettare il proprio turno please
wait your turn
aspettare il tono wait for tone
attendere prego please wait
attenti ai ladri beware of pickpockets
attenti al cane beware of the dog
attenzione ghiaia loose gravel
**attenzione non scendere il gradino
prima dell'apertura della porta** do
not descend steps before doors open
(on buses)
attenzione, prego please be careful
**attenzione, questa macchina non da
resto** this machine does not give
change
attenzione, ... avviso/avvertimento
warning
attesa di ... minuti circa wait approx
... minutes
attrezzatura per pesca subacquea
underwater fishing equipment
attrezzatura per scuba scuba diving
equipment
autonoleggio car rental
autostrada expressway
autunno fall/autumn
avanti cross now

B

bagno restroom/toilets
bagno schiuma foambath
baia bay
balconata balcony, dress circle
balcone balcony
ballo dance
bambini children
bambini solo se accompagnati no
unaccompanied children

banca bank
banco di pesce fishstall *(at market)*
bancomat cash dispenser
barca a remi rowboat
barca a vela sailboat, yacht
batelli di salvataggio lifeboats
batello a vapore steamer
belvedere view point
benvenuti! welcome
benzina gas
bevande analcoliche soft drinks
bevande extra drinks
not included
bevande incluse drinks included
bibite fresche e snacks refreshments
available
biblioteca library
biglietteria ticket office
biglietti tickets
biglietti per oggi tickets for today
biglietto di andata e ritorno return
ticket
biglietto ordinario day ticket
biglietto settimanale weekly ticket
binario platform
biodegradabile disposable
birra beer
borse handbags
bracciole waterwings
bretella expressway junction
burrone profondo canyon

C

cabina bathing cabana/hut
cabina di ponte deck cabin
caduta massi falling rocks
caduta slavine avalanche danger
calcio soccer
calle street *(in Venice)*
calzolaio shoe repairs/cobbler's
cambiare a change at
cambiare per change *(to other
metro lines)*
cambio exchange rate
cambio valute bureau de change

Camera dei Deputati parliament building
camere libere vacancies/accommodations available
camerini fitting rooms
camion truck
campeggio campsite
campi di tennis tennis courts
campo field
campo di battaglia battle site
campo giochi/sportivo sports ground
cancellato cancelled
cancello gate
canna da pesca fishing rod
canoa canoe
canottaggio canoeing, rowing
cantante singer
cantante lirica opera singer
canto Gregoriano Gregorian chant
capella chapel
Capodanno New Year's Day
capolinea terminal
capsule capsules
carne meat
carozza coach
carozza non fumatori (non)smokers compartment
carozza/vagone ristorante dining-car
carrelli carts/trolleys
carta d'imbarco embarkation card
carta riciclata recycled paper
cartelle cliniche medical records
cartoleria stationer's
casa house
casa di cura privata health clinic
casa patrizia stately home
cascata waterfall
casco crash helmet
cassa cashier, checkout
cassa di risparmio savings bank
cassa rapida express checkout
cassette luggage lockers; cassettes
cassieri cashiers
castello castle
catena di montagne mountain range
cavalcavia road bridge

centralino/centralinista operator
centesimo cent
centrifuga dry spin
centro città downtown area
centro commerciale shopping area
centro congressi convention hall
centro direzionale business district
centro sportivo sports center
ceriali cereals
check-in check-in counter
chiamare … per il ricevimento dial … for reception
chiamare … per una linea esterna dial … for an outside line
chiesa church
chilometro kilometer
chirurgia surgery
chiudere il cancello keep gate shut
chiudere la porta please shut the door
chiuso (per restauro) closed (for restoration)
chiuso al traffico closed to traffic
chiuso fino a … closed until …
chiuso per ferie closed for holiday
chiuso per pranzo closed for lunch
chiuso per rinnovo locali closed for repairs
chiusura festiva closed for holidays
chiusura settimanale closed/day off
ciambella rubber ring
ciclismo cycling
ciniglia chenille
cinte belts
cintura di salvataggio lifebelt
cioccolateria confectioner's
circo circus
circonvallazione ring road
città city
città universitaria university
città vecchia old town
cittadini extracomunitari non-EU citizens
cognome surname
collina/colle hill
colonna sonora soundtrack
colori resistenti colorfast**

comando polizia/comando Carabinieri police station
comincia alle ore ... begins at ...
commissioni bank charges
completo full
compreso inclusive
compreso nel prezzo included in the price
compresse tablets
compri due paghi uno buy 2 get 1 free
compriamo a ... currency bought at ...
compro e vendo ... we buy and sell ...
comunicazioni interurbane/ internazionali/intercontinentali (con operatore) long distance calls (with operator): intercity/international/intercontinental
con bagno with private bathroom
con sottotitoli subtitled
con vista sul mare with sea view
concerto concert
conservanti preservatives
consiglio per la consumazione serving suggestion
consultare il proprio medico prima dell'uso consult your doctor before use
consumare entro il ... best before ...
contatore della luce electric meter
contenitore per batterie/vetro/aluminio/latta/plastica container for battery/bottle/ aluminum/tin/plastic/ paper recycling
conto account
conto corrente current account
contorni vari choice of vegetables
contro la forfora against dandruff
controcoperta upper deck
controllo please show your bags before leaving *(in shop);* check/control
controllo valuta currency control
convalidare il biglietto (prima della prossima fermata/prima di salire sul treno) validate your ticket (before next bus stop/before getting on train)
coperto cloudy
corsia d'emergenza emergency lane

corsa di levrieri greyhound racing
corsi di cavallo horseracing
corsia lane
corsia ciclabile cycle track
corsia di sorpasso passing lane
corsia preferenziale do not walk
corso semplice one-way
costa coast
costo per chilo (Kg)/etto/litro/metro price per kilo/330 grams/liter/meter
cotone cotton
crema per le mani hand cream
crociere cruises
cucina cookery
cuffie obbligatorie bathing caps must be worn
cuoio leather
cura intensiva intensive care
curva pericolosa dangerous bend
curve per ... Km bends for ...km

D

da consumarsi entro il ... best before ...
da non prendere per via orale not to be taken orally
da ... a .../dalle ore... alle ore ... from ... to ...
danza dance
danza classica ballet
danza folcloristica folk dancing
dare la precedenza yield/give way
darsena docks
data di nascita date of birth
degustazione vini winetasting
della casa homemade
della stagione in season
deltaplano hang gliding
depositi deposits
deposito ambulanze ambulance station
deposito bagagli left-luggage office
deviazione alternative route, detour/diversion
deviazione per camions/TIR truck route/alternative lorry
di giornata fresh daily

diagnosi e cura treatment room
diapositive slides
diga dam
diocesi diocese
diretto direct
direttore manager
disco orario parking disk
dissolvere in acqua dissolve in water
divieto d'attracco no anchorage
divieto di balneazione no swimming/
bathing
divieto di campeggio no camping
**divieto di ingresso esclusi i mezzi
degli handicappati** access for
disabled person vehicles only
**divieto di ingresso escluso veicoli
autorizzati** authorized vehicles only
divieto di scarico no dumping
divieto di sorpasso no passing
divieto di sosta no stopping
docce showers
dogana customs con.trol
domani tomorrow
domenica Sunday
Domenica delle Palme Palm Sunday
domicilio home address
donne women only, women (toilets)
dopo i pasti after meals
dopobarba aftershave
doposole aftersun
doppiato dubbed
doppio senso two-way traffic
durante i pasti with meals

E

€ euro
edicola newsagent's
edificio pubblico public building
elenco telefonico telephone directory
elicottero helicopter
emergenza emergency
emergenza sanitaria medical
(health) emergency
entrata entrance
Epifania Epiphany (January 6)
equitazione horseback riding

esaurito sold out
**esibire documenti/carta d'identità/
passaporto** proof of identity required
esibire la ricevuta sul paravento
place ticket on windshield
espresso made to order
estate summer
estero foreign
estintore fire extinguisher
estuario estuary
etto 330 grams
extra extra charge/supplement

F

fabbrica factory
fantascienza science fiction
farina wheat flour
farina integrale fermenti lattici vivi
whole wheat flour
farmacia drugstore
faro marina lighthouse
fatto su misura made to measure
fattore 8 factor 8 (sunlotion)
fattoria farm
febbraio February
fermata bus stop
fermata a richiesta request stop
fermata del tram tram stop
fermata service stopping
Ferragosto Assumption Day (August 15)
ferro iron
ferrovia railroad
Festa del Lavoro Labor Day (May 1)
Festa dell'Assunzione Assumption
Day (August 15)
**Festa dell'Immacolata Concezione (8
dicembre)** Immaculate Conception
(December 8)
Festa della liberazione (25 aprile)
Liberation Day (April 25)
festa nazionale national holiday
fibre alimentari fibre *(food)*
fiera fair
fila row
film d'orrore horror film

film per famiglia universal *(film classification)*
filobus trolleybus
filosofia philosophy
fine autostrada/superstrada end of expressway/motorway
fine deviazione end of detour/diversion
fine lavori stradali end of roadworks
finestrino window seat
finire la cura/il trattamento finish the course
fino a ... until ...
fioraio florist's
Firenze Florence
firma signature
fiume river
fon hairdryer
Fondamenta canal-side *(Venice)*
fontana fountain
formaggio cheese
fortezza fortress
fotottico photographic store
fragile – vetro fragile – glass
frana landslide
francobolli stamps
franchigia bagagli luggage allowance
freno d'emergenza emergency brake
fresco fresh
frontiera border crossing
frutta fruit
fruttivendolo greengrocer's
fumetti comics
funivia cable car/gondola
funzione religiosa church service
fuochi d'artificio fireworks
fuori servizio out of order

G

gabinetti restrooms [toilets]
gabinetti pubblici public restrooms
galleria shopping mall (dress) circle; gallery
galleria chiusa (mountain) tunnel closed
galleria d'arte art gallery
gara contest

gas per campeggio camping gas
gennaio January
Genova Genoa
genuino genuine
ghiaccio icy snow
ghiaccio nero black ice
giardini pubblici park
giardino garden
giardino botanico botanical garden
gift omaggio free gift
ginocologo gynecologist
gioaccatoli toystore
giornalaio newsagent's
giorni feriali weekdays
giovedì Thursday
giugno June
gocce drops
goielleria jeweler's
gola gorge
gomma rubber
grassi fat content
grassi vegetali vegetable fats
grotta cave
gruppi groups welcome
guanti, cinte e sciarpe gloves, belts and scarves
guardaroba cloakroom
guida ai piani store guide

H

hockey su ghiaccio ice hockey

I

il cuoco suggerisce ... the chef suggests ...
il migliore del mondo world's best
imbarco ad uscita n° ... boarding at gate no. ...
imbarco immediato boarding now
immigrazione immigration control
in casi di guasti telefonare al numero ... in case of breakdown, phone/contact ...
in funzione sistema di vigilanza/allarme surveillance/alarm system in operation

incrocio crossing
indirizzo address
indirizzo di casa home address
industria cinematografica movies/cinema
informazioni information desk, reception
informazioni elenco abbonati enquiries
informazioni nutirizionali nutritional information
ingoiare intere swallow whole
ingrandimento enlargement service
ingresso access only, entrance
ingresso libero admission free
ingresso per gli handicappati entrance for disabled persons
ingresso per soli residenti access to residents only
inizia alle ore ... commencing ...
inizio autostrada freeway entrance
inizio spettacolo curtain up
innestare la prima marcia prima di lasciare la macchina leave your car in first gear
inserire monete insert coin
inserire carta di credito insert credit card
inserire il denaro nella macchina e ritirare il biglietto insert money in machine and remove ticket
inverno winter
inversione di marcia change direction
irritante per gli occhi e la pelle harmful for eyes and skin
isola pedonale pedestrians only/ pedestrian zone
istituto di credito bank
istruzioni per l'uso instructions for use
itinerario naturale nature trail
itinerario panoramico scenic route
itinerario turistico tourist route
IVA VAT/sales tax
IVA compreso/incluso VAT included

L

l'originale the original
La Befana (6 gennaio) Epiphany (January 6)
la merce non può essere cambiata goods cannot be exchanged
lago (artificiale) (artificial) lake
lana wool
lastri x-ray
latte e latticini dairy products
latteria dairy
lavaggio macchine car wash
lavanderia laundry, washing facilities
lavare a mano hand wash only
lavare in acqua fredda/tiepida wash in cold/warm water
lavori in corso (a ... metri) construction (... m) ahead
leggere attentamente le istruzioni prima dell'uso read instructions carefully before use
legno wood
lettino sun lounger
lettura di poesie poetry reading
levate alle ore ... times of collection
libero vacant, for rent
libreria bookstore
libretto di circolazione/documenti registration papers
lino linen
liquidazione clearance sale
liquori liqueurs
lista menu
Livorno Leghorn
lo chef suggerisce ... the chef suggests ...
locanda guest house
luna park amusement park
lunedì Monday
Lunedì dell'Angelo Easter Monday
luogo di nascita place of birth

M

macchina car
macelleria butcher's

magazzino department store
maggio May
mare sea
mare mosso rough sea
marionette puppets
marmellate e conserve preserves
martedì Tuesday
marzo March
maternità maternity
mattina a.m.
medico doctor
meglio se servito fresco best served chilled
meno di 8 articoli 8 items or less
menù fisso set menu
menù turistico tourist menu
mercato market
mercato coperto covered market
merce da dichiarare goods to declare
mercoledì Wednesday
messa mass
messa vespertina Evensong
metallo metal
metropolitana/metro subway
mezza pensione half board
mimo mime
miniera mine
misura unica one size fits all
mittente sender
mobili ed arredamenti furniture
mobilificio furniture warehouse
molo (boarding) dock (boarding)
molta neve heavy (snow)
monastero monastery
monsignore monseignor
montagna mountain
monumenti antichi ruins
monumento (ai caduti) (war) memorial
monumento di interesse turistico tourist feature
monumento storico ancient monument
mulino mill
mulino a vento windmill
multicine multiplex cinema
municipio town hall

muro wall
museo museum
musica music
musica da camera chamber music
musica dal vivo live music
musica lirica opera

N

Napoli Naples
Natale Christmas
nave ship
nazionalità nationality
nebbia fog
negozio di musica music store/shop
neve snow
neve artificiale artificial snow
neve bagnata wet snow
neve fresca fresh snow
neve ghiacciato icy snow
neve leggera powdery snow
niente flash no flash
niente resto exact change/no change given
niente rimborsi no refunds
nocivo harmful
noleggio for rent
noleggio abiti/vestiti dress rental
nome name
nome dei figli name of children
nome del coniuge name of spouse
nome di famiglia surname
nome di ragazza maiden name
non allacciato disconnected
non appoggiarsi alla porta do not lean against door
non asciugare al sole do not dry in direct sunlight
non avvicinarsi keep clear
non bruciare do not burn
non calpestare il prato/l'erba keep off the grass
non compreso exclusive
non danneggia le pellicole film safe
non esporre a fonti di calore do not expose to heat
non gettare rifiuti do not litter

non incluso not included
non lasciare bagagli incustoditi do not leave baggage unattended
non lasciare oggetti di valore nell'automobile do not leave valuables in your car
non parlare al conducente do not talk to the driver
non più di 4 persone no more than 4 persons
non scongelare prima di cucinare do not defrost before cooking
non si accetta nessuna responsabilità per danni o furto the owners can accept no responsibility for any damage or theft
non si accettano assegni no checks
non si accettano carte di credito no credit cards
non stirare do not iron
non superare 375 kg do not exceed 375 kilos (in elevators)
non toccare do not touch
non usare candeggia do not bleach
nulla da dichiarare nothing to declare
numero di targa license plate number
numero verde toll free number
numeri di emergenza emergency telephone numbers
numeri utili useful numbers
numero del passaporto passport number
numero della carta di credito credit card number
numero di soccorso pubblico di emergenza general emergency number
numero di volo flight number
nuoto swimming

O

occupato occupied/engaged
offerta speciale special offer
officina meccanica car repairs
oggetti elettrici electrical shop/store/appliances
oggetti smarriti lost property

oggi today
ogni ... ore every ... hours
Ognissanti All Saints' Day (November 1)
olio oil; sauces
ombrellone sun umbrella [sunshade]
omeopatico homeopath
ommaggio ...% se spendi più di ... % discount if you spend more than ...
operatore operator
orari timetables
orario opening/business/visiting hours
orario continuato open all day
orario di visite visiting hours
orchestra sinfonica symphony orchestra
24 ore su 24 24-hour service
oreficeria jeweler's
oro gold
ospedale hospital
ospizio hospice
osservatoria observatory
ostello della gioventù youth hostel
ottico optician
ottobre October
ottone brass

P

pacchi packages
padiglione pavilion
padre Father
pagare alla cassa please pay at cash desk
pagare qui please pay here
pagato (grazie) paid (with thanks)
pagine gialle yellow pages
palco (pl. palchi) box
palude marsh, swamp
pane bread
panificio bakery/baker's
paracadutismo parachuting
parcheggio parking (permitted); parking lot
parcheggio libero free parking
parcheggio per biciclette parking for bicycles

parcheggio per soli residenti parking for residents only

parcheggio riservato ai clienti customer parking lot

parcheggio sotterraneo underground garage

parcheggio vietato/divieto di sosta no parking

parrucchiere hairdresser's/hairstylist's

partenze departures

partita match

Pasqua Easter Sunday

passaggio a livello railroad/level crossing

passaggio sotterraneo underground passage

passo carrabile do not block entrance

pasticceria pastry shop

pattini skates

pedaggio toll

pedoni pedestrians

pelle leather

pellicola film

pendenza incline [gradient]

penisola peninsula

pensione completa full board

pensione guest house

per vegetariani suitable for vegetarians

per ... giorni for ... days

percorso del traghetto ferry route

percorso per autobus/pullmans bus route

pericolo danger

pericolo di bufere storm warning

pericolo di burrasche gale warning

pericolo di ghiaccio icy road

pericolo di slavine danger of avalanches

pericoloso dangerous

personale staff only

pesce fish; angling

pesce fresco fresh fish

pesce surgelato frozen fish

pescheria fish store

pesistica weight-lifting

piatti pronti oven to table

piatto del giorno dish of the day

piazza square

picco peak

piccola colazione breakfast

piccoli prezzi grande qualità low prices, top quality

pillole pills

pinacoteca art gallery

pioggia rain

piscina swimming pool

piscina per tuffi diving pool

pista bianca (ski trail)for beginners

pista blu e pista rossa for intermediates *(ski trail)*

pista chiusa closed

pista ciclabile cycle lane/track

pista nera for advanced skiers

pista per principianti for beginners *(ski trail)*

pista pericolosa dangerous trail

platea stalls

polizia police

polizia stradale highway/traffic police

pollame poultry

poltrona n° seat no.

pomata ointment

pomeriggio p.m.

pompa pump

ponte bridge

ponte bassa (altezza ... m.) low bridge (height ... m.)

ponte di coperta upper deck

ponte di passeggiate promenade deck

ponte levatoio drawbridge

porta gate (to town/city); door

porta antincendio fire door

porta automatica automatic door

portiere notturno night porter

porto harbor

posta post office

posto corridoio aisle seat

posto fumatore smoking

posto non fumatore no smoking

posto n° seat no.

posto riservato agli invalidi please give up this seat to the disabled

pozzo well
PP.TT. post office
prato (campeggio) grass (camping site)
prefisso area code
preghiera prayers
prelievi withdrawals
prelievi di sangue blood tests
prendere il biglietto take ticket
prendere la ricevuta dalla cassa automatica pay at the meter
prenotazione biglietti ticket reservation
prenotazioni reservations, advance bookings
prezzi fissi no discounts
prezzi speciali per gruppi special price for groups
prezzo rate
prezzo al litro price per liter/litre
prezzo per chilo (Kg)/etto price per kilo/330 grams
prima classe first class
prima dei pasti before meals
prima di coricarsi before going to bed (medicine dose)
primavera spring
primo piano first floor
prodotti antiallergici antiallergic products
prodotti di bellezza beauty products
proibito circolare nella chiesa durante le funzioni liturgiche/durante la santa messa no entry during services
pronto intervento emergency services
pronto soccorso accident and emergency; medicine box
proprietà privato private property
prossima levata alle ore ... next collection at ...
prossima visita guidata alle ore ... next tour at ...
punto d'imbarco embarkation point
punto d'incontro meeting point
punto di raduno muster station

Q

questa macchina non da resto this machine does not give change
questa sera/stasera this evening
qui si vendono carte telefoniche phone cards on sale here

R

racchetta racket/raquet; ski poles/sticks
raccordo anulare ring-road
rallentare slow down
rallentare, scuola/bambini caution, school/children
reclamo bagagli baggage claim
referti test results
regali gifts
reggersi ai corrimano hold on to the side (escalator)
resto massimo (€2) maximum change given (€.2)
ricambi per auto car accessory/spares shop/store
ricevimento reception
riduzioni reductions
rifugio ski shelter
rilasciato il ... da ... issued on ... by ...
rimozione forzata unauthorized vehicles will be towed away
rio stream
riparazioni repairs
riserva d'acqua reservoir
riserva naturale nature reserve
riservato reserved
ritardo delayed
rocca castle, fortress
roccia (campeggio) stone (camping site)
romanzi novels
rompere il vetro in caso di pericolo break glass in case of emergency
rotatoria (a ... metri) roundabout/circle (... m. ahead)
roulotte trailer/caravan
rubinetto water tap

rupe cliff

sabato Saturday
sabbia mobile quicksand
sala banchetti reception facilities
sala congressi/conferenze conference room
sala d'attesa waiting room
sala da pranzo dining room
sala giochi games room
sala operatoria operating theater
sala passaggeri passenger lounge
sala TV television room
saldi clearance sale
sale salt
salita entrance (get on)
salotto lounge
salvagenti lifejackets
San Gennaro St. Januarius (September 19, Naples)
San Giovanni Battista St. John The Baptist (June 24, Florence)
San Marco Saint Mark's Day (April 25, Venice)
San Pietro e Paolo Saint Paul's and Peter's Day (June 29, Rome)
San Silvestro New Year's Eve
Sant'Ambrogio Saint Ambrose's Day (December 7, Milan)
Santo Stefano Boxing Day (December 26)
sanzioni per i trasgressori trespassers will be prosecuted
sanzioni per i viaggiatori senza biglietto penalty for traveling without a ticket
sanzioni se viaggiate senza biglietto penalty for traveling without ticket
saporito tasty
scadenza della carta di credito credit card expiration date
scala d'emergenza emergency stairs
scala mobile escalator
scarico merci deliveries only
scarpata escarpment

scarponi da sci ski boots
schiuma per la barba shaving cream
sci skis, skiing
sci di fondo cross-country skiing
sci nautico waterskiing
sciovia tow (ski) lift
sconto di ...% se spendi più di ... ... % discount if you spend more than ...
scuola school
scuola rallentare slow, school
sdraia deck-chair
se i sintomi persistono consultare il proprio medico if symptoms persist, consult your doctor
seconda scelta sale
secondo piano second floor
segale rye
seggiovia chairlift
selezionare destinazione/zona select destination/zone
semaforo provvisorio temporary traffic light
senso unico one-way street
sentiero footpath, track
senza grassi fat-free
senza intervallo no intermission
senza piombo unleaded
senza zucchero sugar-free
sereno sunny weather
servizio service charge
servizio compreso/incluso service included
servizio di camera room service
servizio diretto direct service
servizio immediato while you wait
servizio non incluso service not included
servizio notturno night service
seta silk
si accettano gruppi parties welcome
si accettano carte di credito we accept credit cards
si prega consegnare le borse please leave your bags here
si prega controllare il resto please check your change

si prega di aspettare dietro la linea please wait behind barrier

si prega di non consumare cibo nella camera no food in the room please

si prega fare un contributo please make a contribution

si prega mantere il silenzio durante le funzioni religiose quiet, service in progress

si prega pulire la camera make up this room please

si prega rispettare questo luogo sacro please respect this place of worship

si prega tenere il biglietto please retain your ticket

sicurezza security

signore women only; ladies (toilets)

signori gentlemen (toilets)

slittino sledge

soccorso stradale breakdown services

solista soloist

solo ciclisti cyclists only

solo contanti cash only

solo giorni feriali weekdays only

solo giorni festivi Sundays only

solo per gli abbonati season ticket holders only

solo per uso esterno not for internal consumption

solo rasoi shavers only

solo residenti residents only

solo stasera/una serata for 1 night only

solo uso esterno for external use only

sono previste sanzioni per chi non può esibire lo scontrino fiscale/il biglietto you are liable to be fined if you don't keep your receipt/ticket

sopra il livello del mare above sea level

sopraelevata flyover

sorgente spring

spegnere il motore turn off engine

spettacolo spectacular

spettacolo serale evening performance

spettatori spectators

spiaggia beach

spiaggia per nudisti nudist beach

spingere push

spogliatoi changing rooms

SQ subject to availability

squisito delicious

staccare la corrente prima di (togliere) disconnect from electric mains before (removing)

stampa e sviluppo photographic store

stampe prints

stazione degli autobus bus station/terminal

stazione di pedaggio toll booth

stazione di servizio service/filling station

stazione ferroviaro train station

stirare a temperatura bassa cool iron

storia history

storia dell'arte art history

strada road

strada a doppia corsia dual highway

strada a doppio senso traffic from the opposite direction

strada a senso unico one-way street

strada bianca gravel/unpaved road

strada chiusa road closed

strada dissestata uneven road surface

strada in costruzione road under construction

strada nazionale main road/highway

strada principale main street

strada senza uscita cul-de-sac; no through traffic

strada stretta narrow road

straniero(-a) foreign

strappare qui tear here

strisce pedonali pedestrian crossing

studio medico doctor's office [surgery]

succhi di frutta fruit juices

suonare la campanella ring the bell

super four-star (gas)

superstrada expressway

supplemento (notturno, aeroporto, bagagli, festivo) supplement (night-time, airport, baggage, Sunday, holiday)
surgelato frozen
sviluppo developing
svincolo junction/interchange

T

tagliare qui cut here
tangenziale bypass
tavola da sci snowboard
tavola da surf surfboard
tavoli al piano superiore seats upstairs
tassì taxi
teatro per ragazzi children's theater
telefono per solo carte card phone
telefono SOS/di emergenza emergency telephone
teleselezione direct dialing
tenere in frigo keep refrigerated
tenere in un ambiente fresco keep in a cool place
tenere lontano dagli occhi keep away from eyes
tenere lontano dai bambini keep out of reach of children
tenere lontano dal sole do not expose to sunlight
tennis da tavola table tennis
terme baths
tessera season ticket
tessera mensile monthly ticket
tessuti per arredamento upholstered [soft] furnishings
tier tribuna stand/grandstand
tintoria dry cleaner's
tintura per capelli hair dye
tipografia printing & copying
tirare pull
tiro all'arco archery
tomba grave, tomb
Torino Turin
torre tower
tossico poisonous, toxic
traffico intenso delays likely

traffico lento slow traffic
traghetto passenger ferry
transito con catene chains required
transito con catene o pneumatici da neve use chains or snow tires
treno train
trotta harness racing
tuffo deep water diving
tutte le operazioni all transactions

U

ufficio cambi exchange office
ufficio informazioni information office
ufficio postale post office
ufficio prenotazioni ticket reservations
ultima novità brand new
ultima stazione di servizio per ... chilometri last gas station for ... kilometers
ultima vista alle ore ... last entry at ...
una bibita inclusa includes 1 complimentary drink
uomini men only; men (toilets)
usare con cautela take care when using
uscita exit, way out; gate
uscita autostrada freeway/motorway exit
uscita camions truck/lorry exit
uscita d'emergenza emergency/fire exit
uso della cucina cooking facilities

V

vaccinazioni ecografie vaccinations
vaglia postali/telegrafici postal money order and electronic transfers
vagone letto sleeper (train)
validità del passaporto passport expiration date
validità della carta di credito credit card expiration date

valido per (75 minuti) valid for (75 minutes)

valido per le fasce ... valid for zones ...

veicoli lenti slow vehicles

veicoli pesanti heavy vehicles

vela sailing

veleno(so) poison(ous)

velocità massima ... km/ora maximum speed

vendere entro il ... sell by ...

vendiamo a ... currency sold at...

venerdì Friday

venti forti strong winds

venti moderati light winds

verdura vegetables

vernice fresco wet paint

vero genuine

vetro glass

vetro riciclato recycled glass

via street

viaggi/viaggiare travel

viale avenue, boulevard

vicino al mare within easy reach of the sea

vicolo alley

vicolo cieco dead end

videogiochi video games

vietato forbidden

vietato a veicoli con peso superiore a closed to heavy vehicles

vietato accendere il fuoco no fires

vietato ai minori di ... anni no children under ...

vietato ai pedoni no pedestrians

vietato avvicinarsi alle macchine durante la traversata no access to car decks during crossing

vietato di sosta no waiting

vietato fermarsi fino a ... no stopping (between ... and ...)

vietato fotografare no photography

vietato fumare no smoking

vietato gettare rifiuti don't dump rubbish

vietato giocare con la palla no ball games

vietato l'ingresso no entry

vietato l'ingresso dopo l'inizio dello spettacolo no entry once the performance has begun

vietato pescare no fishing

vietato pescare senza autorizzazione fishing by permit only

vietato salire no entry

vietato scendere no exit

vietato sporgersi dalla finestra do not lean out of windows

vietato suonare il clacson use of horn prohibited

vigili del fuoco fire brigade

vigneti vineyards

visite guidate guided tours

vivaio garden center

voi siete qui you are here

voli internazionali international flights

voli nazionali domestic flights

volo numero ... flight number ...

... volte al giorno ... times a day

Z

zona a parcheggio limitato giorni feriali limited parking zone on weekdays

zona fumatore smoking area

zona non fumatori no smoking area

zona pedonale pedestrian zone/precinct

zona riservata a carico e scarico loading bay

zucchero sugar

REFERENCE

GRAMMAR

Regular verbs and their tenses

There are three verb types which follow a regular pattern, their infinitives ending in -**are**, -**ere**, and -**ire**, e.g. *to speak* **parlare**, *to sell* **vendere**, *to finish* **finire**. Here are the most common present, past and future forms:

	PRESENT	PAST	FUTURE
io *I*	parl**o**	ho parlato	parler**ò**
tu *you* (informal)	parl**i**	hai parlato	parler**ai**
lui/lei/Lei *he/she/you* (form.)	parl**a**	ha parlato	parler**à**
noi *we*	parl**iamo**	abbiamo parlato	parler**emo**
voi *you* (pl. inform.)	parl**ate**	avete parlato	parler**ete**
loro/Loro *they/you* (form.)	parl**ano**	hanno parlato	parler**anno**
io *I*	vend**o**	ho venduto	vender**ò**
tu *you* (informal)	vend**i**	hai venduto	vender**ai**
lui/lei/Lei *he/she/you* (form.)	vend**e**	ha venduto	vender**à**
noi *we*	vend**iamo**	abbiamo venduto	vender**emo**
voi *you* (pl. inform.)	vend**ete**	avete venduto	vender**ete**
loro/Loro *they/you* (form.)	vend**ono**	hanno venduto	vender**anno**
io *I*	finis**co**	ho finito	finir**ò**
tu *you* (informal)	finis**ci**	hai finito	finir**ai**
lui/lei/Lei *he/she/you* (form.)	finis**ce**	ha finito	finir**à**
noi *we*	fin**iamo**	abbiamo finito	finir**emo**
voi *you* (pl. inform.)	fin**ite**	avete finito	finir**ete**
loro/Loro *they/you* (form.)	finis**cono**	hanno finito	finir**anno**

Very often, people ommit the pronoun, using only the verb form.

Examples: **Vivo a Roma.** *I live in Rome.*

Parla italiano? *Do you speak Italian?*

There are many irregular verbs whose forms differ considerably.

The most common way to express the past is by using the conjugated form of *to have* **avere** and the past participle of the verb as demonstrated on the previous page. Many verbs, especially verbs related to movement are conjugated with *to be* **essere**. In that case the participle agrees with number and gender of the subject.

avere *to have*	**essere** *to be*
io ho *I have*	**io sono** *I am*
tu hai *you have*	**tu sei** *you are*
lui/lei/Lei ha *he/she/you have*	**lui/lei/Lei è** *he/she/you is*
noi abbiamo *we have*	**noi siamo** *we are*
voi avete *you have*	**voi siete** *you are*
loro/Loro hanno *they/youhave*	**loro/Loro sono** *they/you are*

Examples: **Ho** lavorato. *I worked.*

Lei è andata a Palermo. *She went to Palermo.*

Siamo andate in autobus *We* (fem.) *went by bus.*

Nouns and articles

Generally nouns ending in **-o** are masculine, their plural ending changing to **-i**. Those ending in **-a** are usuallị feminine, their plural ending changing to **-e**. Nouns ending in **-e** can be either gender.

The definite articles are **il** (masc) and **la** (fem). The plural form is **i** (masc) and **le** (fem). When a masculine noun begins with a vowel, **z-**, **sc-**, **sp-**, **st-**, or **gn-** , the singular article changes to **lo**, the plural to **gli**.

Examples:

SINGULAR	PLURAL
il treno *the train*	**i** treni *the trains*
lo studio *the studio*	**gli** studi *the studios*
la casa *the house*	**le** case *the houses*

The indefinite articles also indicate their gender: **un** (masc.) and **uno** when a masculine noun begins with a **z-**, **sc-**, **sp-**, **st-**, or **gn-** or **s-**. The feminine form takes **una** or **un'** when the noun begins with a vowel.

Examples:

SINGULAR	PLURAL
un treno *a train*	**treni** *trains*
uno studio *a studio*	**studi** *studios*
una casa *a house*	**case** *houses*
un' ora *a n hour*	**ore** *hours*

Possessive determiners

Possessives are used to show that the noun belongs to something or someone. They relate to gender and number of the noun that follows:

	SINGULAR		PLURAL	
	MASC.	FEM.	MASC.	FEM.
my	**il mio**	**la mia**	**i miei**	**le mie**
your (inf.)	**il tuo**	**la tua**	**i tuoi**	**le tue**
your (form.)	**il Suo**	**la Sua**	**i Suoi**	**le Sue**
his/her/its	**il suo**	**la sua**	**i suoi**	**le sue**
our	**il nostro**	**la nostra**	**i nostri**	**le nostre**
your (pl, inf.)	**il vostro**	**la vostra**	**i vostri**	**le vostre**
your (pl., form)	**il Loro**	**la Loro**	**i Loro**	**le Loro**
their/	**il loro**	**la loro**	**i loro**	**le loro**

Examples: **Dov'è <u>il Suo</u> biglietto?** *Where is your ticket?*

La vostra corriera parte alle 8. *Your bus leaves at 8.*

La tua casa è bella. *Your (singular) house is pretty.*

Wordorder

The conjugated verb generally comes after the subject.

Example: **Vorrei una birra.** *I'd like a beer.*

Questions are formed by simply raising your voice at the end of the sentence or by reversing the order of subject and verb when using key question words like *how* **come**.

Examples: **Avete cartine?** *Do you have maps?*

Come ci arrivo? *How do I get there?*

Hai visto Carlo? *You saw Carlo?*

Negations

Negative sentences are generally formed by putting *not* **non** before the verb which is to be negated.

Examples: **Non fumiamo.** *We don't smoke.*

Non capisco. *I don't understand.*

Il treno non arriva. *The train doesn't arrive.*

Adjectives

Adjectives describe nouns and agree with them in gender and number. Singular forms end in **-o** (masc), **-a** (fem) or **-e** (masc/fem). Plural forms end in **-i** (masc), **-e** (fem) and **-i** (masc/fem).

Examples: **un ristorante grande** *a large restaurant*
una camicia bianca *a white shirt*
le scarpe italiane *the Italian shoes*

A few common adjectives normally precede the noun:

Examples: **un bel giardino** *a beautiful garden*
la piccola casa *the little house*
una larga strata *a wide street*

Adjectives linked to the subject with a verb also agree in number and gender with the noun they relate to.

Examples: **Il clima è mite.** *The climate is mild.*
Il nostro capo è simpatico . *Our boss is nice.*
Ho visitato molti musei. *I visited many museums.*

Comperatives and superlatives

ADJECTIVE	COMPARATIVE	SUPERLATIVE
ricco	**il più ricco**	**ricchissimo**
rich	*richer*	*the richest*
vecchio	**meno vecchio**	**il meno vecchio**
old	*less old*	*the least old*

Example: **Ha qualcosa di meno caro?** *Do you have anything cheaper?*

Adverbs and adverbial expressions

Adverbs describe verbs. In Italian, the majority are formed by adding **-mente** to the feminine form of the adjective.

ADJECTIVE	FEMININE	ADVERB
lento *slow*	**lenta** *slow*	**lentamente** *slowly*

Adjectives ending in **-re** or **-le** drop the final **-e** before adding **-mente**. Like in English, there are a number of exceptions to the rule, e.g. *good* **buono** / *well* **bene**.

Examples: **Maria guida lentamente.** *Maria drives slowly.*
Roberto guida normalmente. *Robert drives normally.*
Parlo bene italiano. *I speak Italian well.*

Some common adverbial time expressions:

attualmente *presently*
non ancora *not yet*
ancora *still*
finalmente *finally*

NUMBERS

Larger numbers are built up using the components below: e.g.

3 456 789 **tremilioniquattrocentocinquantaseimila
e settecentoottantanove**

Mille, **milione** and **miliardo** have plural forms (**mila**, **milioni**, **miliardi**).

Note that **e** can be used to break larger numbers up.

0	**zero** *dzehro*	40	**quaranta** *kwaranta*
1	**uno** *oono*	50	**cinquanta** *cheengkwanta*
2	**due** *doo-ay*	60	**sessanta** *sayssanta*
3	**tre** *tray*	70	**settanta** *sayttantta*
4	**quattro** *kwattro*	80	**ottanta** *ottanta*
5	**cinque** *cheengkweh*	90	**novanta** *novanta*
6	**sei** *sayee*	100	**cento** *chaynto*
7	**sette** *sehttay*	101	**centouno** *chaynto-oono*
8	**otto** *otto*	200	**duecento** *doo-aychaynto*
9	**nove** *novay*	500	**cinquecento**
10	**dieci** *dee-ehchee*		*cheenkwehchaynto*
11	**undici** *oondeechee*	1000	**mille** *meellay*
12	**dodici** *dodeechee*	10 000	**diecimila**
13	**tredici** *traydeechee*		*deeaycheemeela*
14	**quattordici** *kwattordeechee*	1 000 000	**un milione**
15	**quindici** *kooeendeechee*		*oon meelyonay*
16	**sedici** *saydeechee*	first	**primo** *preemo*
17	**diciassette** *deechassehttay*	second	**secondo** *saykondo*
18	**diciotto** *deechotto*	third	**terzo** *tayrtso*
19	**diciannove** *deechanovay*	fourth	**quarto** *kwarto*
20	**venti** *vayntee*	fifth	**quinto** *kooeento*
21	**ventuno** *vayntoono*	once	**una volta** *oona volta*
30	**trenta** *traynta*	twice	**due volte**
31	**trentuno** *trayntoono*		*doo-ay voltay*

three times	**tre volte**	*tray voltay*
a half	**mezzo**	*maytso*
half a(n) hour	**mezz'ora**	*maytsora*
a quarter	**un quarto**	*oon kwarto*
a third	**un terzo**	*oon tayrtso*
a pair of …	**un paio di …**	*oon paa-eeoo dee*
a dozen …	**una dozzina …**	*oona dotseena*

DAYS

Monday	**lunedì**	*loonaydee*
Tuesday	**martedì**	*martaydee*
Wednesday	**mercoledì**	*mayrkolaydee*
Thursday	**giovedì**	*jovaydee*
Friday	**venerdì**	*vaynayrdee*
Saturday	**sabato**	*sabato*
Sunday	**domenica**	*domayneeka*

MONTHS

January	**gennaio**	*jaynnaaeeo*
February	**febbraio**	*faybbraaeeo*
March	**marzo**	*martso*
April	**aprile**	*apreelay*
May	**maggio**	*madjo*
June	**giugno**	*jooño*
July	**luglio**	*loolyo*
August	**agosto**	*agosto*
September	**settembre**	*sehttehmbray*
October	**ottobre**	*ottobray*
November	**novembre**	*novehmbray*
December	**dicembre**	*deechehmbray*

DATES

It's …	**È …**	*eh*
July 10	**il dieci luglio**	*eel dee-ehchee loolyo*
Tuesday, March 1	**martedì, primo marzo** *martaydee preemo martso*	
yesterday	**ieri**	*ee-ehree*
today	**oggi**	*odjee*
tomorrow	**domani**	*domaanee*
this/last …	**questo(-a)/l'ultimo(-a) …** *kwaysto(-a)/loolteemo(-a)*	
next week	**la prossima settimana** *la prosseema saytteemaana*	

220

SEASONS

spring	**la primavera** *la preemavayra*
summer	**l'estate** *laystaatay*
fall/autumn	**l'autunno** *lowtoonno*
winter	**l'inverno** *leenvayrno*

GREETINGS

Happy birthday!	**Buon compleanno!** *bwon komplayanno*
Merry Christmas!	**Buon Natale!** *bwon nataalay*
Happy New Year!	**Felice Anno Nuovo! Buon anno!** *fayleechay anno noo-ovo/bwon anno*
Happy Easter!	**Buona Pasqua!** *bwona paskwa*
Best wishes!	**Tanti auguri!** *tantee owgooree*
Congratulations!	**Congratulazioni!** *kongraatoolatseeonee*
Good luck!/All the best!	**Buona fortuna!** *bwona fortoona*
Have a good trip!	**Buon viaggio!** *bwon veeadjo*

PUBLIC HOLIDAYS

There are a number of regional holidays observed in Italy. National holidays are listed below.

January 1	**Capodanno or Primo dell'Anno**	New Year's Day
January 6	**Epifania/Befana**	Epiphany
April 25	**Anniversario della Liberazione (1945)**	Liberation Day
May 1	**Festa del Lavoro**	Labor Day
August 15	**Ferragosto**	Assumption Day
November 1	**Ognissanti**	All Saints' Day
December 8	**L'Immacolata Concezione**	Immaculate Conception
December 25	**Natale**	Christmas
December 26	**Santo Stefano**	St Stephen's Day
Movable dates:	**Lunedì di Pasqua/Pasquetta**	Easter Monday

Except for April 25, all Italian holidays are celebrated in the **Ticino** (Italian-speaking Switzerland), as well as: March 19 (**San Giuseppe**), August 1st (National Holiday), and the holidays of **Ascensione** (Ascension Day) and **Corpus Domini**.

221

The official time system uses the 24-hour clock. However, in ordinary conversation, time is generally expressed as shown below, often with the addition of **di mattina** (morning), **di pomeriggio** (afternoon) or **di sera** (evening).

Excuse me. Can you tell me the time?	**Scusi, può dirmi che ora è?** *skoozee pwo deermee kay ora eh*
It's five past one.	**È l'una e cinque.** *eh loona ay cheenkway*
It's …	**Sono le …** *sono lay*
ten past two	**due e dieci** *doo-ay ay dee-ehchee*
a quarter past three	**tre e un quarto** *tray ay oon kwarto*
twenty past four	**quattro e venti** *kwattro ay vayntee*
twenty-five past five	**cinque e venticinque** *cheenkway ay vaynteecheenkway*
half past six	**sei e trenta** *seh-ee ay traynta*
twenty-five to seven	**sei e trentacinque** *seh-ee ay traynta cheenkway*
twenty to eight	**otto meno venti** *otto mayno vayntee*
a quarter to nine	**nove meno un quarto** *novay mayno oon kwarto*
ten to ten	**dieci meno dieci** *dee-ehchee mayno dee-ehchee*

It's twelve o'clock (noon/midnight).	**È mezzogiorno/mezzanotte.** *eh maytsojorno/ maytsanottay mittaag/mitternakht*	
at dawn	**all'alba** *allalba*	
in the morning	**al mattino** *al matteeno*	
during the day	**durante il giorno** *doorantay eel jorno*	
before/after lunch	**prima di pranzo** *preema/dopo dee prandzo*	
in the afternoon	**nel pomeriggio** *nayl pomayreedjo*	
in the evening	**di sera** *dee sayra*	
at night	**di notte** *dee nottay*	
I'll be ready in five minutes.	**Sarò pronto(-a) fra cinque minuti.** *saro pronto(-a) fra cheenkway meenootee*	
He'll be back in a quarter of an hour.	**Ritorna fra un quarto d'ora.** *reetorno fra oon kwarto dora*	
She arrived half an hour ago.	**È arrivata mezz'ora fa.** *eh arreevaata maytsora fa*	
The train leaves at …	**il treno parte …** *eel trayno partay*	
13:04	**alle tredici e zero quattro** *allay traydeechee ay dzayro kwattro*	
0:40	**alle zero e quaranta** *allay dzayro ay kwaraanta*	
10 minutes late/early	**con dieci minuti di ritardo/di anticipo** *kon dee-ehchee meenootee dee reetaardo/dee anteecheepo*	
5 minutes fast/slow	**cinque minuti avanti/indietro** *cheenkway meenootee avaantee/eendeeaytro*	
from 9:00 to 5:00	**dalle nove alle cinque** *dallay novay allay cheenkway*	
between 8:00 and 2:00	**fra le otto e le due** *fra lay otto ay lay doo-ay*	
I'll be leaving by …	**Partirò entro …** *parteero ayntro*	
Will you be back before …?	**Ritornerà prima di …?** *reetornayra preema dee*	
We'll be here until …	**Saremo qui entro le …** *saraymo kwee entroh leh*	

ITALIA